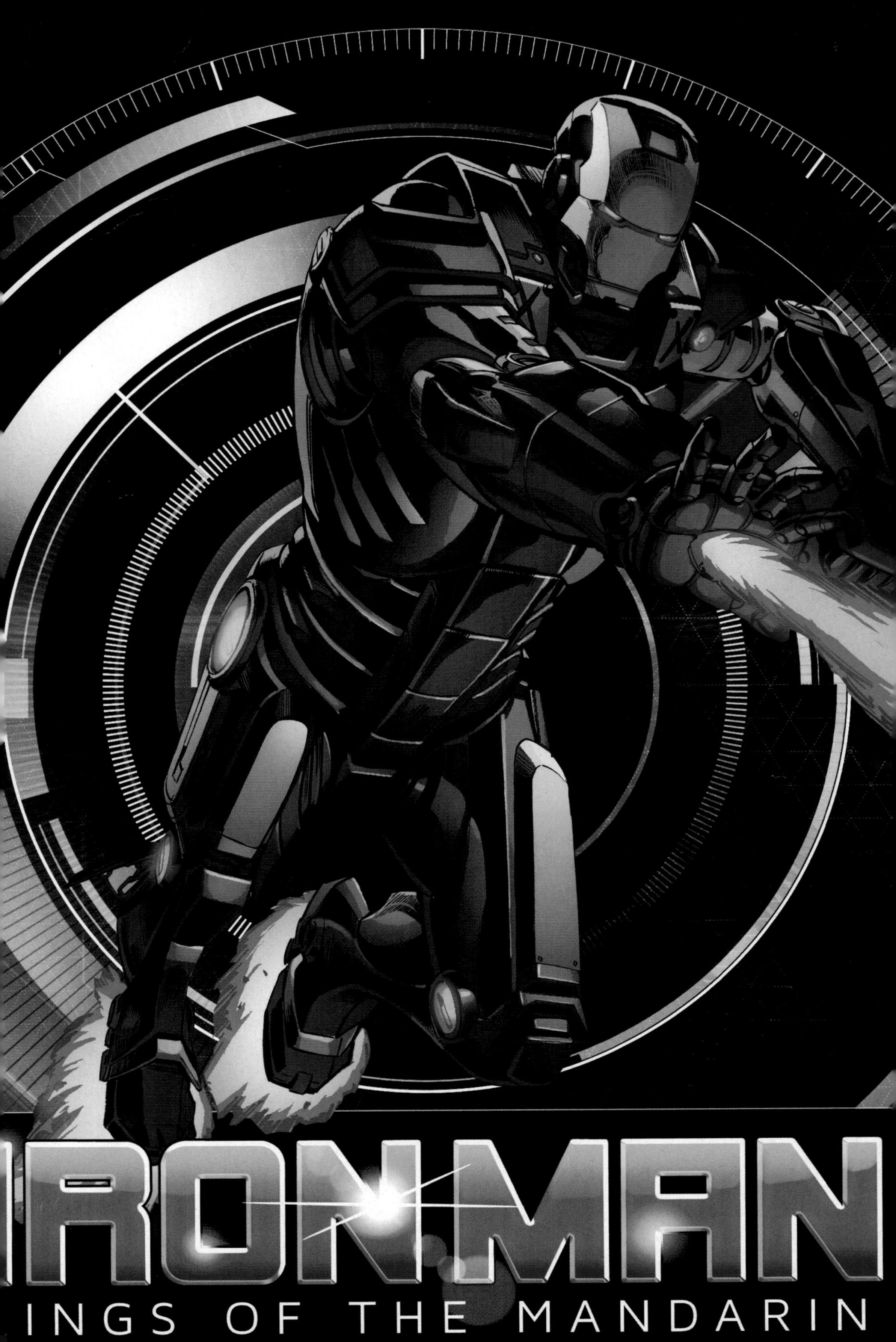

IRON MAN

INGS OF THE MANDARIN

Tony Stark is a technological visionary...a famous, wealthy and unparalled inventor. With the world's most advanced and powerful suit of armor, Stark valiantly protects the innocent as an invincible bright knight known as...

IRON MAN
RINGS OF THE MANDARIN

KIERON GILLEN
WRITER

LUKE ROSS
ARTIST, #23-25 & #26, PP. 14-20

JOE BENNETT
PENCILER, #26, PP. 1-13; #27, PP. 8-14; #28, PP. 1-11

CLIFF RICHARDS
PENCILER, #27, PP. 1-7 & 15-20; #28, PP. 12-14 & 19-20

DERLIS SANTACRU
PENCILER, #28, PP. 15-18

SCOTT HANNA
INKER, #16, PP. 1-13; #27; #28, PP. 1-16 & 18

RICK MAGYAR
INKER, #28, PP. 17 & 19-2

GURU-eFX
COLORIST

VC'S JOE CARAMAGNA
LETTERER

MIKE DEL MUNDO
COVER ART, #23-26

CHRISTIAN WARD
COVER ART, #27

IN-HYUK LEE
COVER ART, #28

EMILY SHAW
ASSISTANT EDITOR

MARK PANICCIA
EDITOR

COLLECTION EDITOR: **SARAH BRUNSTAD**
ASSOCIATE MANAGING EDITOR: **ALEX STARBUCK**
EDITORS, SPECIAL PROJECTS: **MARK D. BEAZLEY & JENNIFER GRÜNWALD**
SENIOR EDITOR, SPECIAL PROJECTS: **JEFF YOUNGQUIST**
SVP PRINT, SALES & MARKETING: **DAVID GABRIEL**
BOOK DESIGNER: **RODOLFO MURAGUCHI**

EDITOR IN CHIEF: **AXEL ALONSO**
CHIEF CREATIVE OFFICER: **JOE QUESADA**
PUBLISHER: **DAN BUCKLEY**
EXECUTIVE PRODUCER: **ALAN FINE**

IRON MAN VOL. 5: RINGS OF THE MANDARIN. Contains material originally published in magazine form as IRON MAN #23-28. First printing 2014. ISBN# 978-0-7851-5482-2. Published by MARVEL WORLDWID INC., a subsidiary of MARVEL ENTERTAINMENT, LLC. OFFICE OF PUBLICATION: 135 West 50th Street, New York, NY 10020. Printed in the U.S.A. ALAN FINE, EVP - Office of the Presider Marvel Worldwide, Inc. and EVP & CMO Marvel Characters B.V.; DAN BUCKLEY, Publisher & President - Print, Animation & Digital Divisions; JOE QUESADA, Chief Creative Officer; TOM BREVOORT, SVP of Publishin DAVID BOGART, SVP of Operations & Procurement, Publishing; C.B. CEBULSKI, SVP of Creator & Content Development; DAVID GABRIEL, SVP Print, Sales & Marketing; JIM O'KEEFE, VP of Operations & Logistic DAN CARR, Executive Director of Publishing Technology; SUSAN CRESPI, Editorial Operations Manager; ALEX MORALES, Publishing Operations Manager; STAN LEE, Chairman Emeritus. For information regardir advertising in Marvel Comics or on Marvel.com, please contact Niza Disla, Director of Marvel Partnerships, at ndisla@marvel.com. For Marvel subscription inquiries, please call 800-217-9158. **Manufacture**

Are you sitting comfortably?

Then I'll begin.

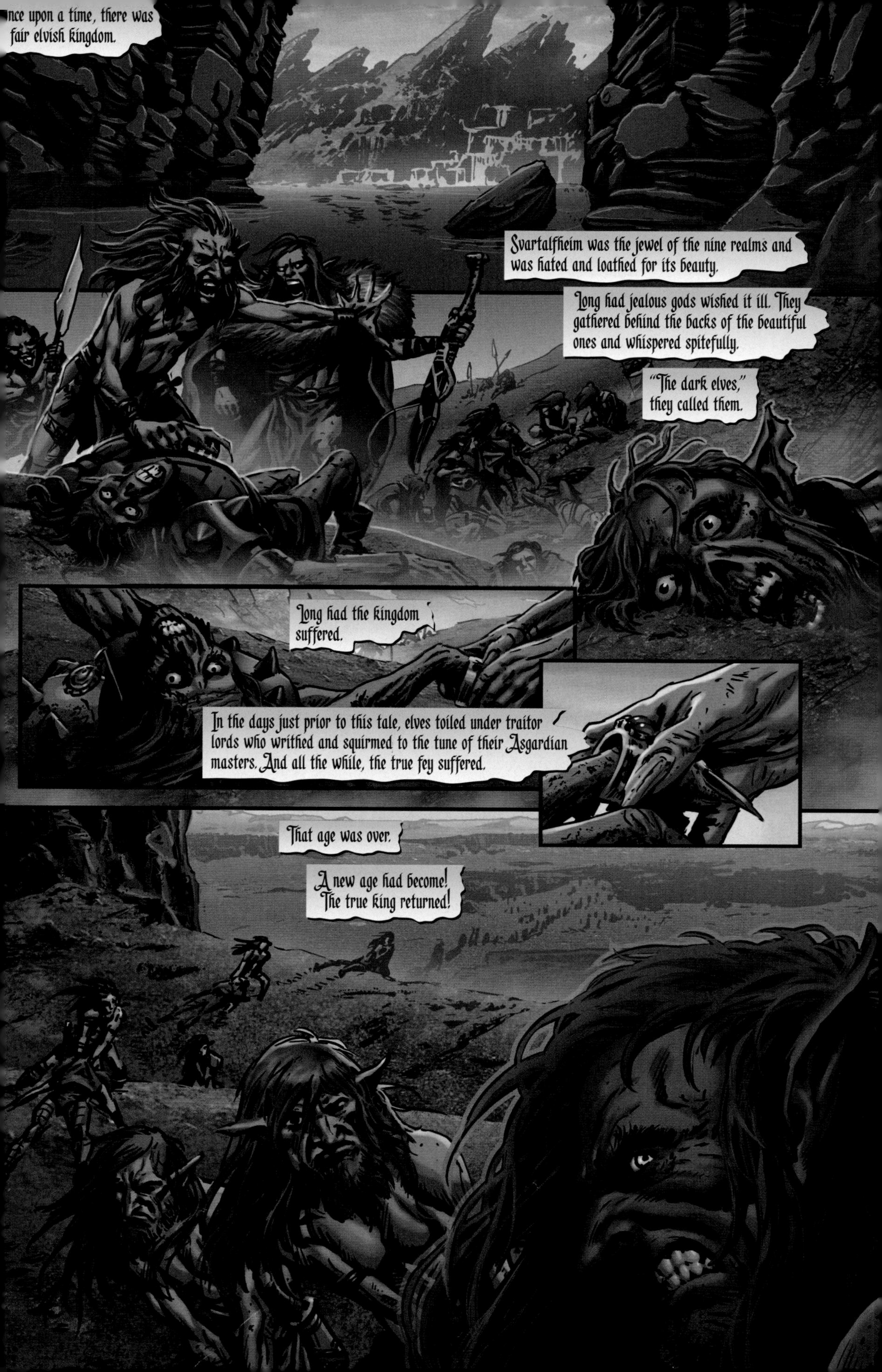
nce upon a time, there was
fair elvish kingdom.
Svartalfheim was the jewel of the nine realms and was hated and loathed for its beauty.
Long had jealous gods wished it ill. They gathered behind the backs of the beautiful ones and whispered spitefully.
"The dark elves," they called them.
Long had the kingdom suffered.
In the days just prior to this tale, elves toiled under traitor lords who writhed and squirmed to the tune of their Asgardian masters. And all the while, the true fey suffered.
That age was over.
A new age had become! The true king returned!

Malekith the Accursed sat on the ebony throne!

(Accursed, as he was cursed by his enemy and his enemy were all who would wish ill upon the elves of Svartalfheim!)

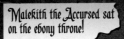

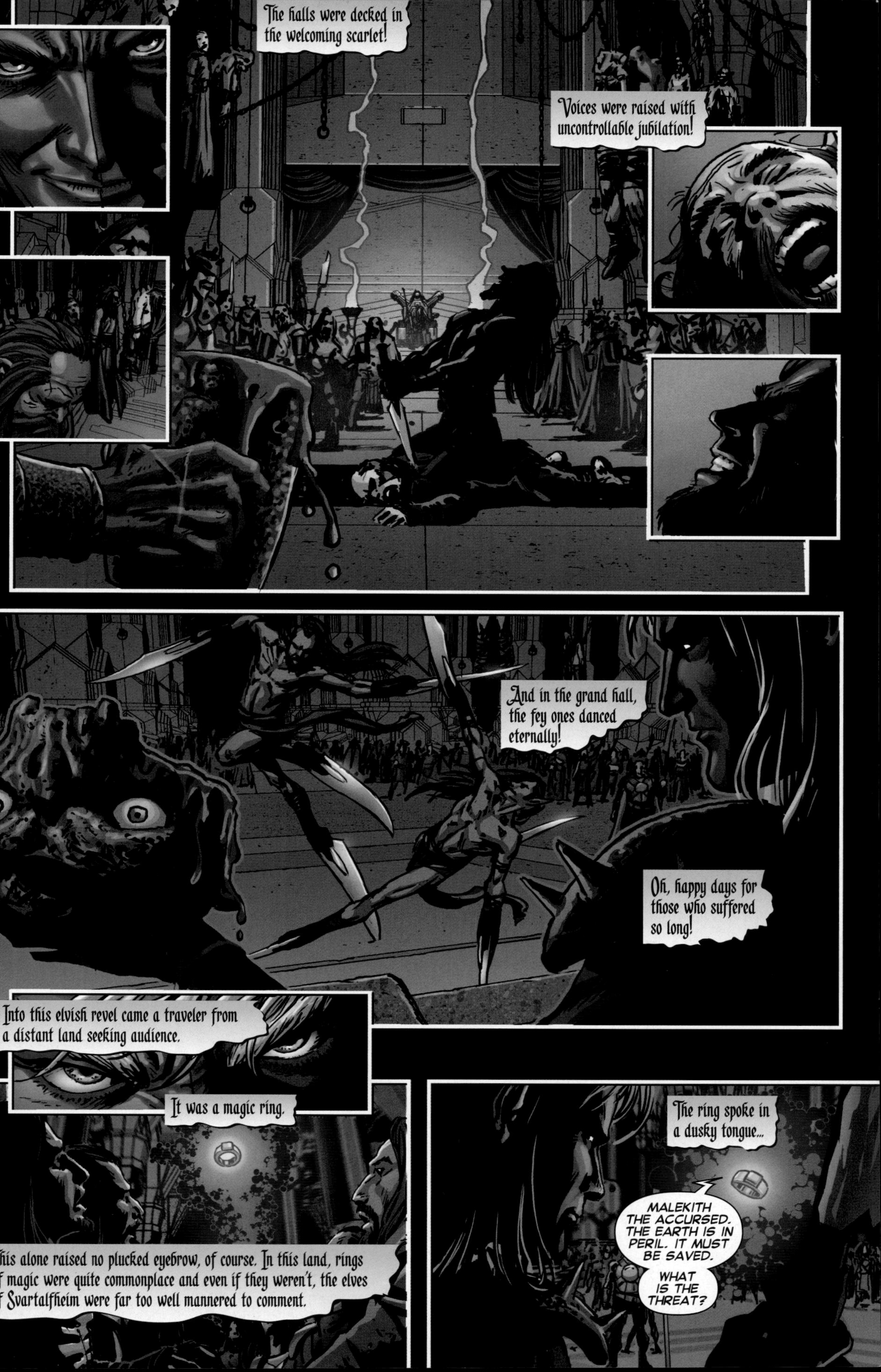
The halls were decked in the welcoming scarlet!
Voices were raised with uncontrollable jubilation!
And in the grand hall, the fey ones danced eternally!
Oh, happy days for those who suffered so long!
Into this elvish revel came a traveler from a distant land seeking audience.
It was a magic ring.
This alone raised no plucked eyebrow, of course. In this land, rings of magic were quite commonplace and even if they weren't, the elves of Svartalfheim were far too well mannered to comment.
The ring spoke in a dusky tongue...
MALEKITH THE ACCURSED. THE EARTH IS IN PERIL. IT MUST BE SAVED.
WHAT IS THE THREAT?

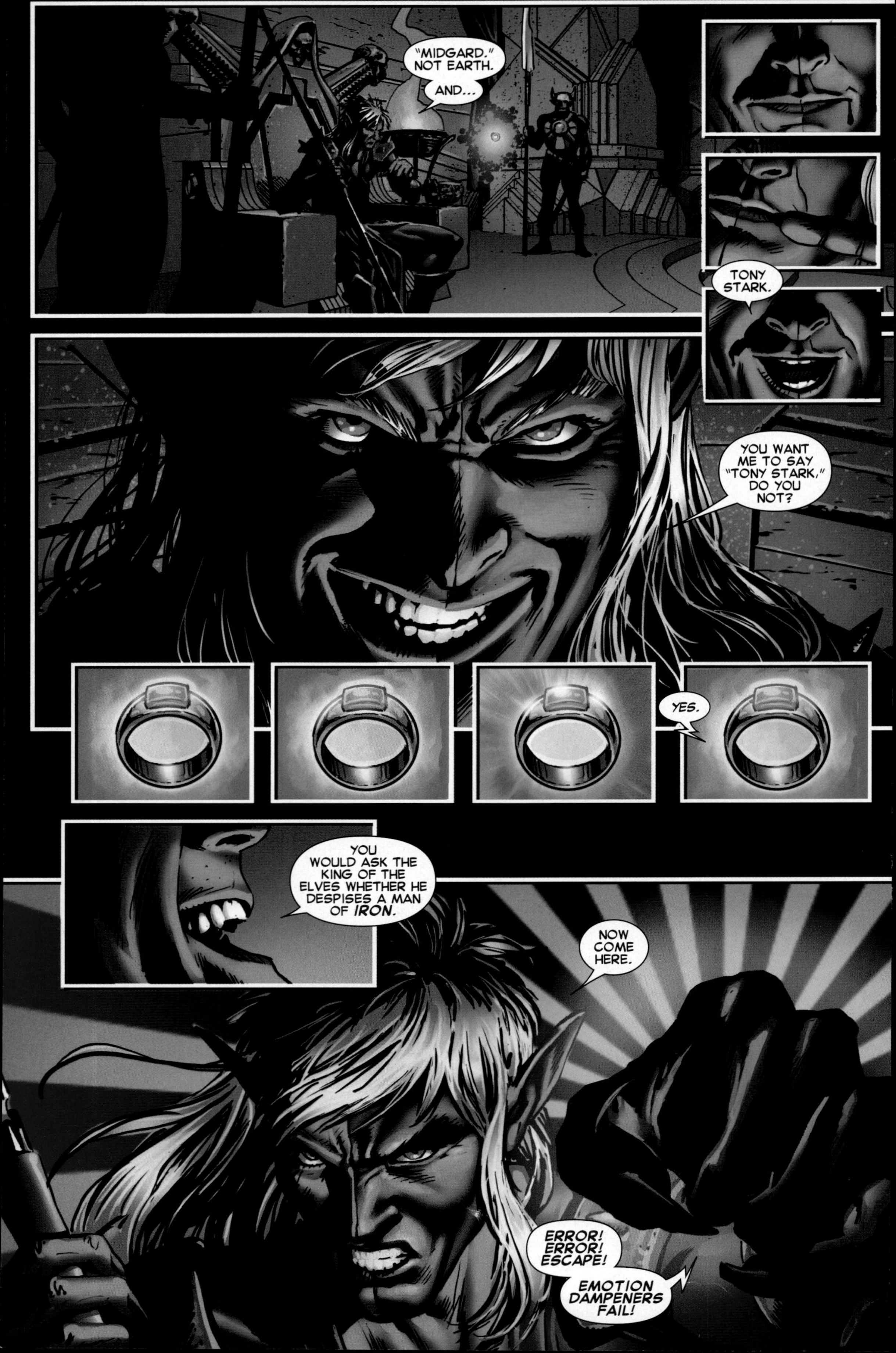
"MIDGARD." NOT EARTH.
AND...
TONY STARK.
YOU WANT ME TO SAY "TONY STARK," DO YOU NOT?
YES.
YOU WOULD ASK THE KING OF THE ELVES WHETHER HE DESPISES A MAN OF IRON.
NOW COME HERE.
ERROR! ERROR! ESCAPE!
EMOTION DAMPENERS FAIL!

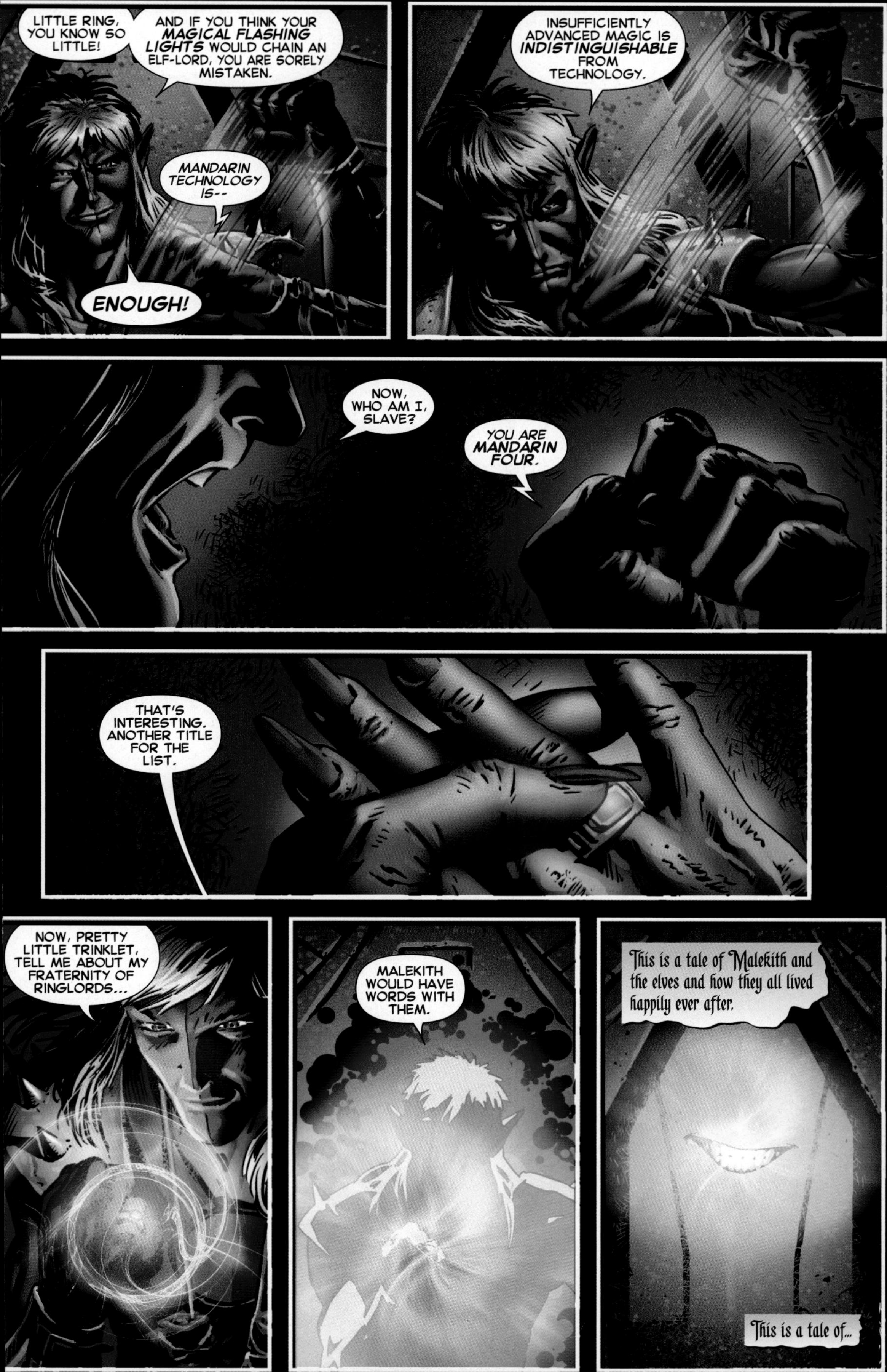
LITTLE RING, YOU KNOW SO LITTLE!
AND IF YOU THINK YOUR MAGICAL FLASHING LIGHTS WOULD CHAIN AN ELF-LORD, YOU ARE SORELY MISTAKEN.
MANDARIN TECHNOLOGY IS--
ENOUGH!
INSUFFICIENTLY ADVANCED MAGIC IS INDISTINGUISHABLE FROM TECHNOLOGY.
NOW, WHO AM I, SLAVE?
YOU ARE MANDARIN FOUR.
THAT'S INTERESTING. ANOTHER TITLE FOR THE LIST.
NOW, PRETTY LITTLE TRINKLET, TELL ME ABOUT MY FRATERNITY OF RINGLORDS...
MALEKITH WOULD HAVE WORDS WITH THEM.
This is a tale of Malekith and the elves and how they all lived happily ever after.
This is a tale of...

IRO

Rings OF THE

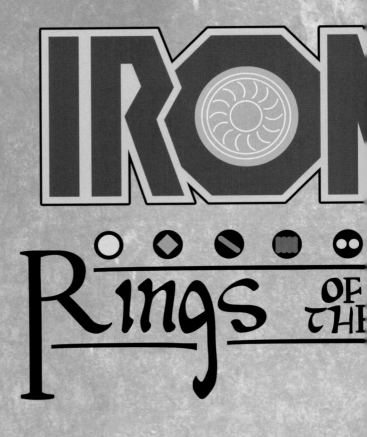

MAN

MANDARIN

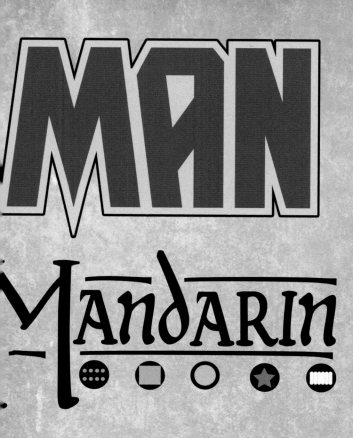

NEW YORK.

I'M TONY STARK. I RECENTLY DISCOVERED I WAS ADOPTED AND HAD A SECRET BROTHER, ARNO.

THIS STORY HAS NOTHING TO DO WITH THAT.

I'M A MULTIMEDIA ICON. AS A GOOD CAPITALIST, I TURN THAT INTO HOT, HOT CASH TO FUND MY FAVORITE PROJECTS.

(WHICH IS BASICALLY SAVING THE WORLD. AND SPORTS CARS.)

THE COMMERCIALIZATION OF IRON MAN HAS LEAD TO PRODUCTS YOU WOULDN'T BELIEVE. RELEVANTLY?

A MUSICAL.

MY PEOPLE HIRED A DIRECTOR/ COMPOSER/ CONDUCTOR/ GENERAL ARTISTE.

HE TURNED ME INTO A PERVERT, APPARENTLY.

THE MAN IN THE IRON MASK TONY STARK STORY!

THAT DOESN'T BOTHER ME. YOU HIRE AN ARTIST, DON'T BE SURPRISED WHEN YOU GET ART. MY PEOPLE MESSED UP.

AND THEY REPLACED HIM. HE TOOK IT...POORLY.

THAT'S A BUSINESS SUIT PROBLEM. I ALSO HAVE AN IRON MAN SUIT PROBLEM...

THE MANDARIN'S RINGS ARE FINDING OWNERS WHO HAVE ISSUES WITH ME, AND GIVING THEM A LITTLE EMOTIONAL PUSH INTO ACTING OUT AND ATTACKING ME AND MINE...

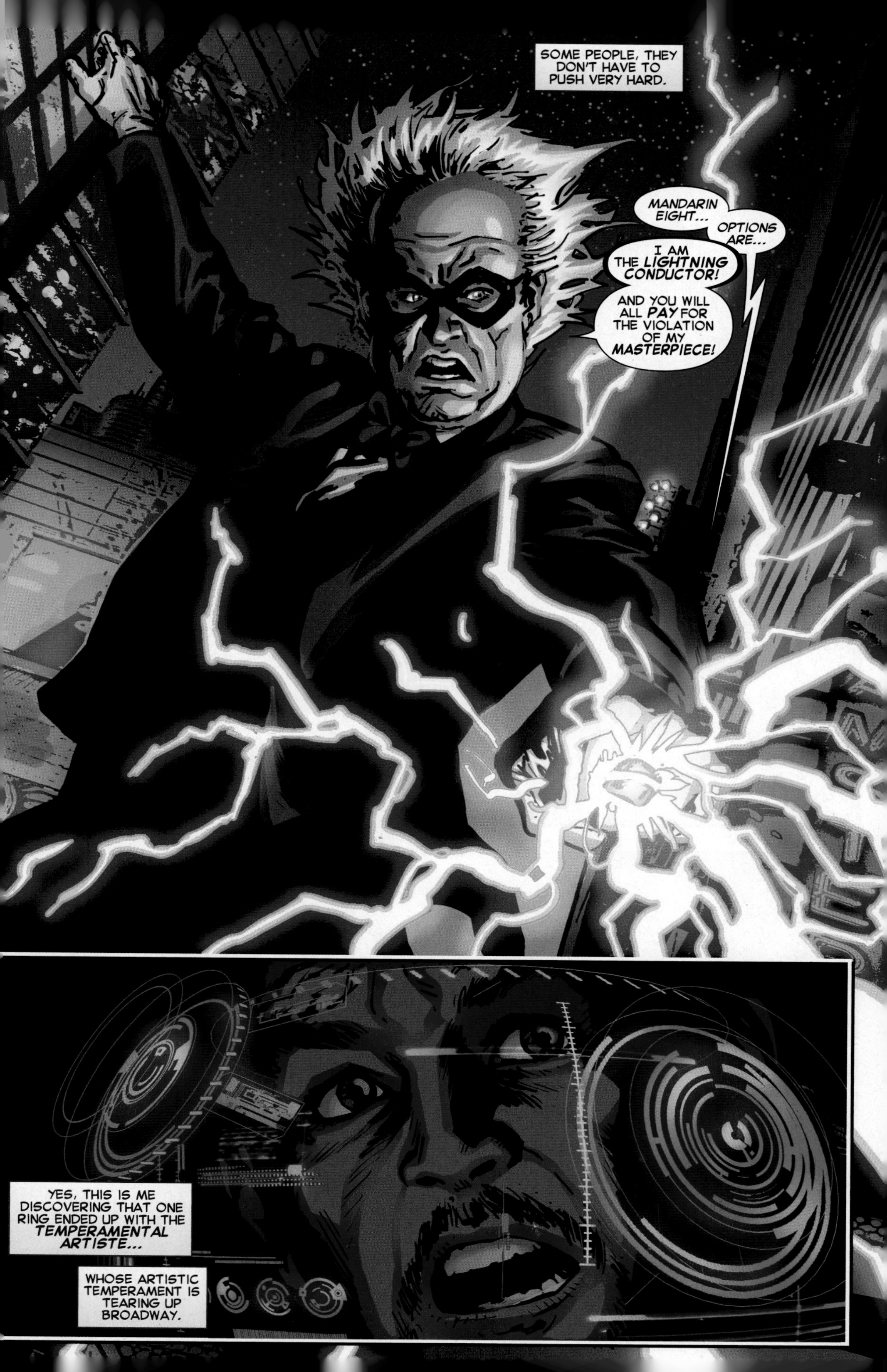
SOME PEOPLE, THEY DON'T HAVE TO PUSH VERY HARD.
MANDARIN EIGHT...
OPTIONS ARE...
I AM THE LIGHTNING CONDUCTOR!
AND YOU WILL ALL PAY FOR THE VIOLATION OF MY MASTERPIECE!
YES, THIS IS ME DISCOVERING THAT ONE RING ENDED UP WITH THE TEMPERAMENTAL ARTISTE...
WHOSE ARTISTIC TEMPERAMENT IS TEARING UP BROADWAY.

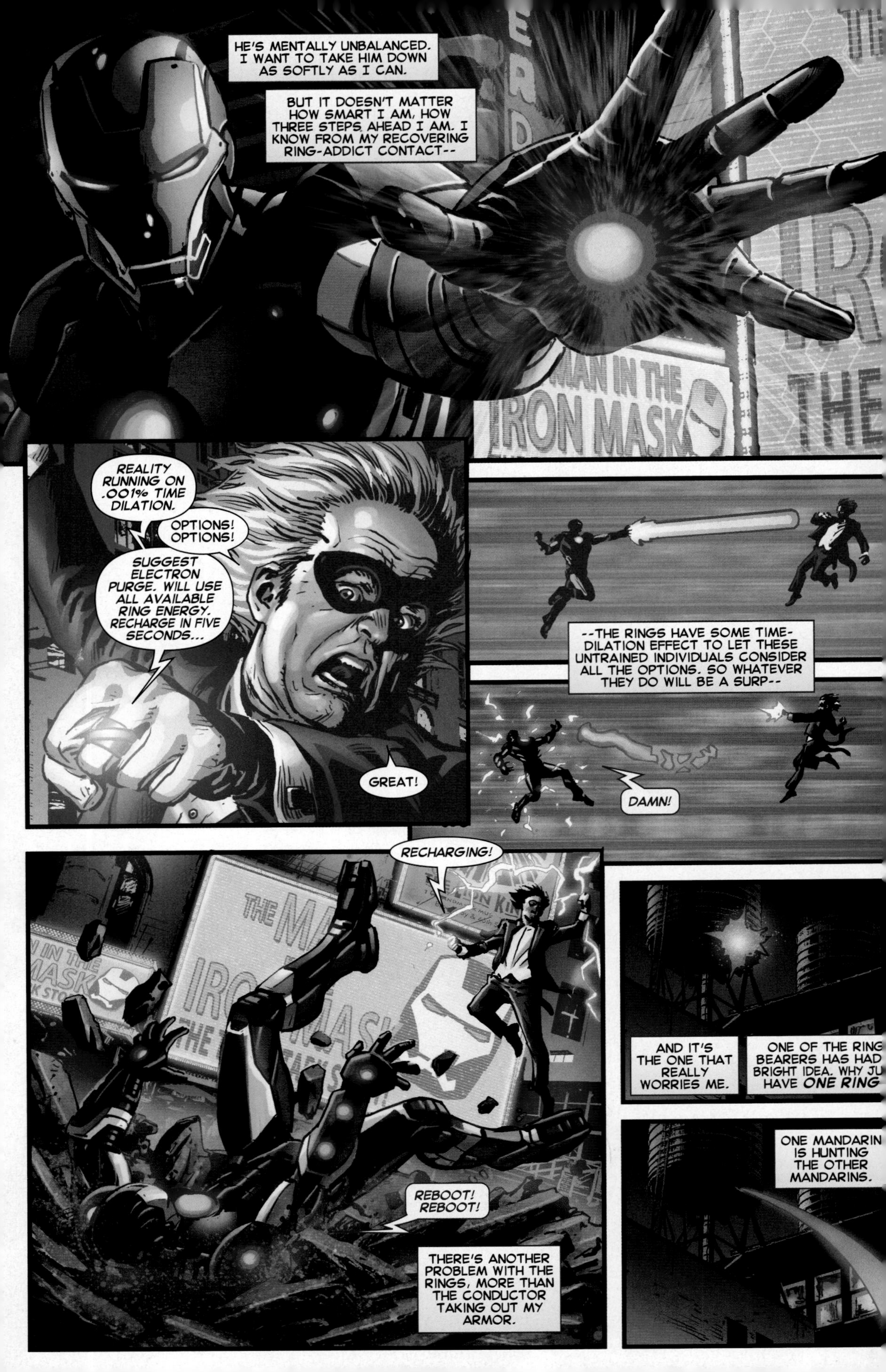
HE'S MENTALLY UNBALANCED. I WANT TO TAKE HIM DOWN AS SOFTLY AS I CAN.
BUT IT DOESN'T MATTER HOW SMART I AM, HOW THREE STEPS AHEAD I AM. I KNOW FROM MY RECOVERING RING-ADDICT CONTACT--
MAN IN THE IRON MASK
THE
REALITY RUNNING ON .001% TIME DILATION.
OPTIONS! OPTIONS!
SUGGEST ELECTRON PURGE. WILL USE ALL AVAILABLE RING ENERGY. RECHARGE IN FIVE SECONDS...
GREAT!
--THE RINGS HAVE SOME TIME-DILATION EFFECT TO LET THESE UNTRAINED INDIVIDUALS CONSIDER ALL THE OPTIONS. SO WHATEVER THEY DO WILL BE A SURP--
DAMN!
RECHARGING!
REBOOT! REBOOT!
THERE'S ANOTHER PROBLEM WITH THE RINGS, MORE THAN THE CONDUCTOR TAKING OUT MY ARMOR.
ONE OF THE RING BEARERS HAS HAD BRIGHT IDEA. WHY JU HAVE ONE RING
AND IT'S THE ONE THAT REALLY WORRIES ME.
ONE MANDARIN IS HUNTING THE OTHER MANDARINS.

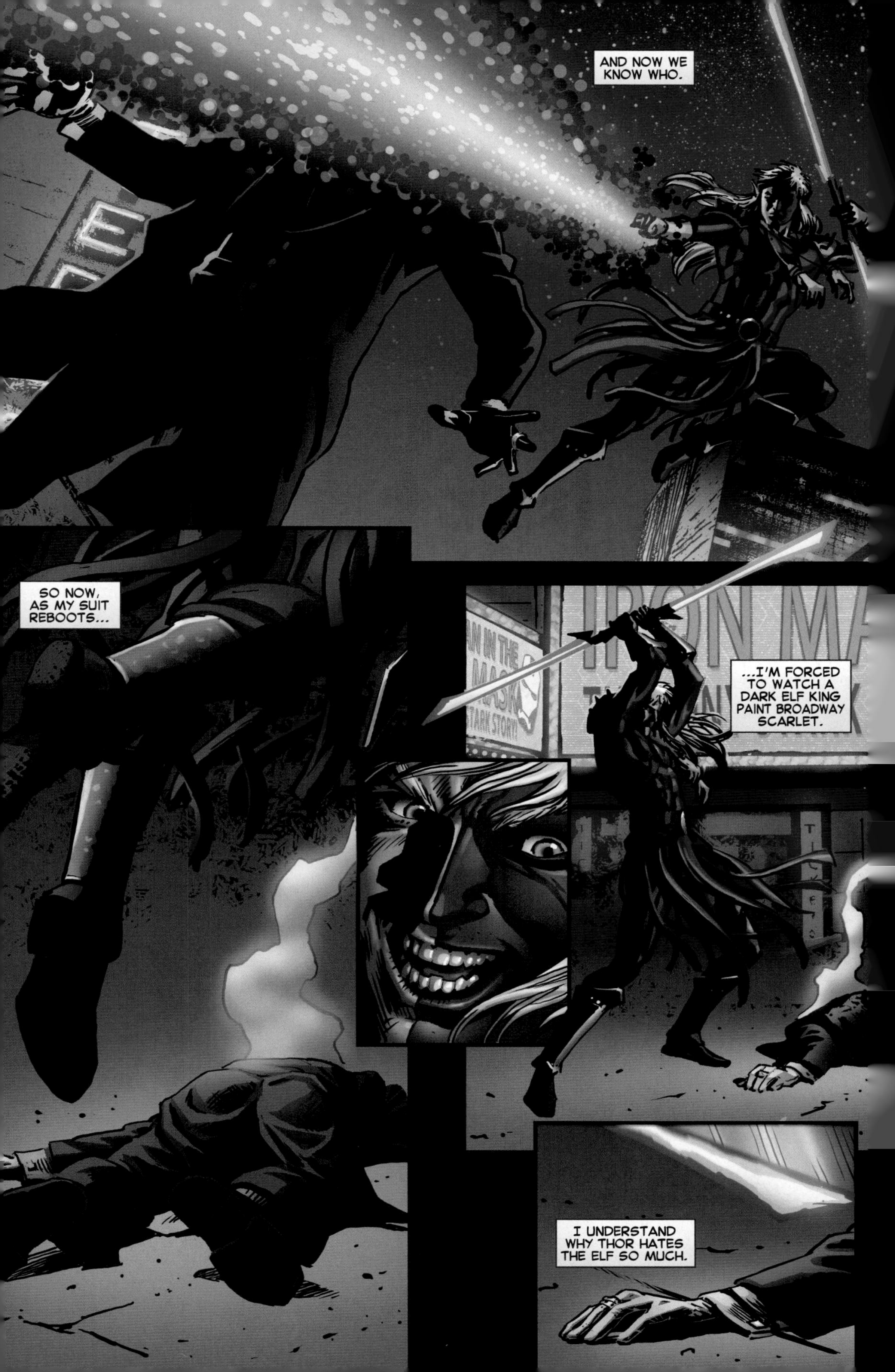
AND NOW WE KNOW WHO.
SO NOW, AS MY SUIT REBOOTS...
...I'M FORCED TO WATCH A DARK ELF KING PAINT BROADWAY SCARLET.
I UNDERSTAND WHY THOR HATES THE ELF SO MUCH.

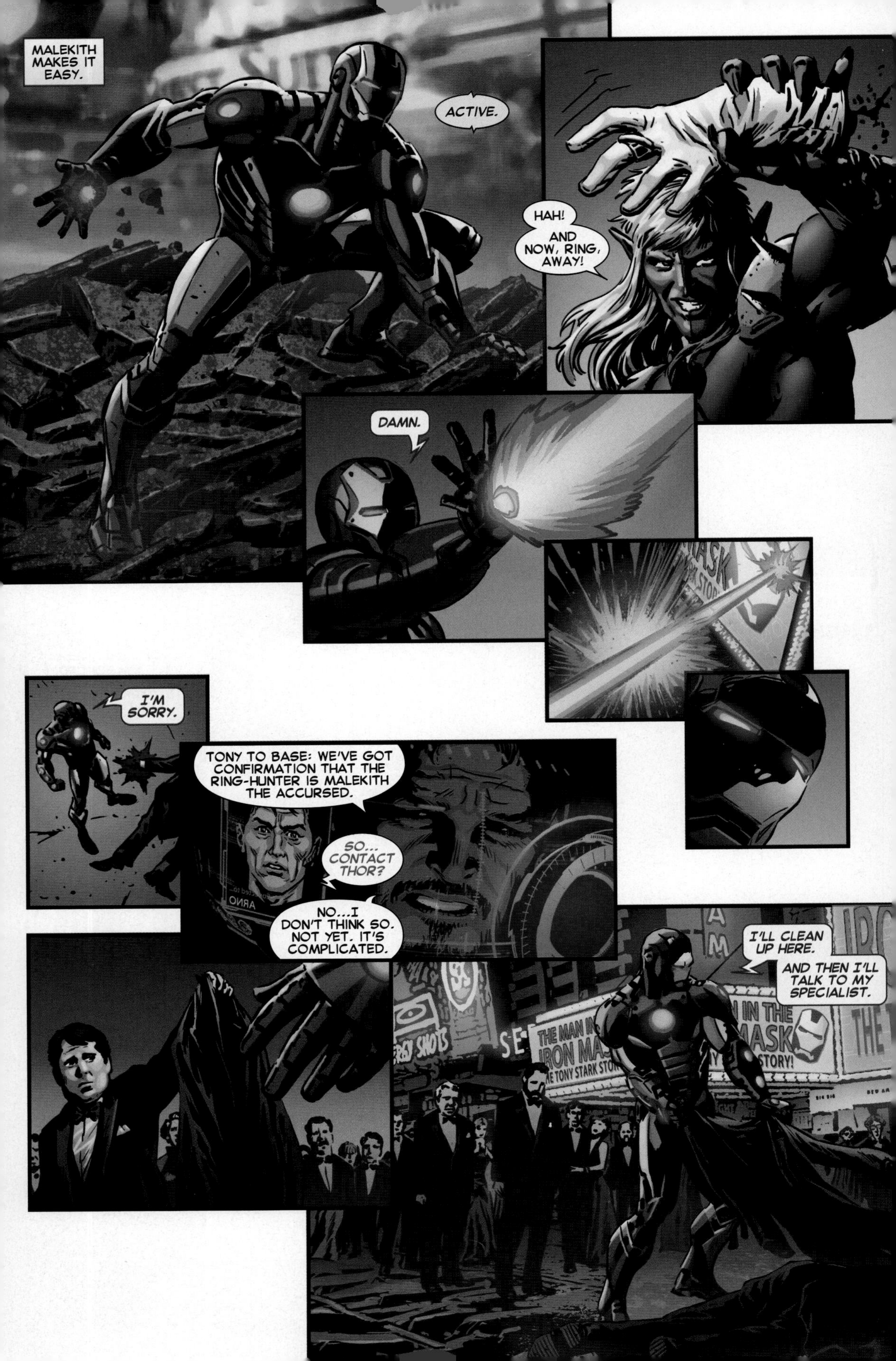

MALEKITH MAKES IT EASY.
ACTIVE.
HAH!
AND NOW, RING, AWAY!
DAMN.
I'M SORRY.
TONY TO BASE: WE'VE GOT CONFIRMATION THAT THE RING-HUNTER IS MALEKITH THE ACCURSED.
SO... CONTACT THOR?
NO...I DON'T THINK SO. NOT YET. IT'S COMPLICATED.
I'LL CLEAN UP HERE.
AND THEN I'LL TALK TO MY SPECIALIST.
THE MAN IN THE IRON MASK
THE TONY STARK STORY!

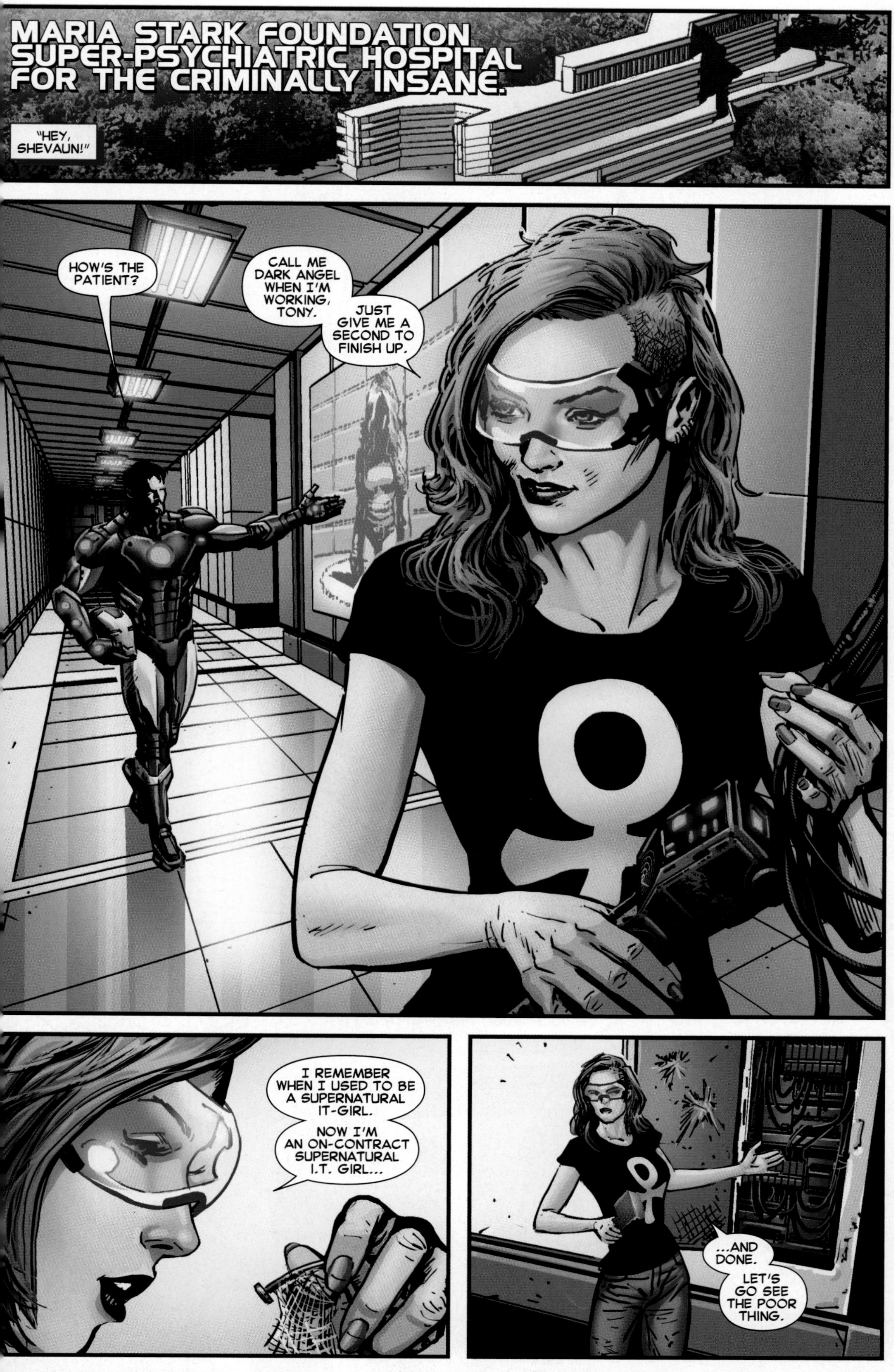
MARIA STARK FOUNDATION
SUPER-PSYCHIATRIC HOSPITAL
FOR THE CRIMINALLY INSANE.
"HEY, SHEVAUN!"
HOW'S THE PATIENT?
CALL ME DARK ANGEL WHEN I'M WORKING, TONY.
JUST GIVE ME A SECOND TO FINISH UP.
I REMEMBER WHEN I USED TO BE A SUPERNATURAL IT-GIRL.
NOW I'M AN ON-CONTRACT SUPERNATURAL I.T. GIRL...
...AND DONE.
LET'S GO SEE THE POOR THING.

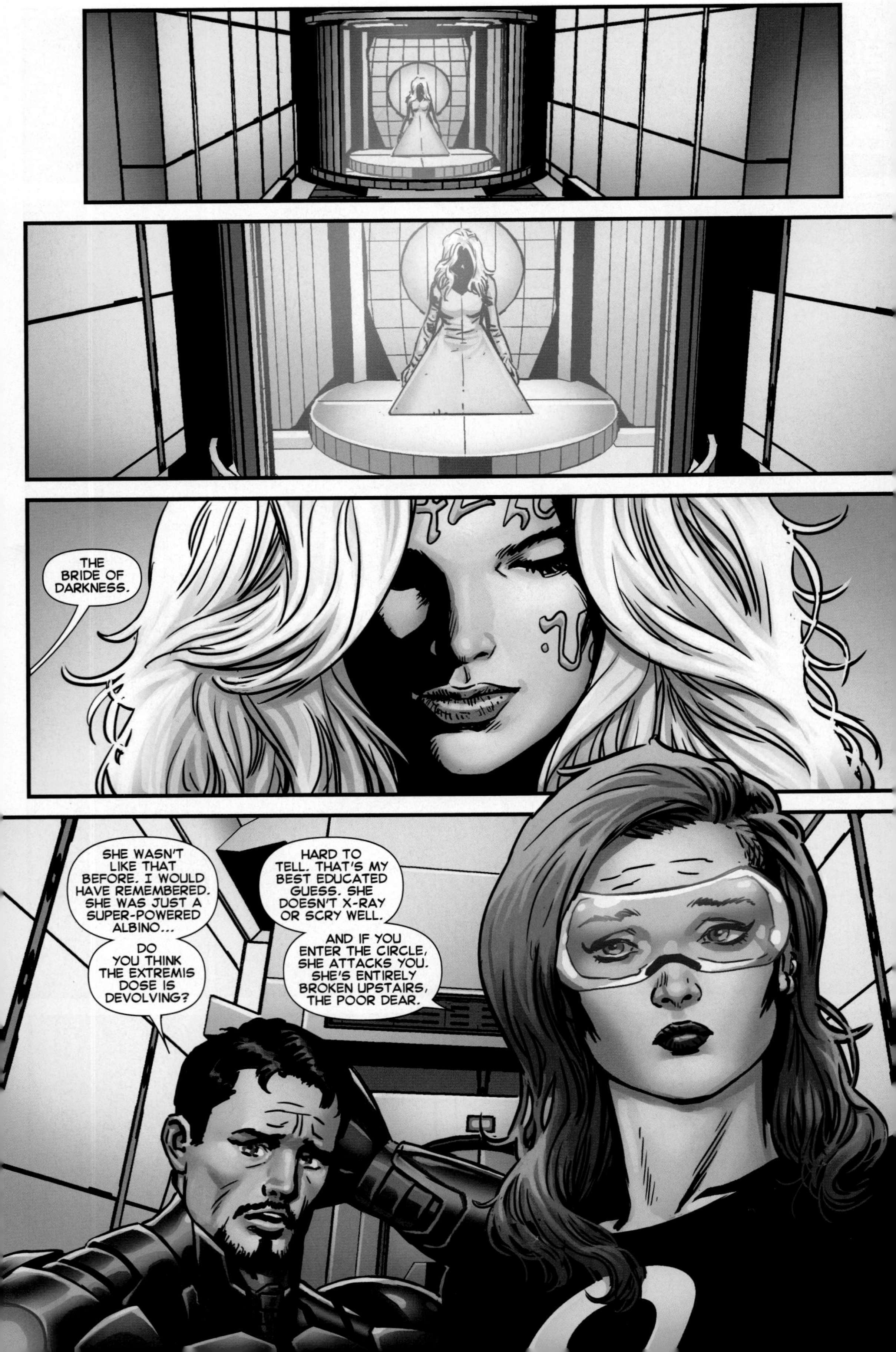
THE BRIDE OF DARKNESS.
SHE WASN'T LIKE THAT BEFORE. I WOULD HAVE REMEMBERED. SHE WAS JUST A SUPER-POWERED ALBINO...
DO YOU THINK THE EXTREMIS DOSE IS DEVOLVING?
HARD TO TELL. THAT'S MY BEST EDUCATED GUESS. SHE DOESN'T X-RAY OR SCRY WELL.
AND IF YOU ENTER THE CIRCLE, SHE ATTACKS YOU. SHE'S ENTIRELY BROKEN UPSTAIRS, THE POOR DEAR.

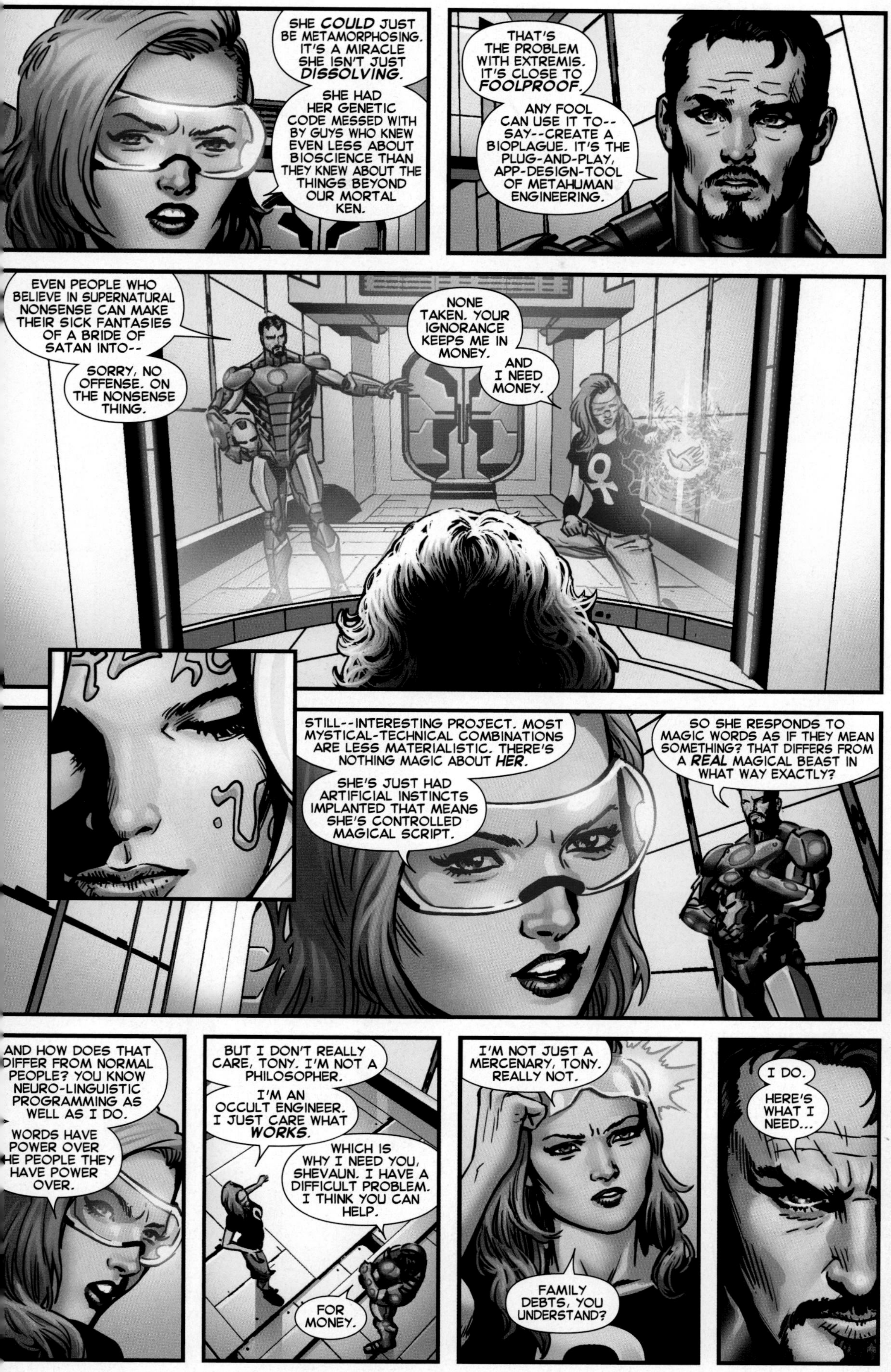
SHE COULD JUST BE METAMORPHOSING. IT'S A MIRACLE SHE ISN'T JUST DISSOLVING.
SHE HAD HER GENETIC CODE MESSED WITH BY GUYS WHO KNEW EVEN LESS ABOUT BIOSCIENCE THAN THEY KNEW ABOUT THE THINGS BEYOND OUR MORTAL KEN.
THAT'S THE PROBLEM WITH EXTREMIS. IT'S CLOSE TO FOOLPROOF.
ANY FOOL CAN USE IT TO--SAY--CREATE A BIOPLAGUE. IT'S THE PLUG-AND-PLAY, APP-DESIGN-TOOL OF METAHUMAN ENGINEERING.
EVEN PEOPLE WHO BELIEVE IN SUPERNATURAL NONSENSE CAN MAKE THEIR SICK FANTASIES OF A BRIDE OF SATAN INTO--
SORRY, NO OFFENSE. ON THE NONSENSE THING.
NONE TAKEN. YOUR IGNORANCE KEEPS ME IN MONEY.
AND I NEED MONEY.
STILL--INTERESTING PROJECT. MOST MYSTICAL-TECHNICAL COMBINATIONS ARE LESS MATERIALISTIC. THERE'S NOTHING MAGIC ABOUT HER.
SHE'S JUST HAD ARTIFICIAL INSTINCTS IMPLANTED THAT MEANS SHE'S CONTROLLED MAGICAL SCRIPT.
SO SHE RESPONDS TO MAGIC WORDS AS IF THEY MEAN SOMETHING? THAT DIFFERS FROM A REAL MAGICAL BEAST IN WHAT WAY EXACTLY?
AND HOW DOES THAT DIFFER FROM NORMAL PEOPLE? YOU KNOW NEURO-LINGUISTIC PROGRAMMING AS WELL AS I DO.
WORDS HAVE POWER OVER THE PEOPLE THEY HAVE POWER OVER.
BUT I DON'T REALLY CARE, TONY. I'M NOT A PHILOSOPHER.
I'M AN OCCULT ENGINEER. I JUST CARE WHAT WORKS.
WHICH IS WHY I NEED YOU, SHEVAUN. I HAVE A DIFFICULT PROBLEM. I THINK YOU CAN HELP.
FOR MONEY.
I'M NOT JUST A MERCENARY, TONY. REALLY NOT.
FAMILY DEBTS, YOU UNDERSTAND?
I DO.
HERE'S WHAT I NEED...

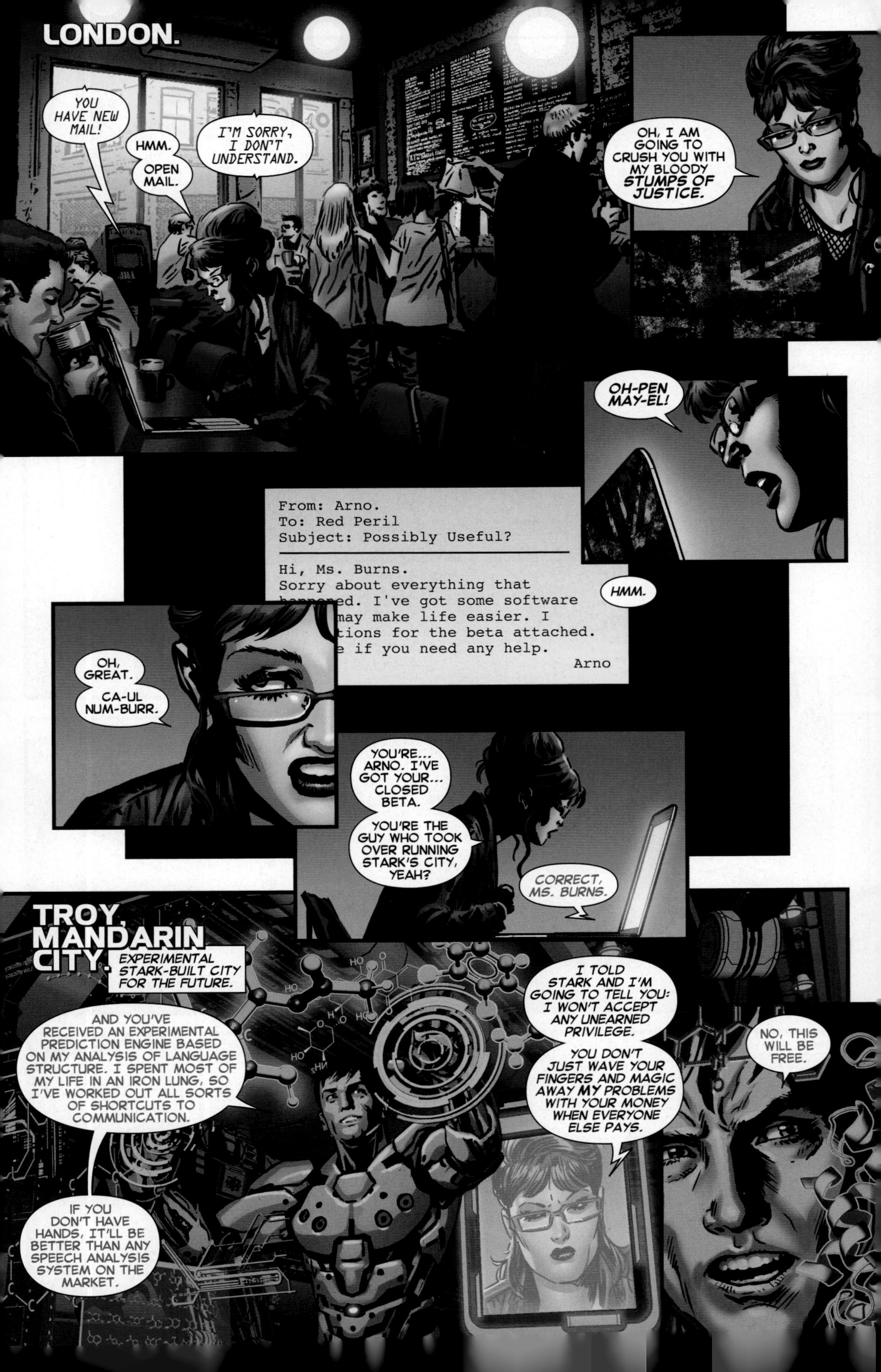
LONDON.
YOU HAVE NEW MAIL!
HMM.
OPEN MAIL.
I'M SORRY, I DON'T UNDERSTAND.
OH, I AM GOING TO CRUSH YOU WITH MY BLOODY STUMPS OF JUSTICE.
OH-PEN MAY-EL!
From: Arno.
To: Red Peril
Subject: Possibly Useful?
Hi, Ms. Burns.
Sorry about everything that
ed. I've got some software
may make life easier. I
tions for the beta attached.
e if you need any help.
Arno
HMM.
OH, GREAT.
CA-UL NUM-BURR.
YOU'RE... ARNO. I'VE GOT YOUR... CLOSED BETA.
YOU'RE THE GUY WHO TOOK OVER RUNNING STARK'S CITY, YEAH?
CORRECT, MS. BURNS.
TROY, MANDARIN CITY.
EXPERIMENTAL STARK-BUILT CITY FOR THE FUTURE.
AND YOU'VE RECEIVED AN EXPERIMENTAL PREDICTION ENGINE BASED ON MY ANALYSIS OF LANGUAGE STRUCTURE. I SPENT MOST OF MY LIFE IN AN IRON LUNG, SO I'VE WORKED OUT ALL SORTS OF SHORTCUTS TO COMMUNICATION.
IF YOU DON'T HAVE HANDS, IT'LL BE BETTER THAN ANY SPEECH ANALYSIS SYSTEM ON THE MARKET.
I TOLD STARK AND I'M GOING TO TELL YOU: I WON'T ACCEPT ANY UNEARNED PRIVILEGE.
YOU DON'T JUST WAVE YOUR FINGERS AND MAGIC AWAY MY PROBLEMS WITH YOUR MONEY WHEN EVERYONE ELSE PAYS.
NO, THIS WILL BE FREE.

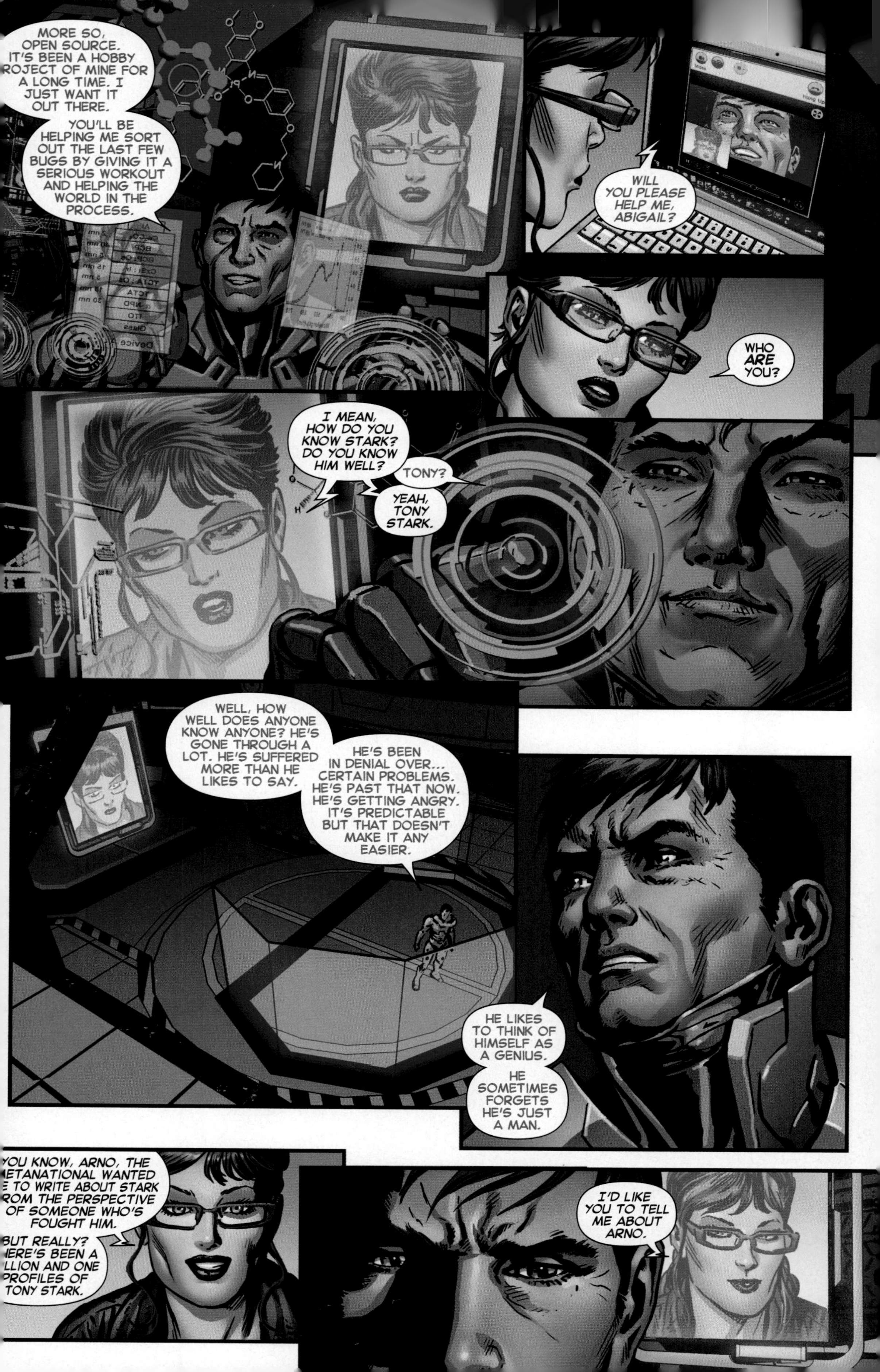
MORE SO, OPEN SOURCE. IT'S BEEN A HOBBY ROJECT OF MINE FOR A LONG TIME. I JUST WANT IT OUT THERE.
YOU'LL BE HELPING ME SORT OUT THE LAST FEW BUGS BY GIVING IT A SERIOUS WORKOUT AND HELPING THE WORLD IN THE PROCESS.
WILL YOU PLEASE HELP ME, ABIGAIL?
WHO ARE YOU?
I MEAN, HOW DO YOU KNOW STARK? DO YOU KNOW HIM WELL?
TONY?
YEAH, TONY STARK.
WELL, HOW WELL DOES ANYONE KNOW ANYONE? HE'S GONE THROUGH A LOT. HE'S SUFFERED MORE THAN HE LIKES TO SAY.
HE'S BEEN IN DENIAL OVER... CERTAIN PROBLEMS. HE'S PAST THAT NOW. HE'S GETTING ANGRY. IT'S PREDICTABLE BUT THAT DOESN'T MAKE IT ANY EASIER.
HE LIKES TO THINK OF HIMSELF AS A GENIUS.
HE SOMETIMES FORGETS HE'S JUST A MAN.
YOU KNOW, ARNO, THE ETANATIONAL WANTED E TO WRITE ABOUT STARK ROM THE PERSPECTIVE OF SOMEONE WHO'S FOUGHT HIM.
BUT REALLY? HERE'S BEEN A LLION AND ONE PROFILES OF TONY STARK.
I'D LIKE YOU TO TELL ME ABOUT ARNO.

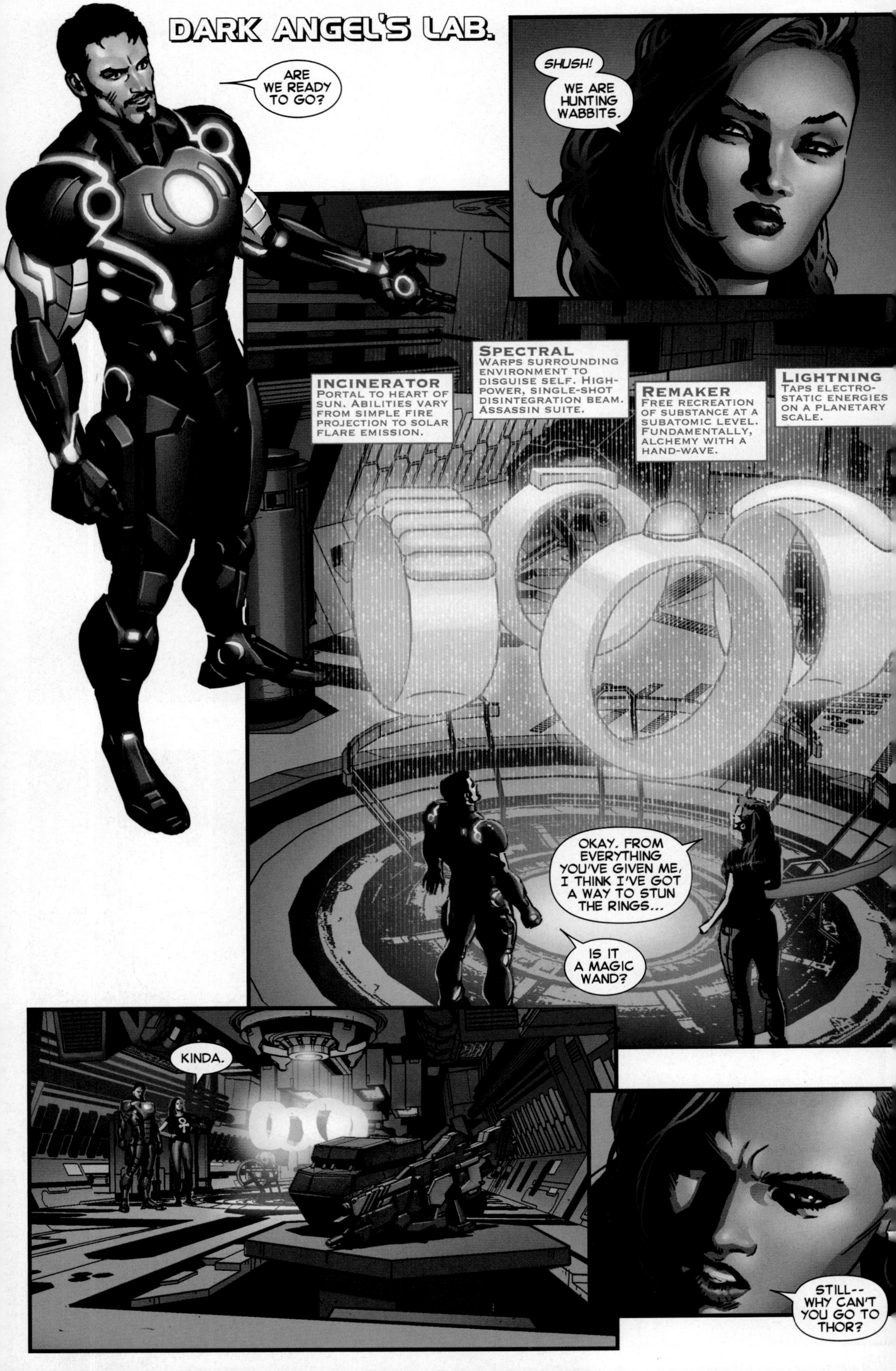
DARK ANGEL'S LAB.
ARE WE READY TO GO?
SHUSH!
WE ARE HUNTING WABBITS.
INCINERATOR Portal to heart of sun. Abilities vary from simple fire projection to solar flare emission.
SPECTRAL Warps surrounding environment to disguise self. High-power, single-shot disintegration beam. Assassin suite.
REMAKER Free recreation of substance at a subatomic level. Fundamentally, alchemy with a hand-wave.
LIGHTNING Taps electro-static energies on a planetary scale.
OKAY. FROM EVERYTHING YOU'VE GIVEN ME, I THINK I'VE GOT A WAY TO STUN THE RINGS...
IS IT A MAGIC WAND?
KINDA.
STILL-- WHY CAN'T YOU GO TO THOR?

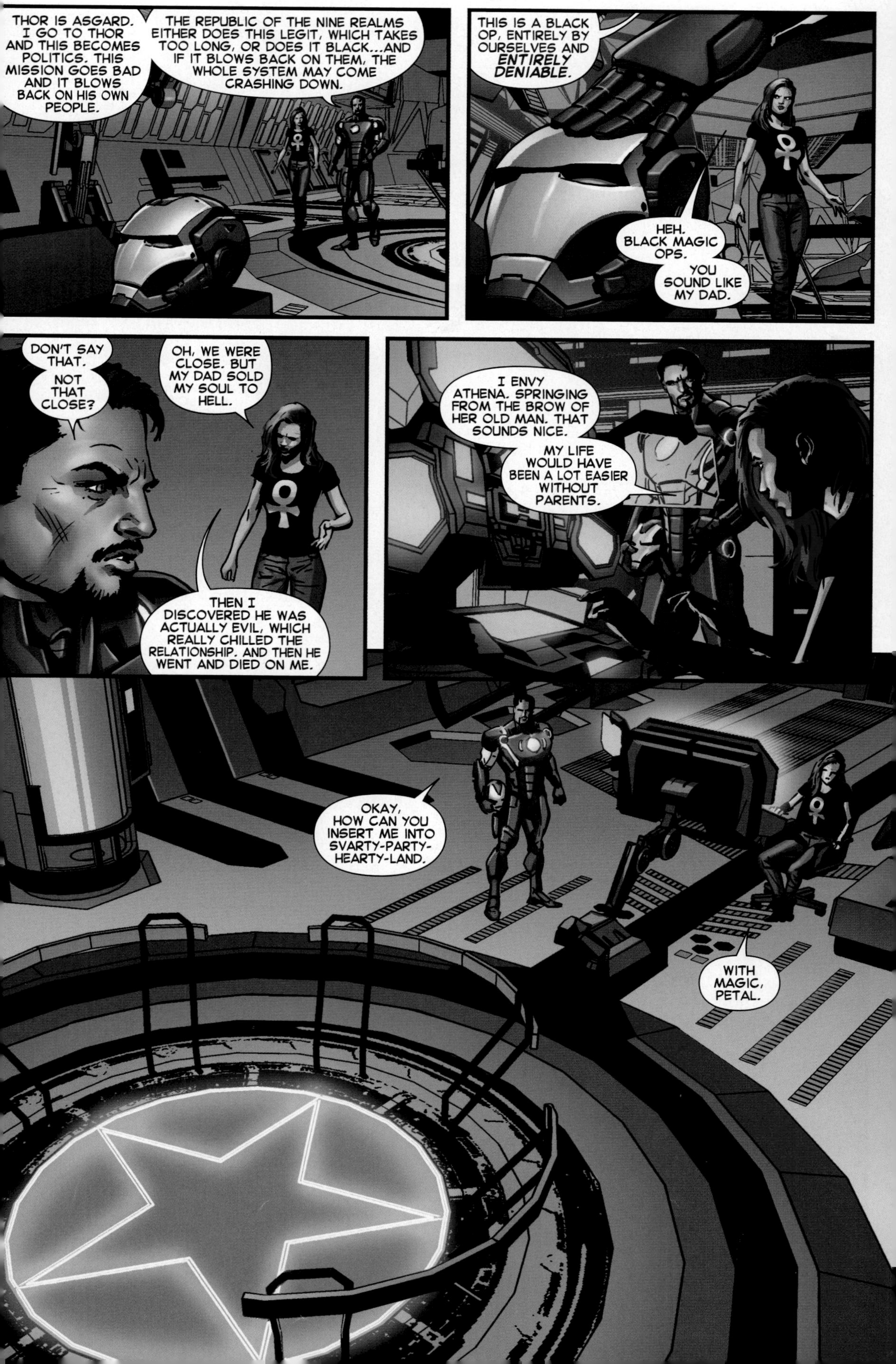
THOR IS ASGARD. I GO TO THOR AND THIS BECOMES POLITICS. THIS MISSION GOES BAD AND IT BLOWS BACK ON HIS OWN PEOPLE.
THE REPUBLIC OF THE NINE REALMS EITHER DOES THIS LEGIT, WHICH TAKES TOO LONG, OR DOES IT BLACK...AND IF IT BLOWS BACK ON THEM, THE WHOLE SYSTEM MAY COME CRASHING DOWN.
THIS IS A BLACK OP, ENTIRELY BY OURSELVES AND *ENTIRELY DENIABLE.*
HEH. BLACK MAGIC OPS.
YOU SOUND LIKE MY DAD.
DON'T SAY THAT.
NOT THAT CLOSE?
OH, WE WERE CLOSE. BUT MY DAD SOLD MY SOUL TO HELL.
THEN I DISCOVERED HE WAS ACTUALLY EVIL, WHICH REALLY CHILLED THE RELATIONSHIP. AND THEN HE WENT AND DIED ON ME.
I ENVY ATHENA. SPRINGING FROM THE BROW OF HER OLD MAN. THAT SOUNDS NICE.
MY LIFE WOULD HAVE BEEN A LOT EASIER WITHOUT PARENTS.
OKAY, HOW CAN YOU INSERT ME INTO SVARTY-PARTY-HEARTY-LAND.
WITH MAGIC, PETAL.

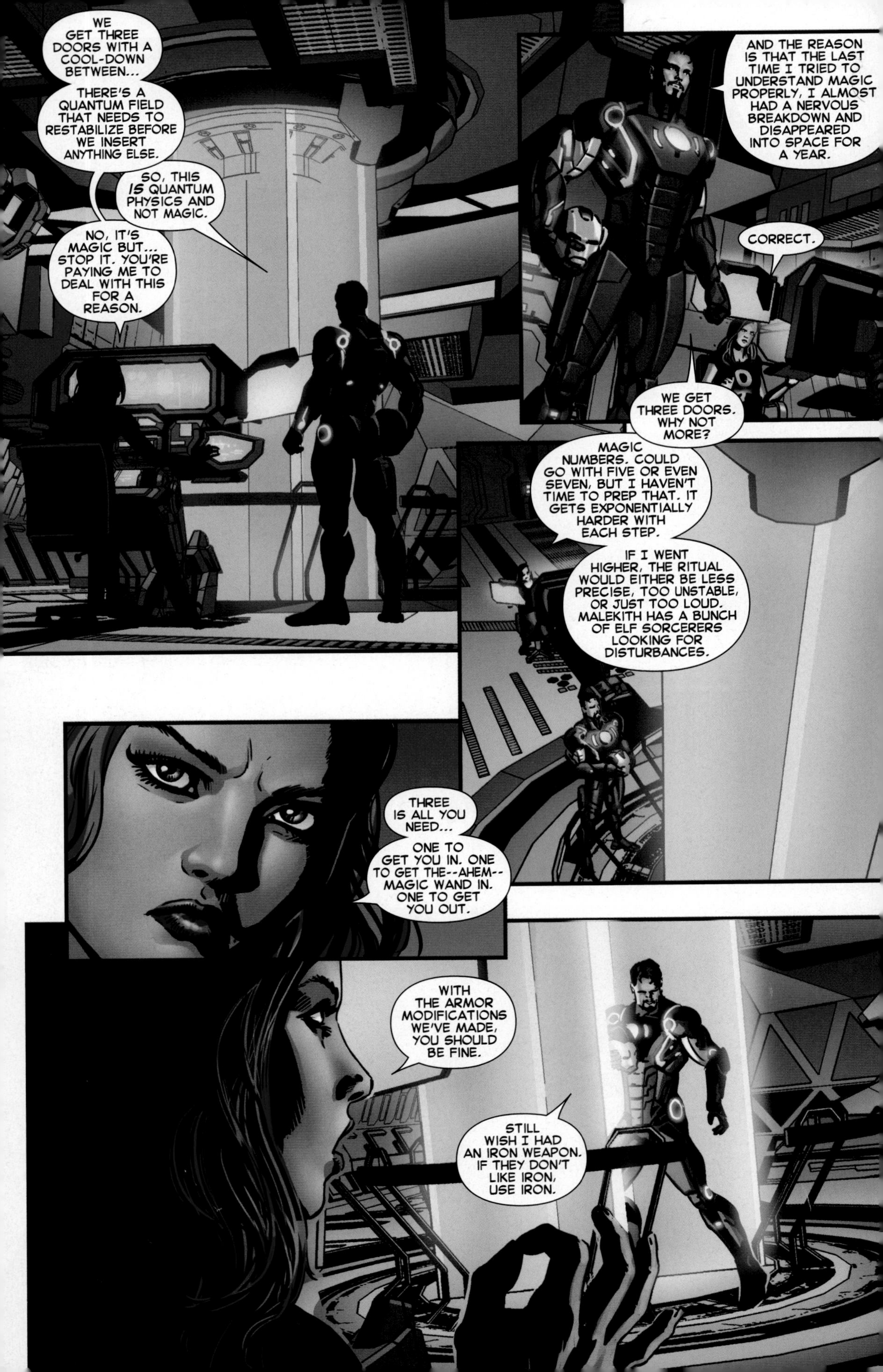
WE GET THREE DOORS WITH A COOL-DOWN BETWEEN...
THERE'S A QUANTUM FIELD THAT NEEDS TO RESTABILIZE BEFORE WE INSERT ANYTHING ELSE.
SO, THIS *IS* QUANTUM PHYSICS AND NOT MAGIC.
NO, IT'S MAGIC BUT... STOP IT. YOU'RE PAYING ME TO DEAL WITH THIS FOR A REASON.
AND THE REASON IS THAT THE LAST TIME I TRIED TO UNDERSTAND MAGIC PROPERLY, I ALMOST HAD A NERVOUS BREAKDOWN AND DISAPPEARED INTO SPACE FOR A YEAR.
CORRECT.
WE GET THREE DOORS. WHY NOT MORE?
MAGIC NUMBERS. COULD GO WITH FIVE OR EVEN SEVEN, BUT I HAVEN'T TIME TO PREP THAT. IT GETS EXPONENTIALLY HARDER WITH EACH STEP.
IF I WENT HIGHER, THE RITUAL WOULD EITHER BE LESS PRECISE, TOO UNSTABLE, OR JUST TOO LOUD. MALEKITH HAS A BUNCH OF ELF SORCERERS LOOKING FOR DISTURBANCES.
THREE IS ALL YOU NEED...
ONE TO GET YOU IN. ONE TO GET THE--AHEM--MAGIC WAND IN. ONE TO GET YOU OUT.
WITH THE ARMOR MODIFICATIONS WE'VE MADE, YOU SHOULD BE FINE.
STILL WISH I HAD AN IRON WEAPON. IF THEY DON'T LIKE IRON, USE IRON.

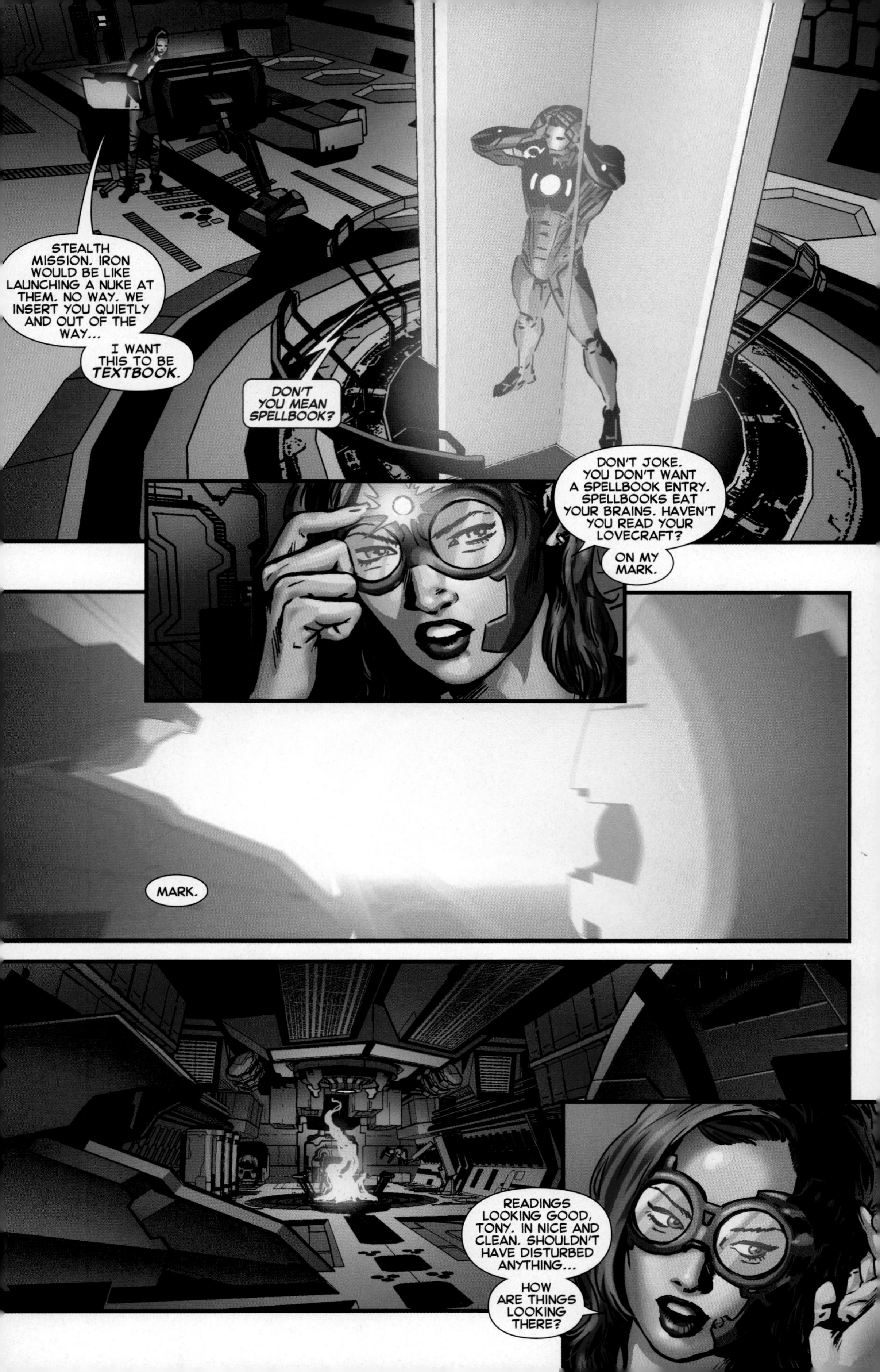
STEALTH MISSION. IRON WOULD BE LIKE LAUNCHING A NUKE AT THEM. NO WAY. WE INSERT YOU QUIETLY AND OUT OF THE WAY...
I WANT THIS TO BE *TEXTBOOK*.
DON'T YOU MEAN SPELLBOOK?
DON'T JOKE. YOU DON'T WANT A SPELLBOOK ENTRY. SPELLBOOKS EAT YOUR BRAINS. HAVEN'T YOU READ YOUR LOVECRAFT?
ON MY MARK.
MARK.
READINGS LOOKING GOOD, TONY. IN NICE AND CLEAN. SHOULDN'T HAVE DISTURBED ANYTHING...
HOW ARE THINGS LOOKING THERE?

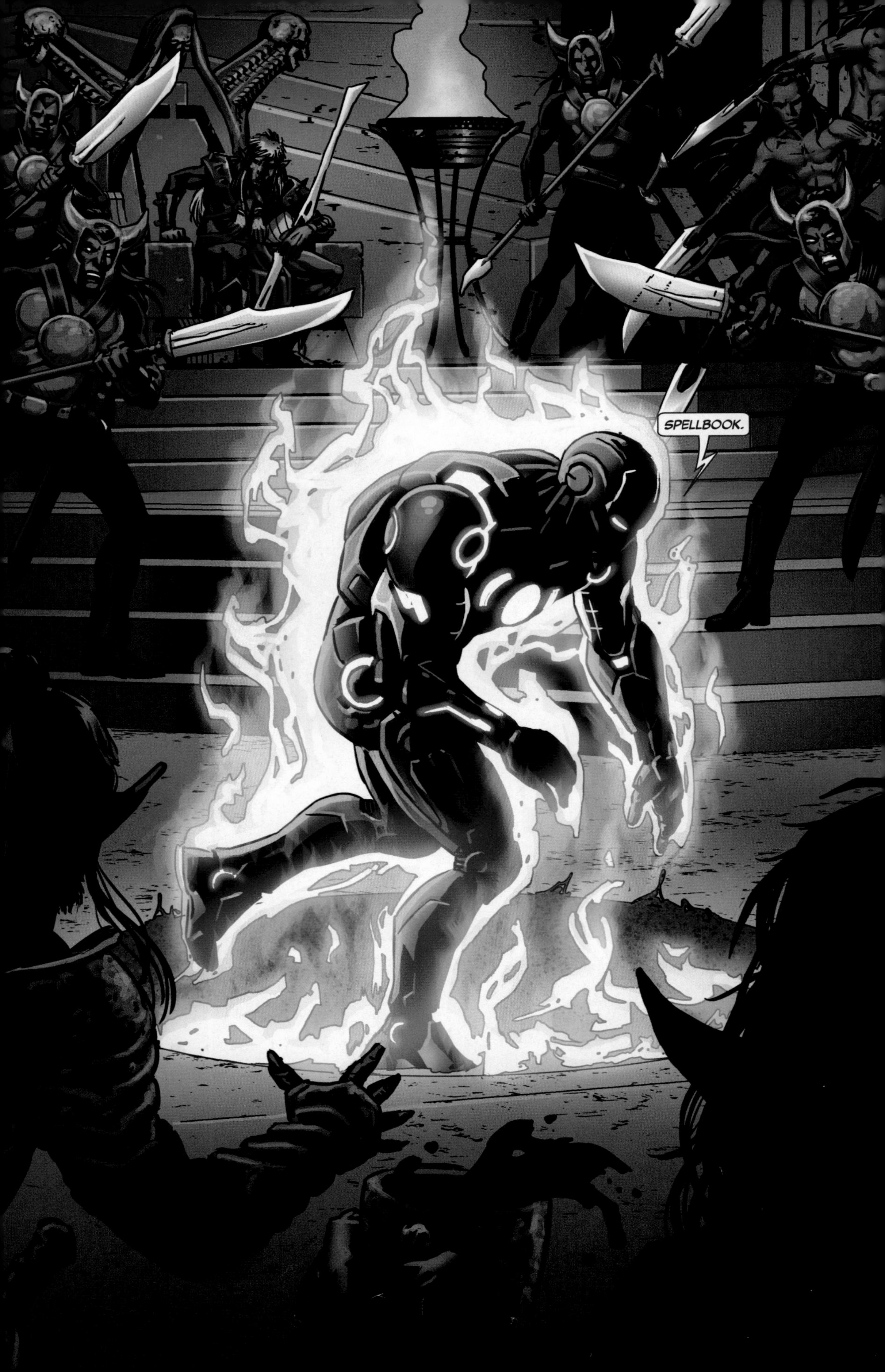
SPELLBOOK.

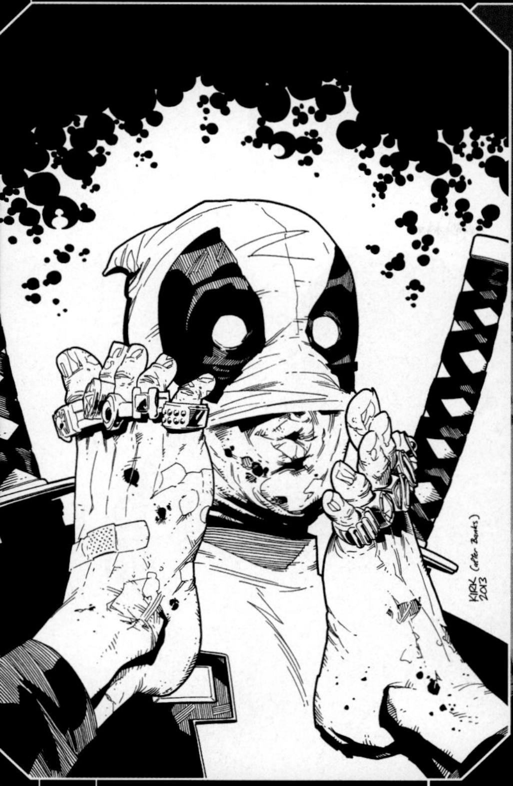
KIRK (after Banks)
2013

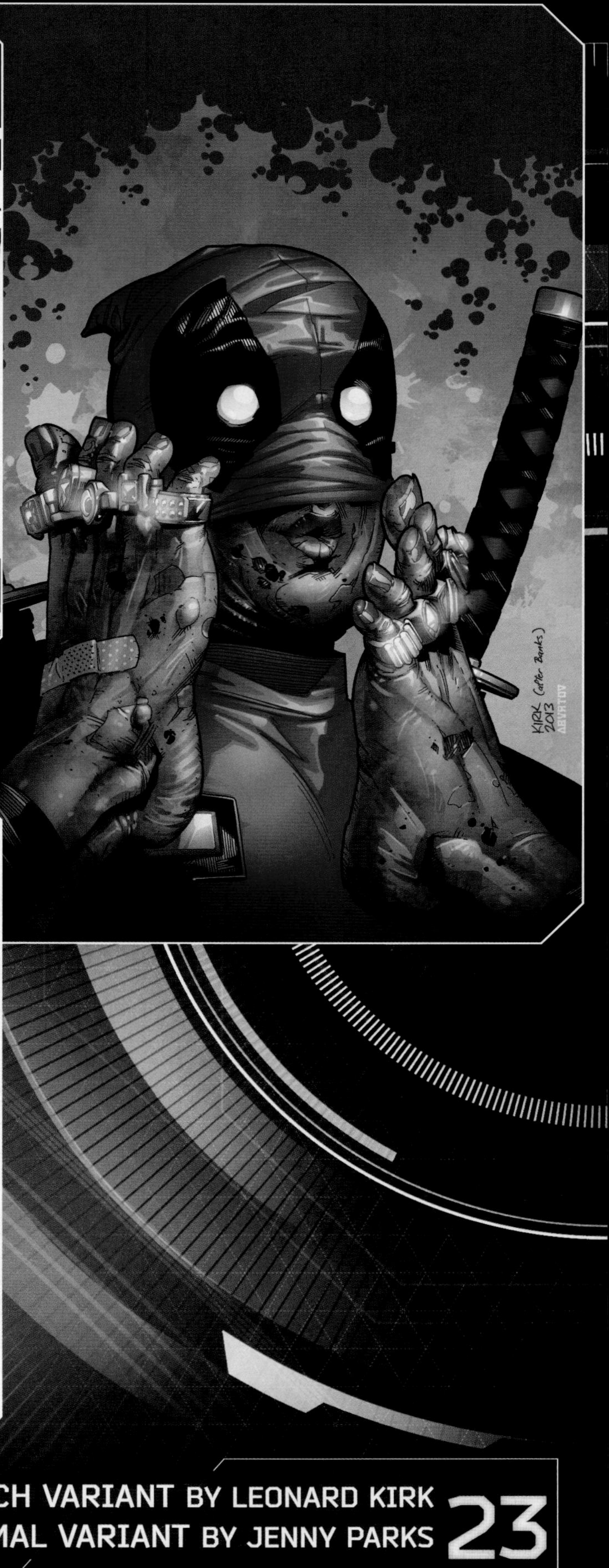
KIRK (after Banks)
2013

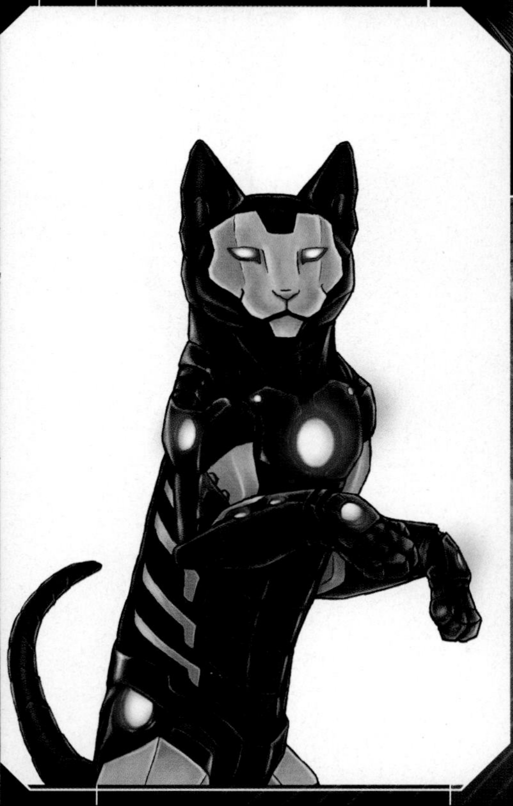

EADPOOL & DEADPOOL SKETCH VARIANT BY LEONARD KIRK
& ANIMAL VARIANT BY JENNY PARKS

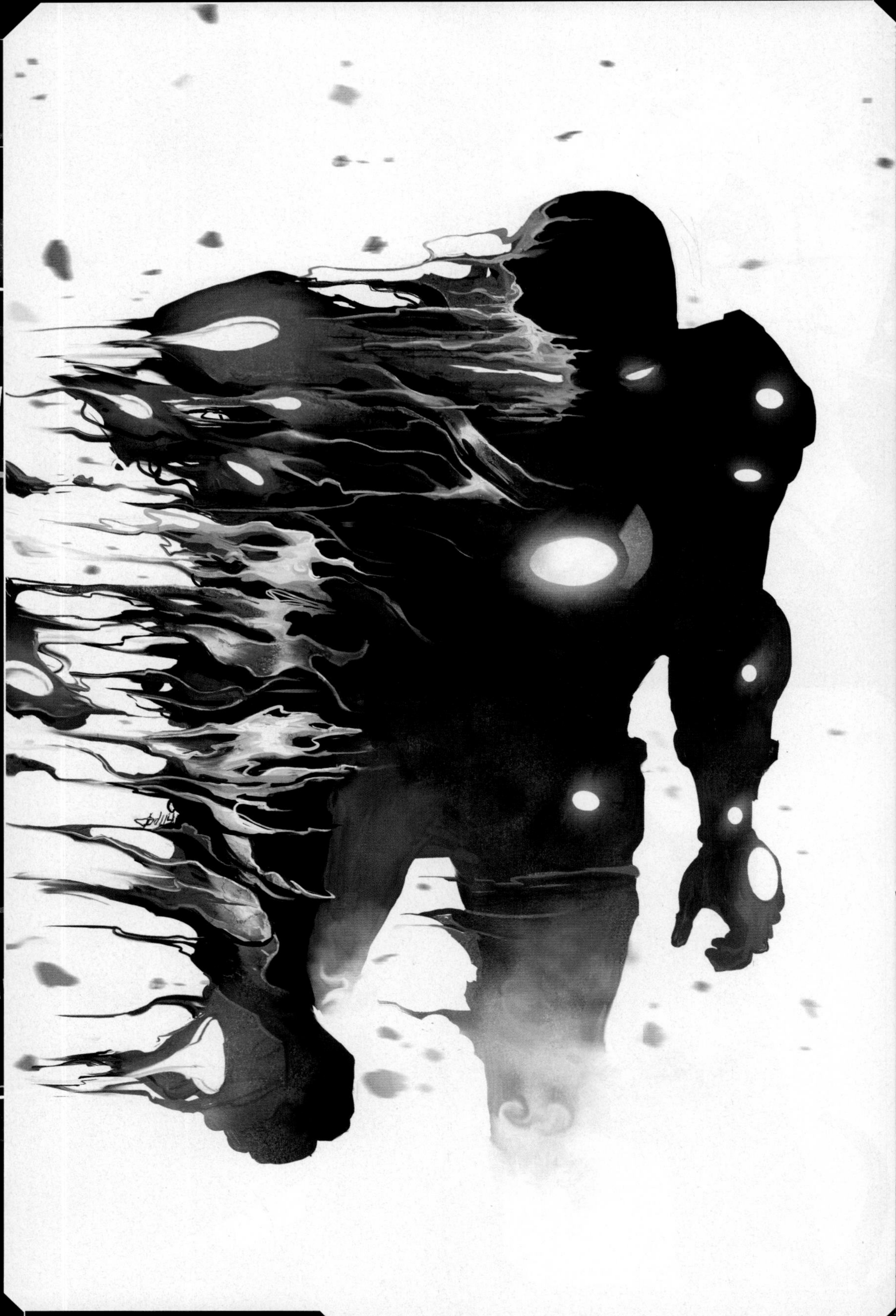

24 RINGS OF THE MANDARIN CHAPTER 2

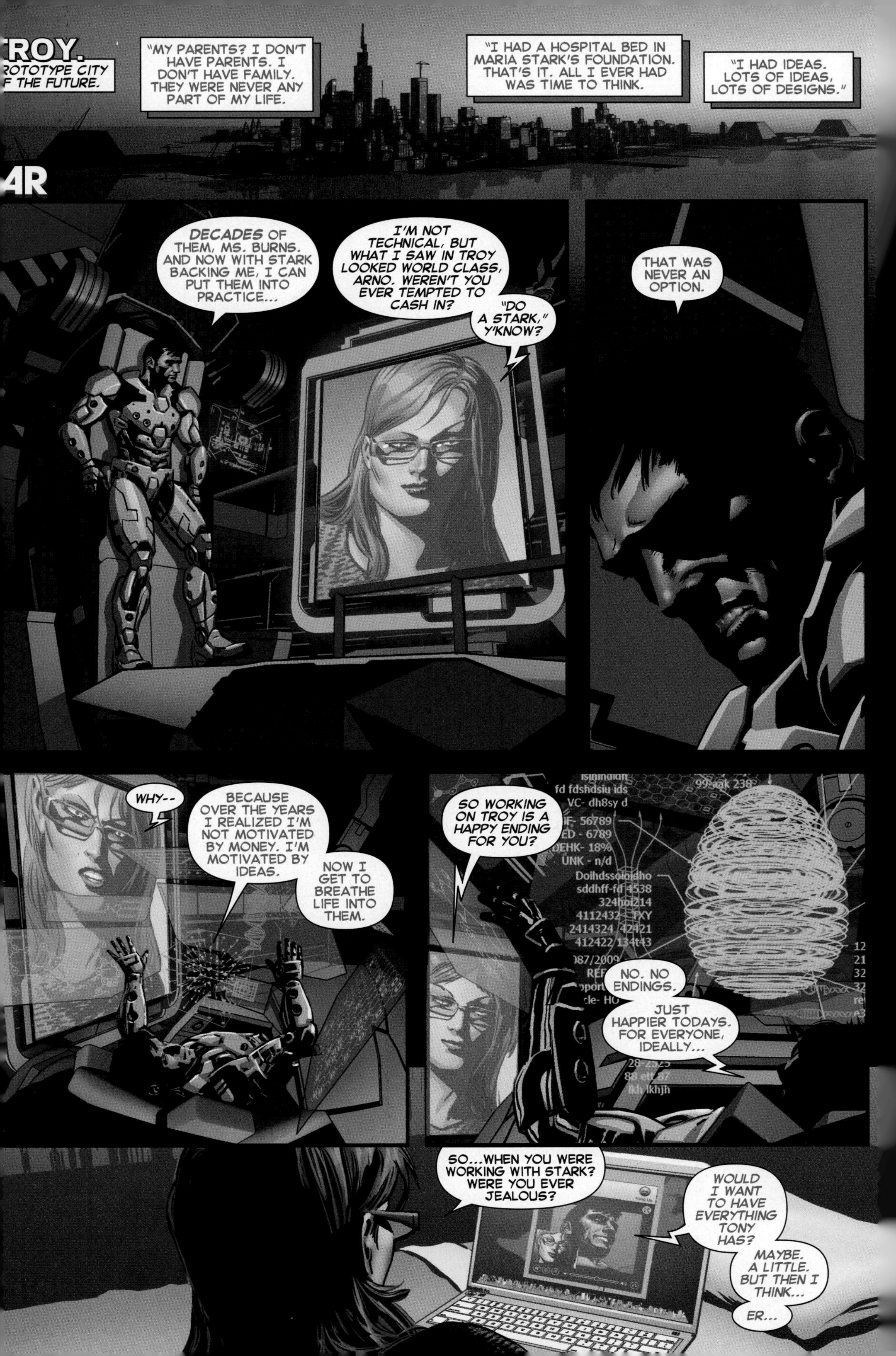
ROY.
ROTOTYPE CITY
F THE FUTURE.
"MY PARENTS? I DON'T HAVE PARENTS. I DON'T HAVE FAMILY. THEY WERE NEVER ANY PART OF MY LIFE.
"I HAD A HOSPITAL BED IN MARIA STARK'S FOUNDATION. THAT'S IT. ALL I EVER HAD WAS TIME TO THINK.
"I HAD IDEAS. LOTS OF IDEAS, LOTS OF DESIGNS."
DECADES OF THEM, MS. BURNS. AND NOW WITH STARK BACKING ME, I CAN PUT THEM INTO PRACTICE...
I'M NOT TECHNICAL, BUT WHAT I SAW IN TROY LOOKED WORLD CLASS, ARNO. WEREN'T YOU EVER TEMPTED TO CASH IN?
"DO A STARK," Y'KNOW?
THAT WAS NEVER AN OPTION.
WHY--
BECAUSE OVER THE YEARS I REALIZED I'M NOT MOTIVATED BY MONEY. I'M MOTIVATED BY IDEAS.
NOW I GET TO BREATHE LIFE INTO THEM.
SO WORKING ON TROY IS A HAPPY ENDING FOR YOU?
NO. NO ENDINGS.
JUST HAPPIER TODAYS. FOR EVERYONE, IDEALLY...
SO...WHEN YOU WERE WORKING WITH STARK? WERE YOU EVER JEALOUS?
WOULD I WANT TO HAVE EVERYTHING TONY HAS?
MAYBE. A LITTLE. BUT THEN I THINK...
ER...

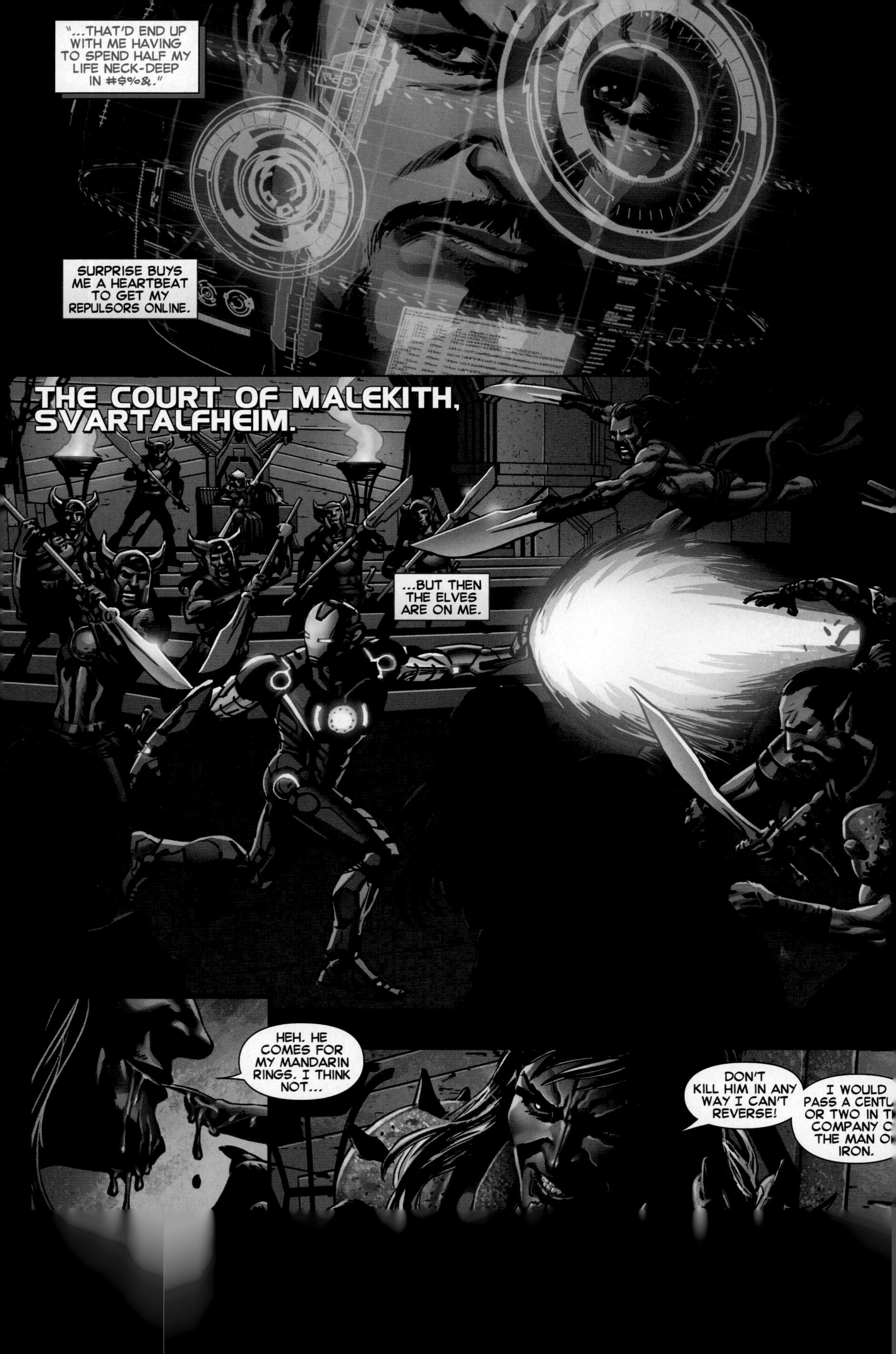
"...THAT'D END UP WITH ME HAVING TO SPEND HALF MY LIFE NECK-DEEP IN #$%&."
SURPRISE BUYS ME A HEARTBEAT TO GET MY REPULSORS ONLINE.
THE COURT OF MALEKITH, SVARTALFHEIM.
...BUT THEN THE ELVES ARE ON ME.
HEH. HE COMES FOR MY MANDARIN RINGS. I THINK NOT...
DON'T KILL HIM IN ANY WAY I CAN'T REVERSE!
I WOULD PASS A CENTL OR TWO IN T COMPANY O THE MAN O IRON.

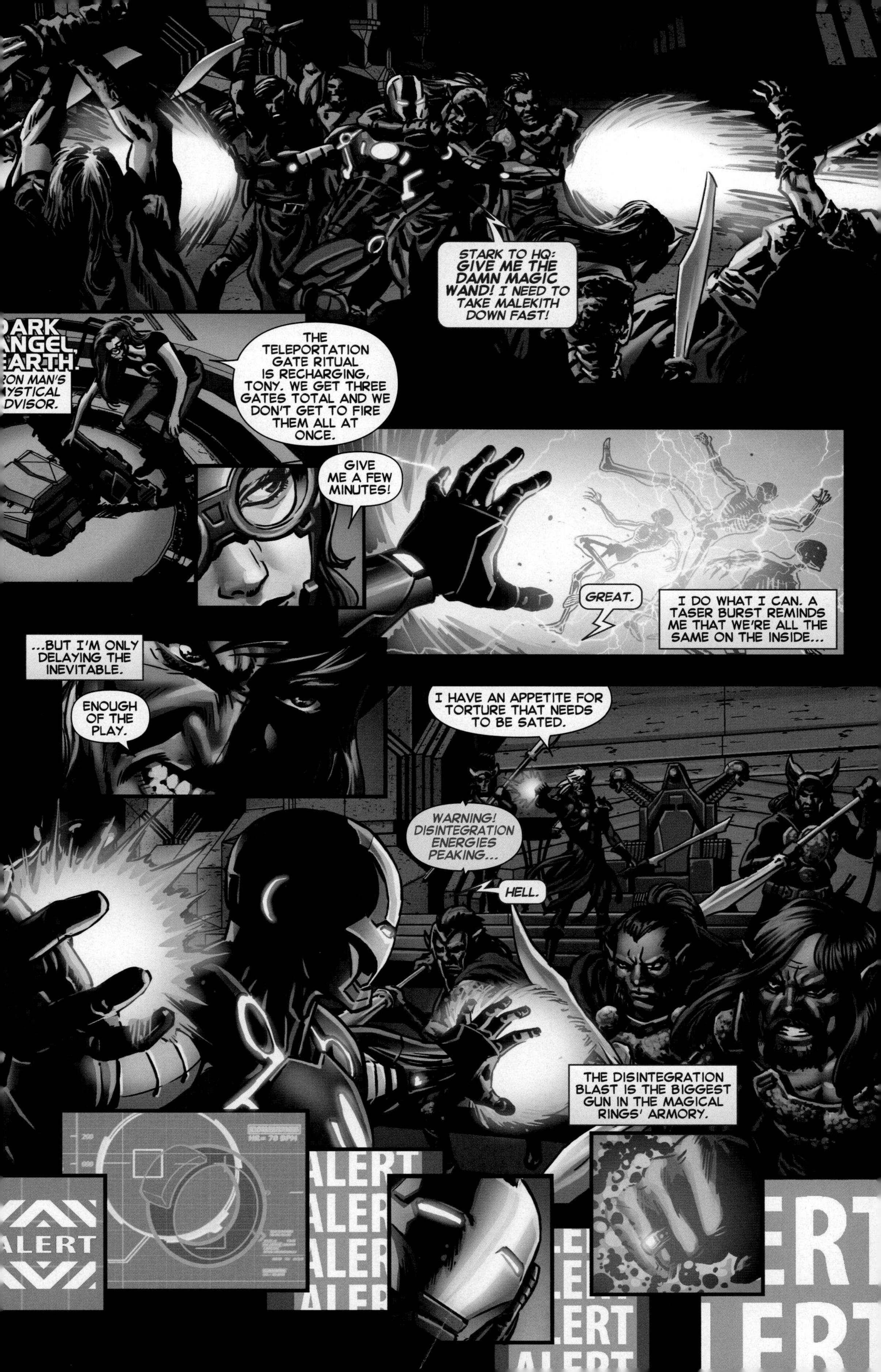
STARK TO HQ: GIVE ME THE DAMN MAGIC WAND! I NEED TO TAKE MALEKITH DOWN FAST!
ARK ANGEL, EARTH. RON MAN'S YSTICAL DVISOR.
THE TELEPORTATION GATE RITUAL IS RECHARGING, TONY. WE GET THREE GATES TOTAL AND WE DON'T GET TO FIRE THEM ALL AT ONCE.
GIVE ME A FEW MINUTES!
GREAT.
I DO WHAT I CAN. A TASER BURST REMINDS ME THAT WE'RE ALL THE SAME ON THE INSIDE...
...BUT I'M ONLY DELAYING THE INEVITABLE.
ENOUGH OF THE PLAY.
I HAVE AN APPETITE FOR TORTURE THAT NEEDS TO BE SATED.
WARNING! DISINTEGRATION ENERGIES PEAKING...
HELL.
THE DISINTEGRATION BLAST IS THE BIGGEST GUN IN THE MAGICAL RINGS' ARMORY.
ALERT
ALERT
ALERT
ALERT
ALERT

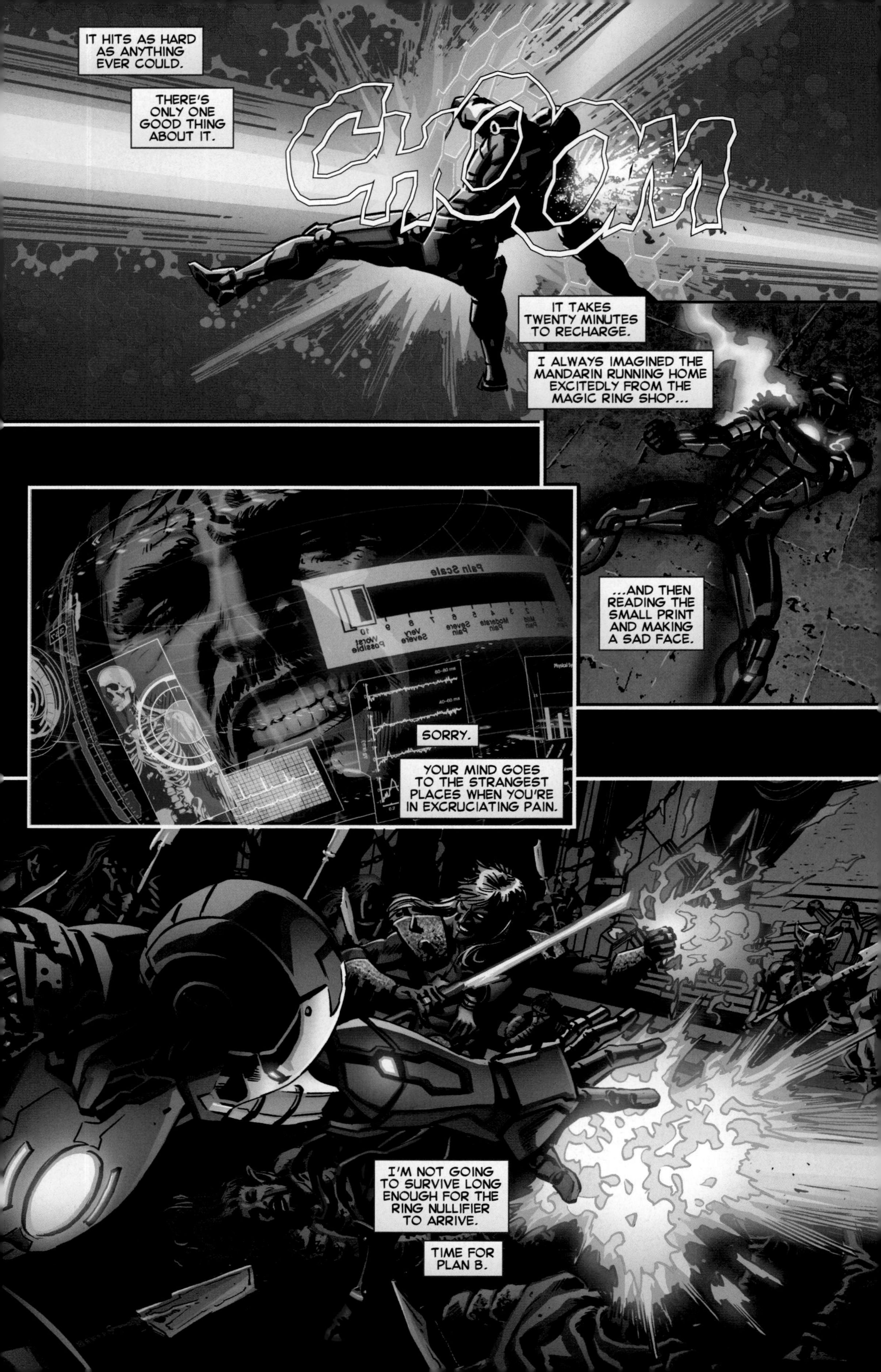
IT HITS AS HARD AS ANYTHING EVER COULD.
THERE'S ONLY ONE GOOD THING ABOUT IT.
CHOOM
IT TAKES TWENTY MINUTES TO RECHARGE.
I ALWAYS IMAGINED THE MANDARIN RUNNING HOME EXCITEDLY FROM THE MAGIC RING SHOP...
...AND THEN READING THE SMALL PRINT AND MAKING A SAD FACE.
SORRY.
YOUR MIND GOES TO THE STRANGEST PLACES WHEN YOU'RE IN EXCRUCIATING PAIN.
I'M NOT GOING TO SURVIVE LONG ENOUGH FOR THE RING NULLIFIER TO ARRIVE.
TIME FOR PLAN B.

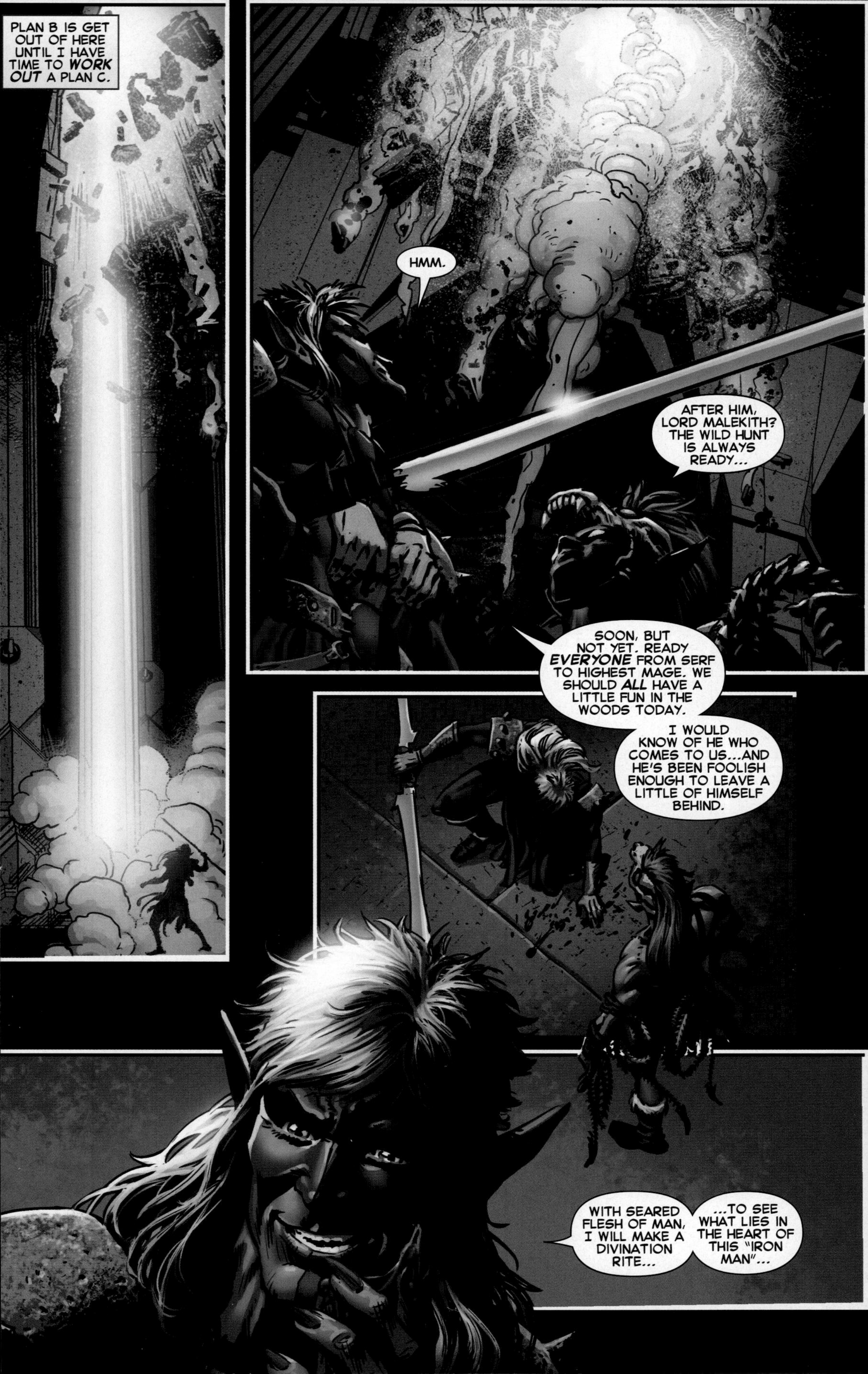
PLAN B IS GET OUT OF HERE UNTIL I HAVE TIME TO WORK OUT A PLAN C.
HMM.
AFTER HIM, LORD MALEKITH? THE WILD HUNT IS ALWAYS READY...
SOON, BUT NOT YET. READY EVERYONE FROM SERF TO HIGHEST MAGE. WE SHOULD ALL HAVE A LITTLE FUN IN THE WOODS TODAY.
I WOULD KNOW OF HE WHO COMES TO US...AND HE'S BEEN FOOLISH ENOUGH TO LEAVE A LITTLE OF HIMSELF BEHIND.
WITH SEARED FLESH OF MAN, I WILL MAKE A DIVINATION RITE...
...TO SEE WHAT LIES IN THE HEART OF THIS "IRON MAN"...

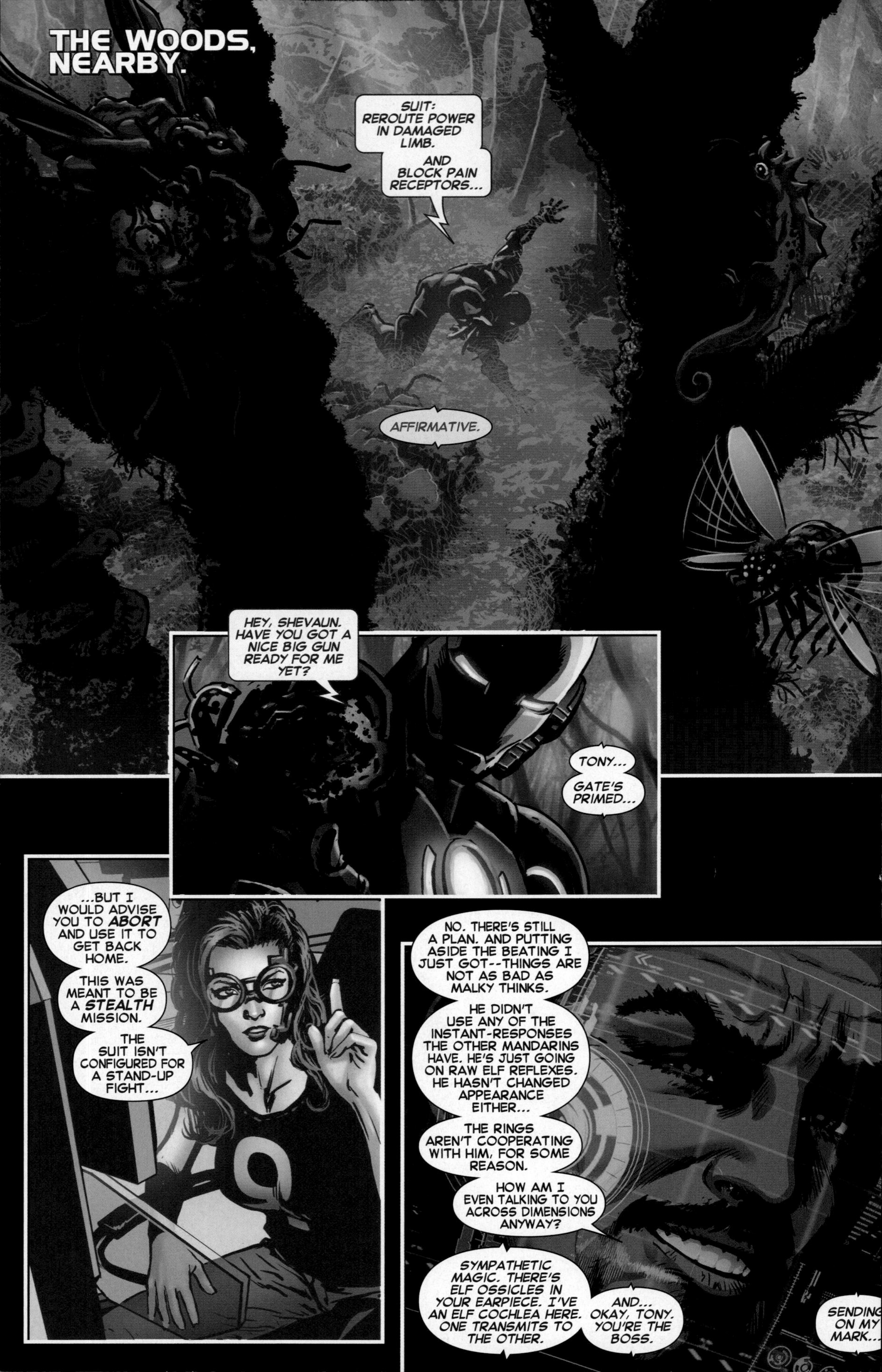
THE WOODS, NEARBY.
SUIT: REROUTE POWER IN DAMAGED LIMB.
AND BLOCK PAIN RECEPTORS...
AFFIRMATIVE.
HEY, SHEVAUN. HAVE YOU GOT A NICE BIG GUN READY FOR ME YET?
TONY...
GATE'S PRIMED...
...BUT I WOULD ADVISE YOU TO ABORT AND USE IT TO GET BACK HOME.
THIS WAS MEANT TO BE A STEALTH MISSION.
THE SUIT ISN'T CONFIGURED FOR A STAND-UP FIGHT...
NO. THERE'S STILL A PLAN. AND PUTTING ASIDE THE BEATING I JUST GOT--THINGS ARE NOT AS BAD AS MALKY THINKS.
HE DIDN'T USE ANY OF THE INSTANT-RESPONSES THE OTHER MANDARINS HAVE. HE'S JUST GOING ON RAW ELF REFLEXES. HE HASN'T CHANGED APPEARANCE EITHER...
THE RINGS AREN'T COOPERATING WITH HIM, FOR SOME REASON.
HOW AM I EVEN TALKING TO YOU ACROSS DIMENSIONS ANYWAY?
SYMPATHETIC MAGIC. THERE'S ELF OSSICLES IN YOUR EARPIECE. I'VE AN ELF COCHLEA HERE. ONE TRANSMITS TO THE OTHER.
AND... OKAY, TONY. YOU'RE THE BOSS.
SENDING ON MY MARK...

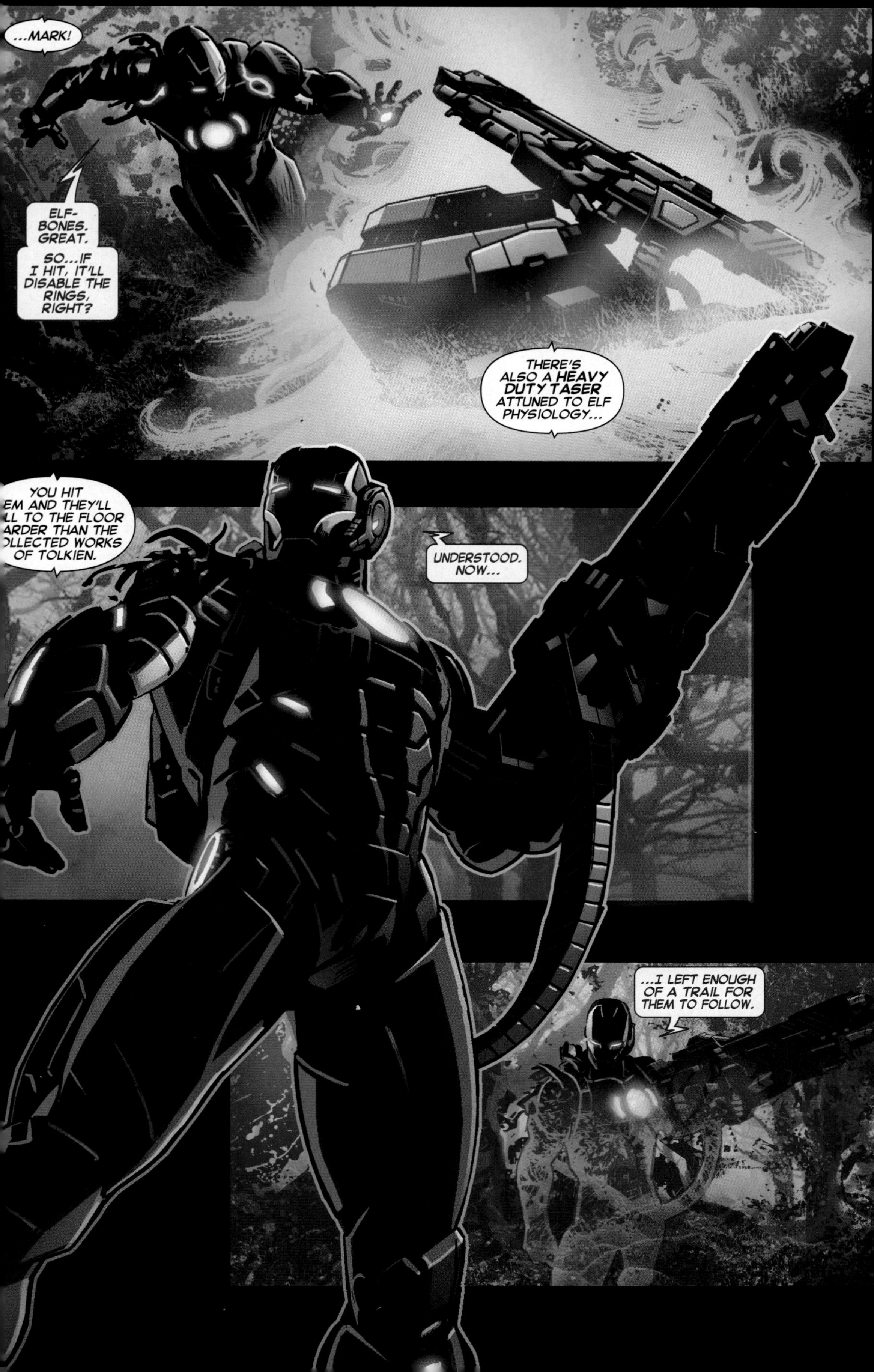
...MARK!
ELF-BONES. GREAT.
SO...IF I HIT, IT'LL DISABLE THE RINGS, RIGHT?
THERE'S ALSO A **HEAVY DUTY TASER** ATTUNED TO ELF PHYSIOLOGY...
YOU HIT EM AND THEY'LL LL TO THE FLOOR ARDER THAN THE OLLECTED WORKS OF TOLKIEN.
UNDERSTOOD. NOW...
...I LEFT ENOUGH OF A TRAIL FOR THEM TO FOLLOW.

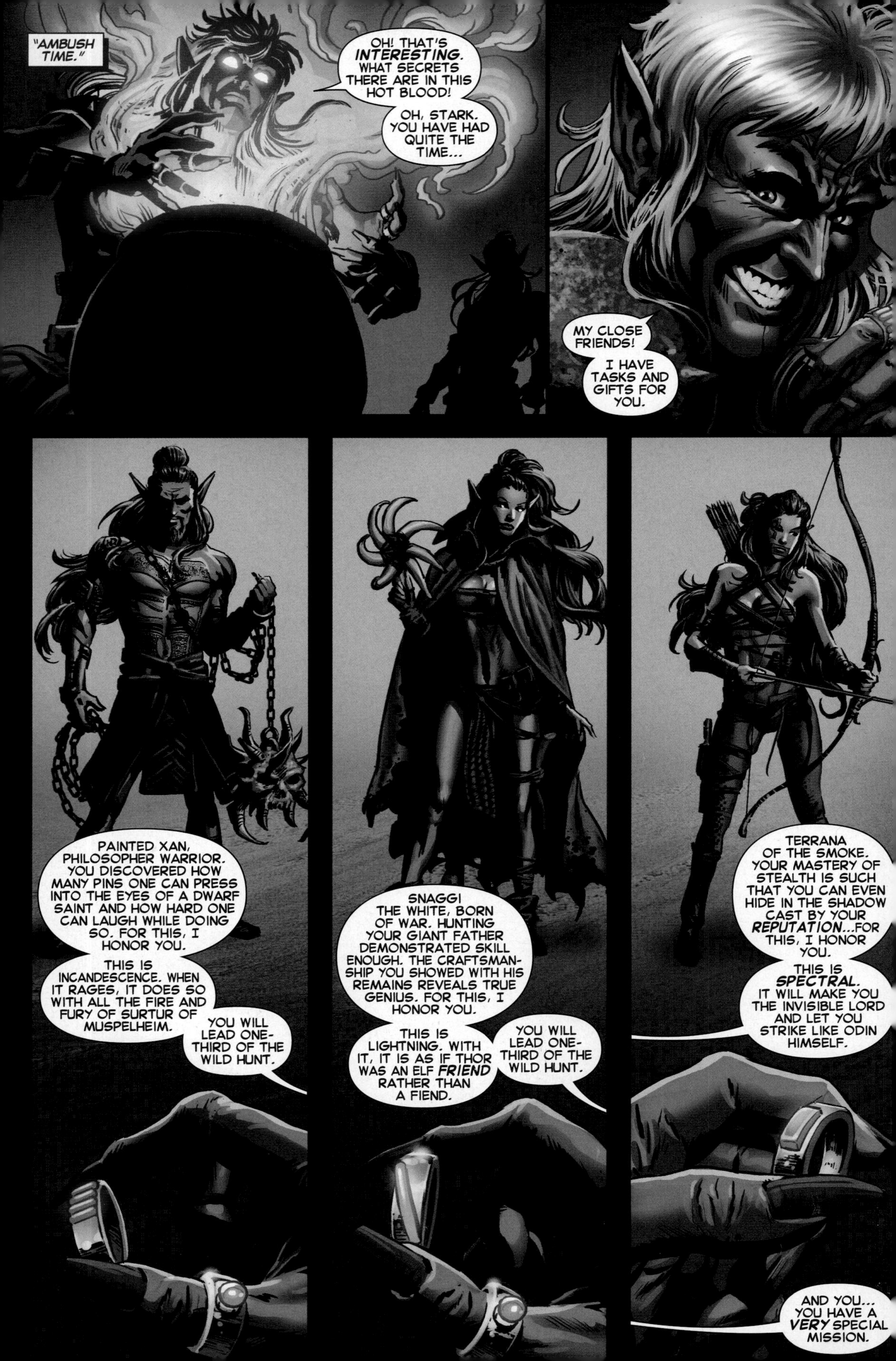
"AMBUSH TIME."
OH! THAT'S *INTERESTING.* WHAT SECRETS THERE ARE IN THIS HOT BLOOD!
OH, STARK. YOU HAVE HAD QUITE THE TIME...
MY CLOSE FRIENDS!
I HAVE TASKS AND GIFTS FOR YOU.
PAINTED XAN, PHILOSOPHER WARRIOR. YOU DISCOVERED HOW MANY PINS ONE CAN PRESS INTO THE EYES OF A DWARF SAINT AND HOW HARD ONE CAN LAUGH WHILE DOING SO. FOR THIS, I HONOR YOU.
THIS IS INCANDESCENCE. WHEN IT RAGES, IT DOES SO WITH ALL THE FIRE AND FURY OF SURTUR OF MUSPELHEIM.
YOU WILL LEAD ONE-THIRD OF THE WILD HUNT.
SNAGGI THE WHITE, BORN OF WAR. HUNTING YOUR GIANT FATHER DEMONSTRATED SKILL ENOUGH. THE CRAFTSMANSHIP YOU SHOWED WITH HIS REMAINS REVEALS TRUE GENIUS. FOR THIS, I HONOR YOU.
THIS IS LIGHTNING. WITH IT, IT IS AS IF THOR WAS AN ELF *FRIEND* RATHER THAN A FIEND.
YOU WILL LEAD ONE-THIRD OF THE WILD HUNT.
TERRANA OF THE SMOKE. YOUR MASTERY OF STEALTH IS SUCH THAT YOU CAN EVEN HIDE IN THE SHADOW CAST BY YOUR *REPUTATION*...FOR THIS, I HONOR YOU.
THIS IS *SPECTRAL.* IT WILL MAKE YOU THE INVISIBLE LORD AND LET YOU STRIKE LIKE ODIN HIMSELF.
AND YOU... YOU HAVE A *VERY* SPECIAL MISSION.

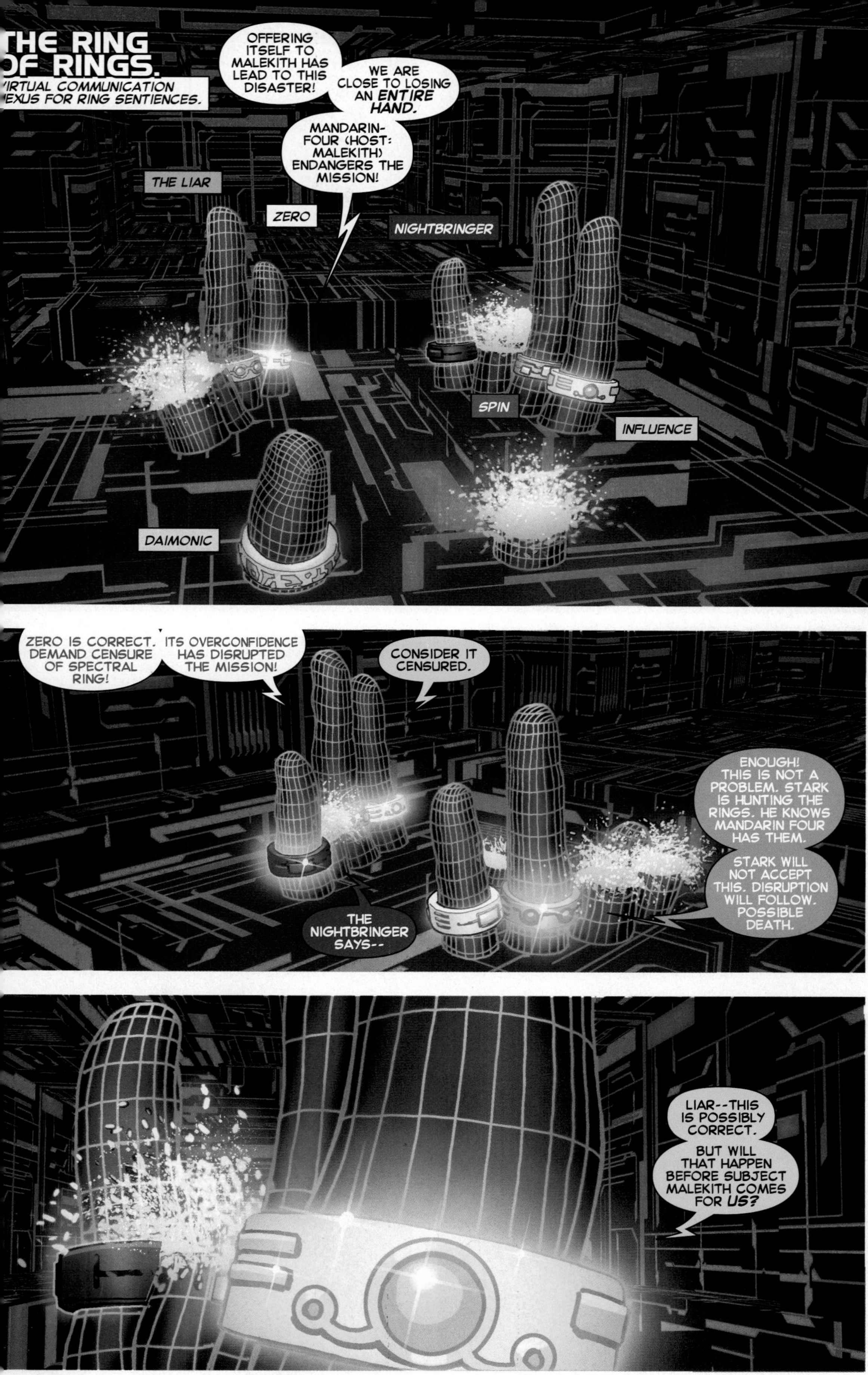

THE RING OF RINGS.
VIRTUAL COMMUNICATION NEXUS FOR RING SENTIENCES.
OFFERING ITSELF TO MALEKITH HAS LEAD TO THIS DISASTER!
WE ARE CLOSE TO LOSING AN ENTIRE HAND.
MANDARIN-FOUR (HOST: MALEKITH) ENDANGERS THE MISSION!
THE LIAR
ZERO
NIGHTBRINGER
SPIN
INFLUENCE
DAIMONIC
ZERO IS CORRECT. DEMAND CENSURE OF SPECTRAL RING!
ITS OVERCONFIDENCE HAS DISRUPTED THE MISSION!
CONSIDER IT CENSURED.
THE NIGHTBRINGER SAYS--
ENOUGH! THIS IS NOT A PROBLEM. STARK IS HUNTING THE RINGS. HE KNOWS MANDARIN FOUR HAS THEM.
STARK WILL NOT ACCEPT THIS. DISRUPTION WILL FOLLOW. POSSIBLE DEATH.
LIAR--THIS IS POSSIBLY CORRECT.
BUT WILL THAT HAPPEN BEFORE SUBJECT MALEKITH COMES FOR US?

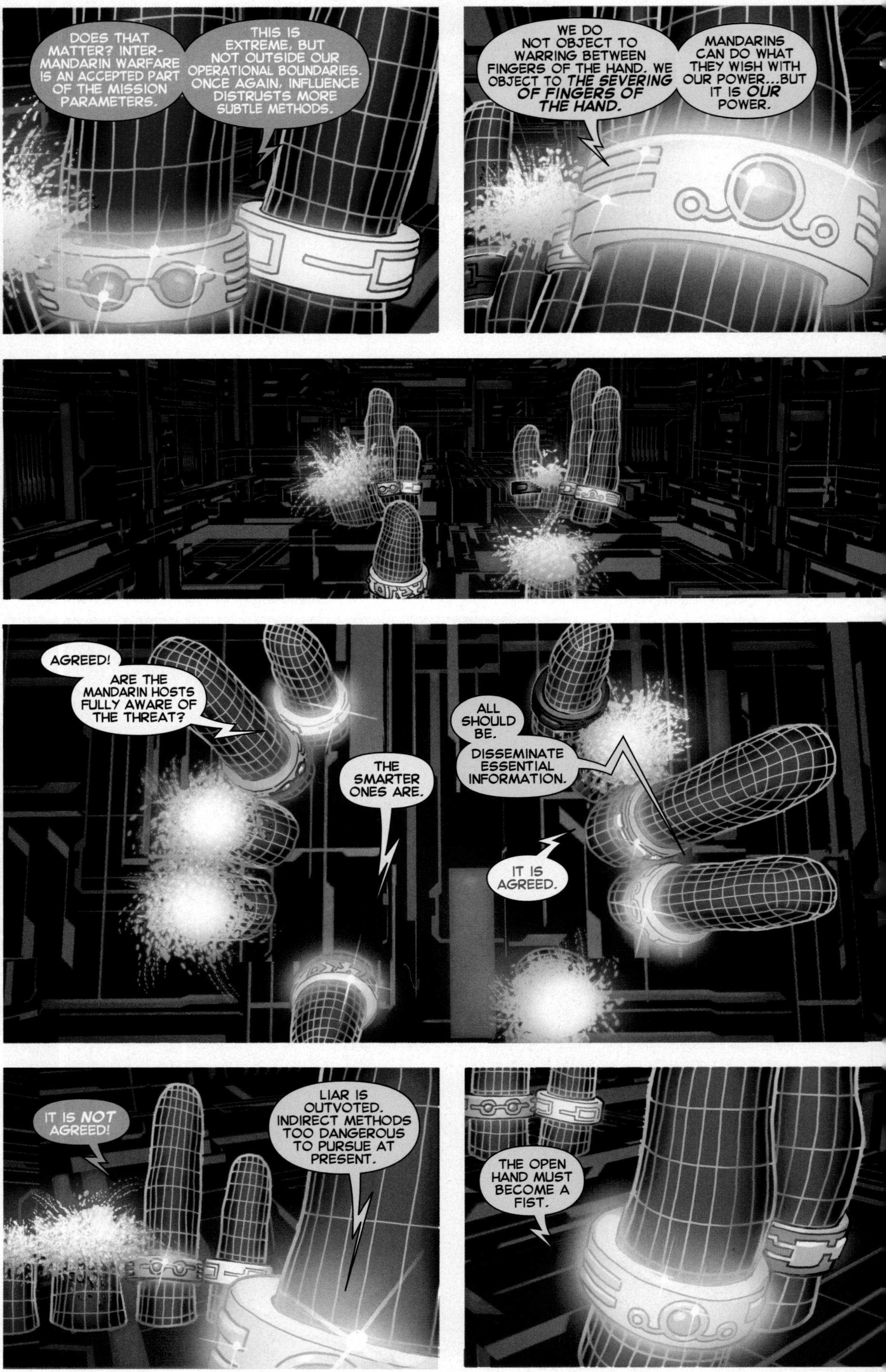
DOES THAT MATTER? INTER-MANDARIN WARFARE IS AN ACCEPTED PART OF THE MISSION PARAMETERS.
THIS IS EXTREME, BUT NOT OUTSIDE OUR OPERATIONAL BOUNDARIES. ONCE AGAIN, INFLUENCE DISTRUSTS MORE SUBTLE METHODS.
WE DO NOT OBJECT TO WARRING BETWEEN FINGERS OF THE HAND. WE OBJECT TO *THE SEVERING OF FINGERS OF THE HAND.*
MANDARINS CAN DO WHAT THEY WISH WITH OUR POWER...BUT IT IS *OUR* POWER.
AGREED!
ARE THE MANDARIN HOSTS FULLY AWARE OF THE THREAT?
THE SMARTER ONES ARE.
ALL SHOULD BE.
DISSEMINATE ESSENTIAL INFORMATION.
IT IS AGREED.
IT IS *NOT* AGREED!
LIAR IS OUTVOTED. INDIRECT METHODS TOO DANGEROUS TO PURSUE AT PRESENT.
THE OPEN HAND MUST BECOME A FIST.

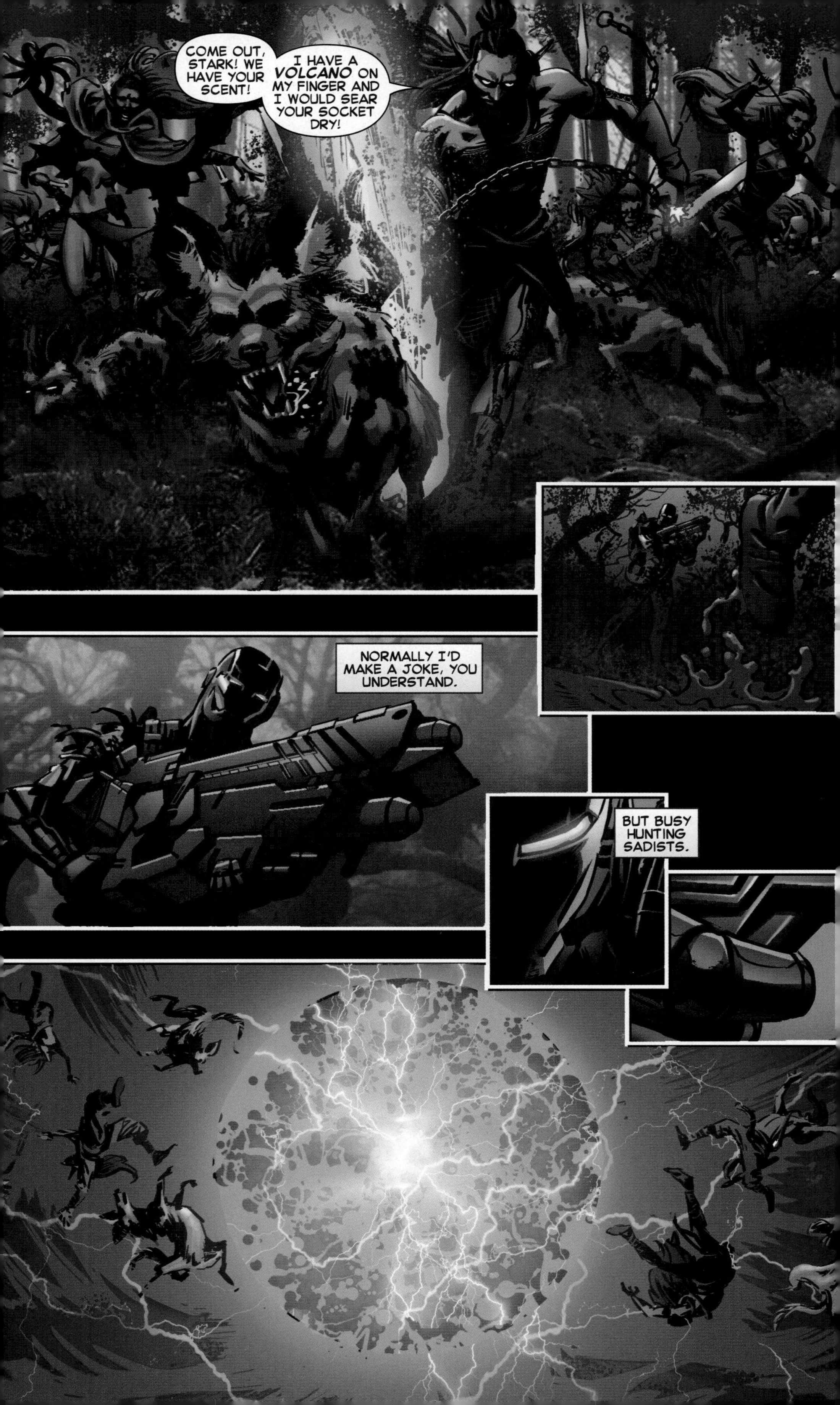
COME OUT, STARK! WE HAVE YOUR SCENT!
I HAVE A VOLCANO ON MY FINGER AND I WOULD SEAR YOUR SOCKET DRY!
NORMALLY I'D MAKE A JOKE, YOU UNDERSTAND.
BUT BUSY HUNTING SADISTS.

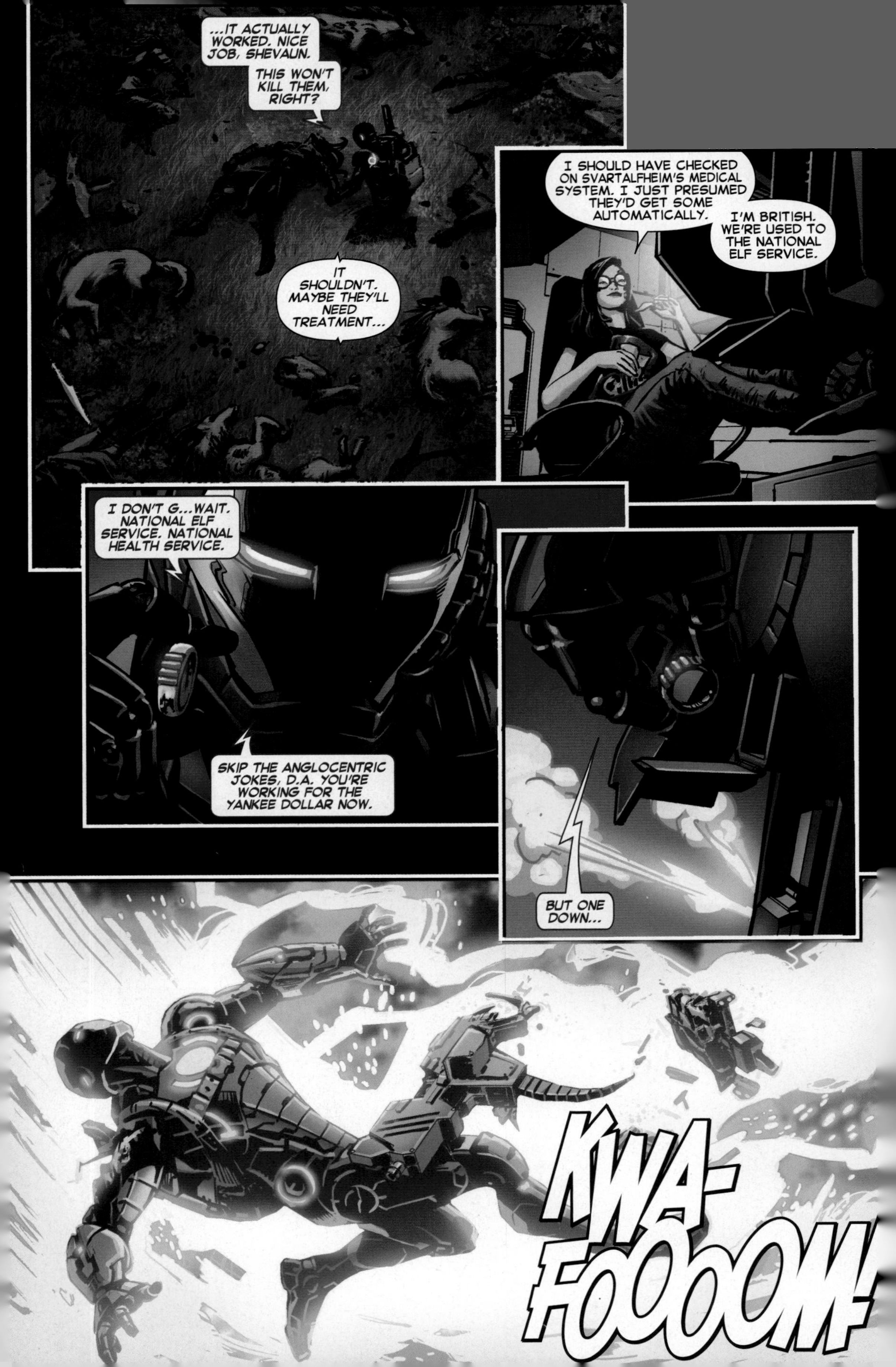
...IT ACTUALLY WORKED. NICE JOB, SHEVAUN.
THIS WON'T KILL THEM, RIGHT?
IT SHOULDN'T. MAYBE THEY'LL NEED TREATMENT...
I SHOULD HAVE CHECKED ON SVARTALFHEIM'S MEDICAL SYSTEM. I JUST PRESUMED THEY'D GET SOME AUTOMATICALLY.
I'M BRITISH. WE'RE USED TO THE NATIONAL ELF SERVICE.
I DON'T G...WAIT. NATIONAL ELF SERVICE. NATIONAL HEALTH SERVICE.
SKIP THE ANGLOCENTRIC JOKES, D.A. YOU'RE WORKING FOR THE YANKEE DOLLAR NOW.
BUT ONE DOWN...
KWA-FOOOOOM!

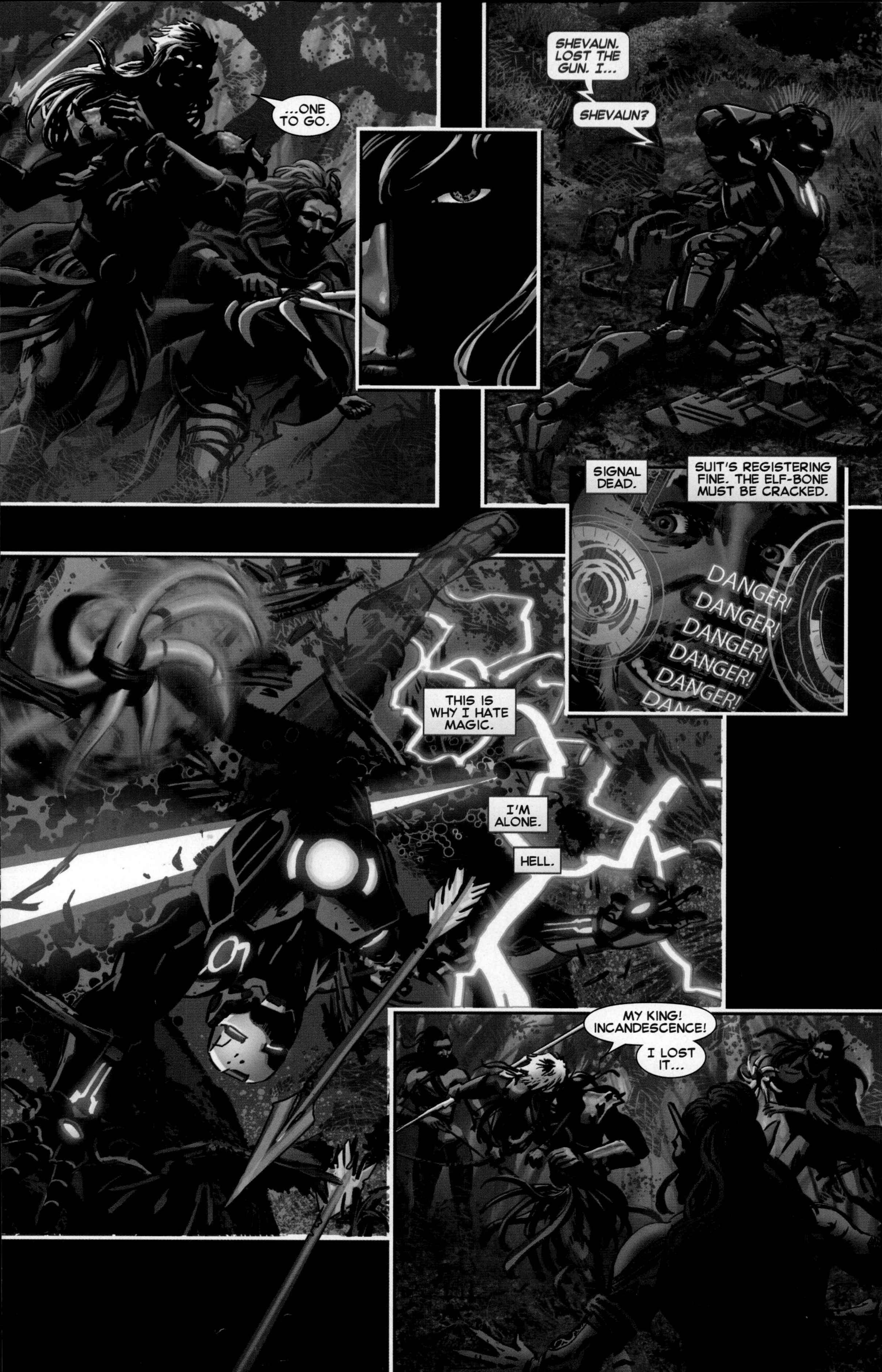
...ONE TO GO.
SHEVAUN. LOST THE GUN. I...
SHEVAUN?
SIGNAL DEAD.
SUIT'S REGISTERING FINE. THE ELF-BONE MUST BE CRACKED.
DANGER!
DANGER!
DANGER!
DANGER!
DANGER!
DANGER!
THIS IS WHY I HATE MAGIC.
I'M ALONE.
HELL.
MY KING! INCANDESCENCE!
I LOST IT...

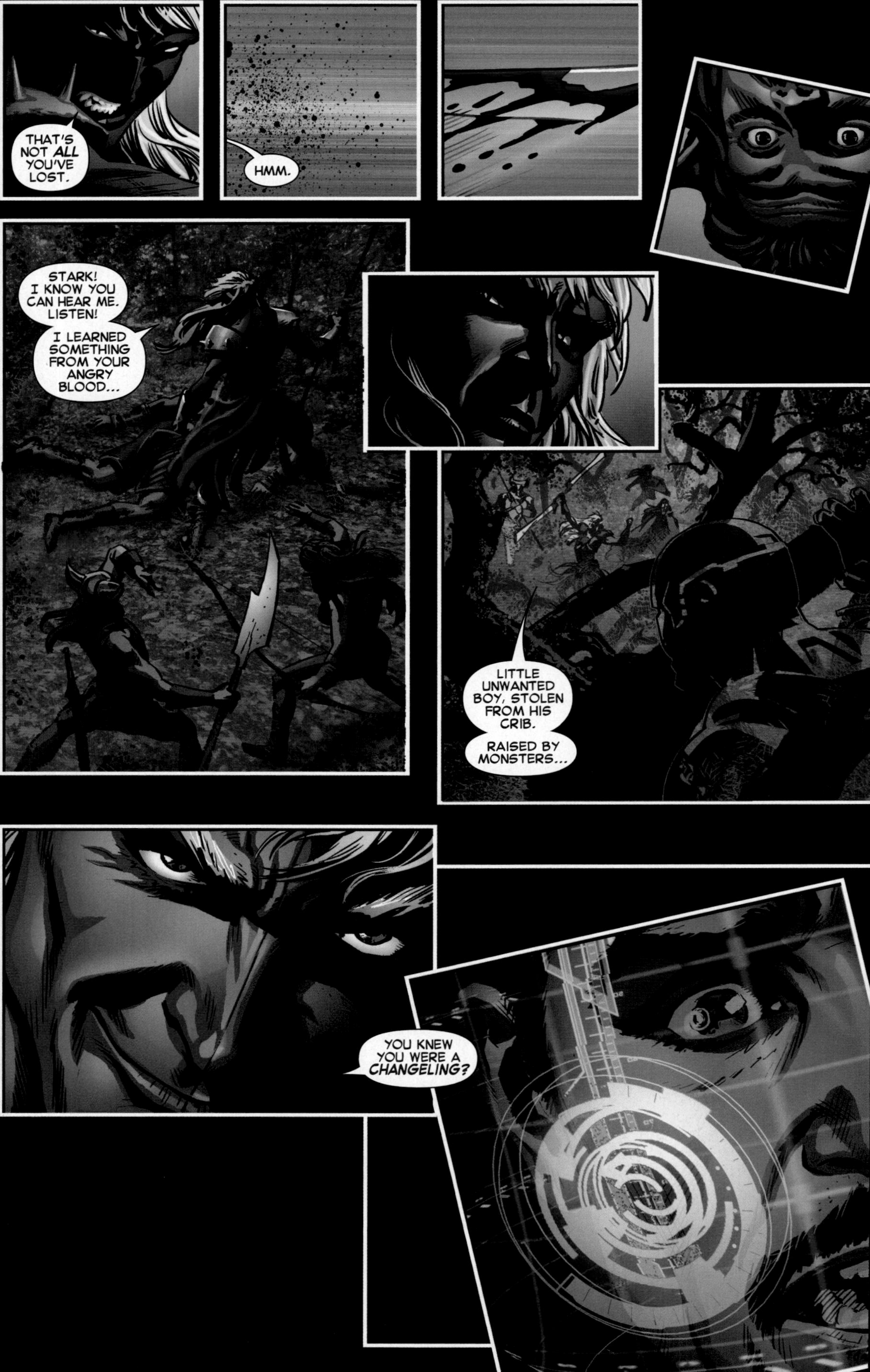
THAT'S NOT ALL YOU'VE LOST.
HMM.
STARK! I KNOW YOU CAN HEAR ME. LISTEN!
I LEARNED SOMETHING FROM YOUR ANGRY BLOOD...
LITTLE UNWANTED BOY, STOLEN FROM HIS CRIB.
RAISED BY MONSTERS...
YOU KNEW YOU WERE A CHANGELING?

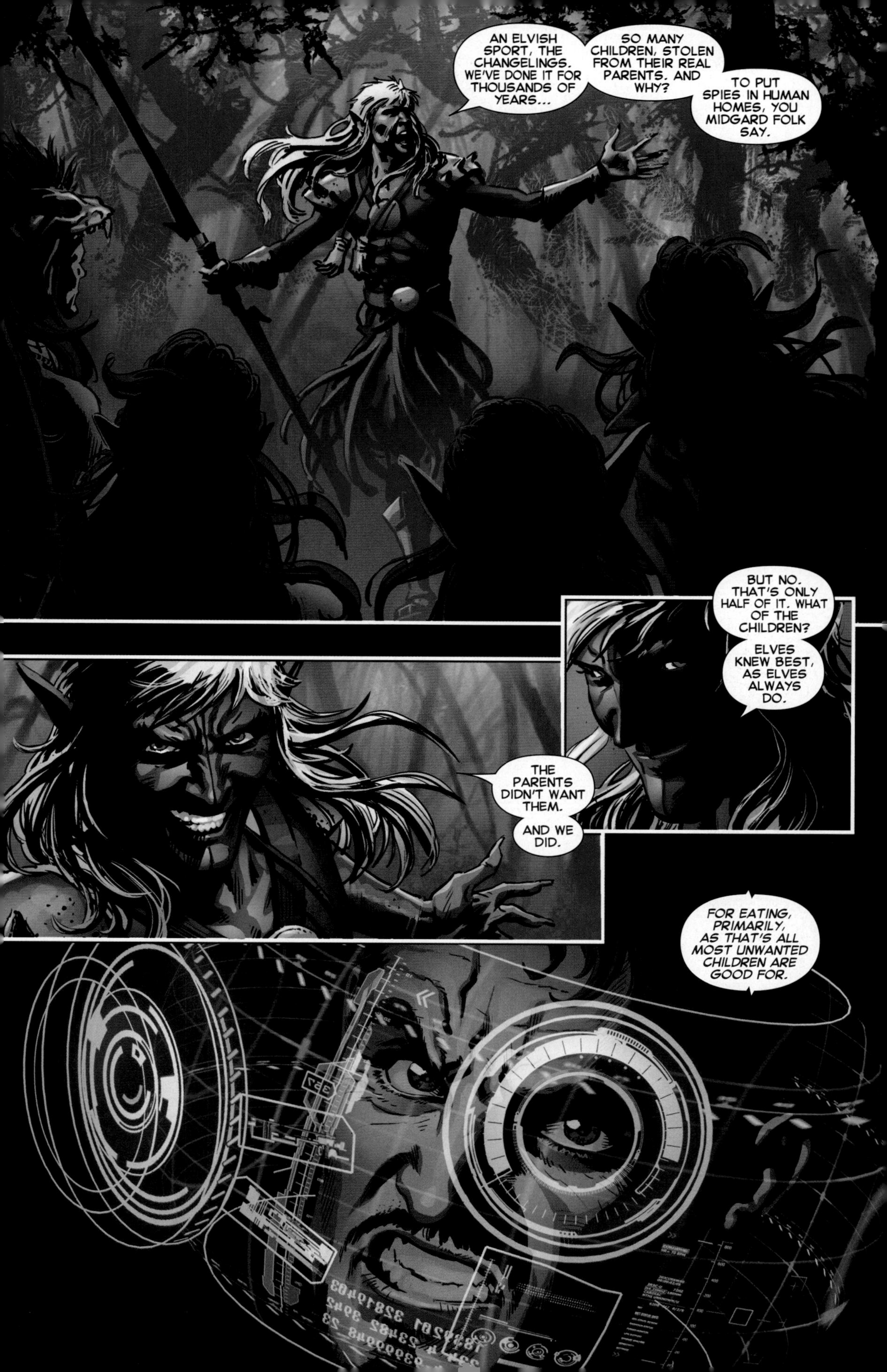
AN ELVISH SPORT, THE CHANGELINGS. WE'VE DONE IT FOR THOUSANDS OF YEARS...
SO MANY CHILDREN, STOLEN FROM THEIR REAL PARENTS. AND WHY?
TO PUT SPIES IN HUMAN HOMES, YOU MIDGARD FOLK SAY.
BUT NO. THAT'S ONLY HALF OF IT. WHAT OF THE CHILDREN?
ELVES KNEW BEST, AS ELVES ALWAYS DO.
THE PARENTS DIDN'T WANT THEM.
AND WE DID.
FOR EATING, PRIMARILY, AS THAT'S ALL MOST UNWANTED CHILDREN ARE GOOD FOR.

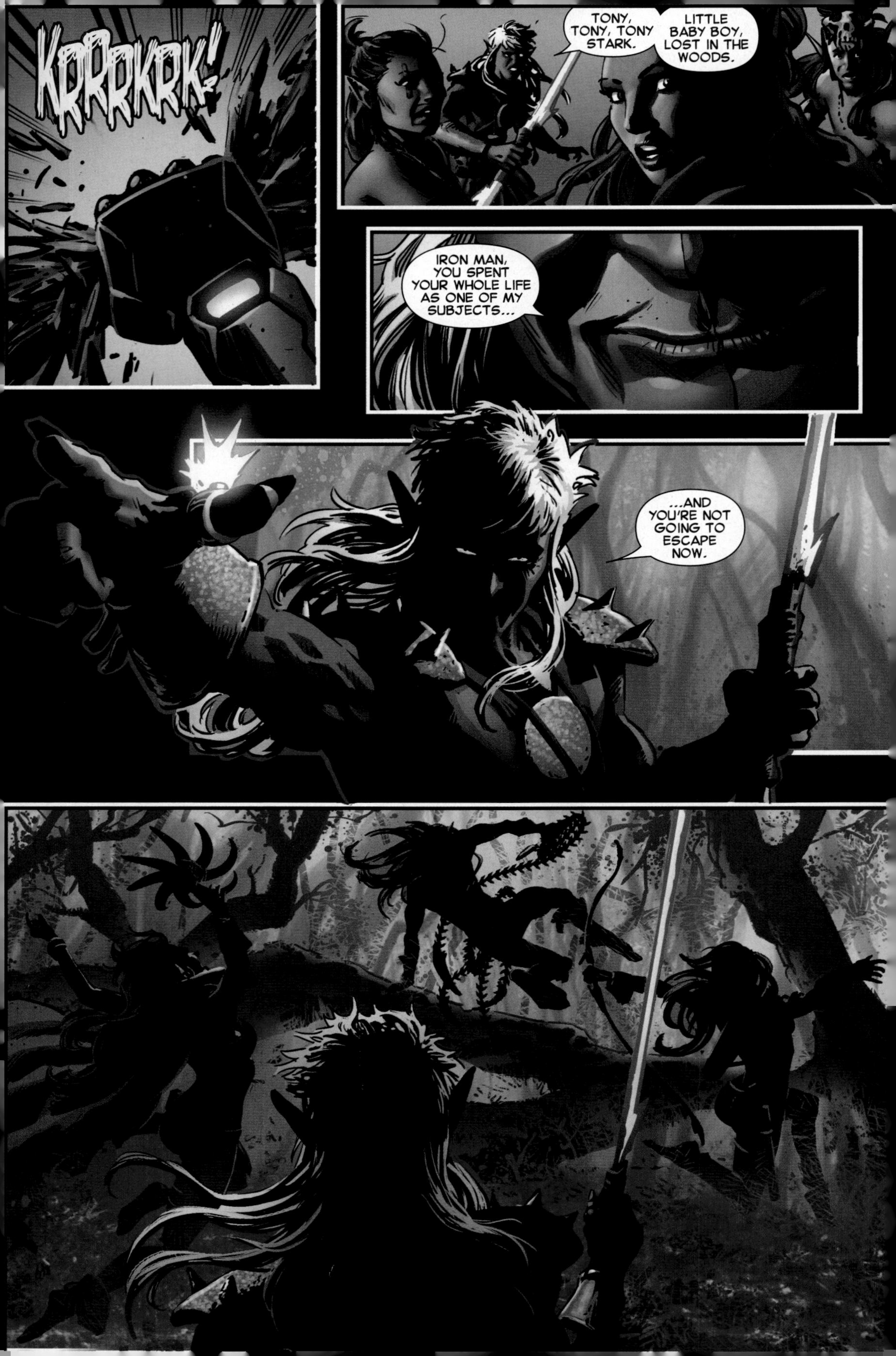
KRRRKRK!
TONY, TONY, TONY STARK.
LITTLE BABY BOY, LOST IN THE WOODS.
IRON MAN, YOU SPENT YOUR WHOLE LIFE AS ONE OF MY SUBJECTS...
...AND YOU'RE NOT GOING TO ESCAPE NOW.

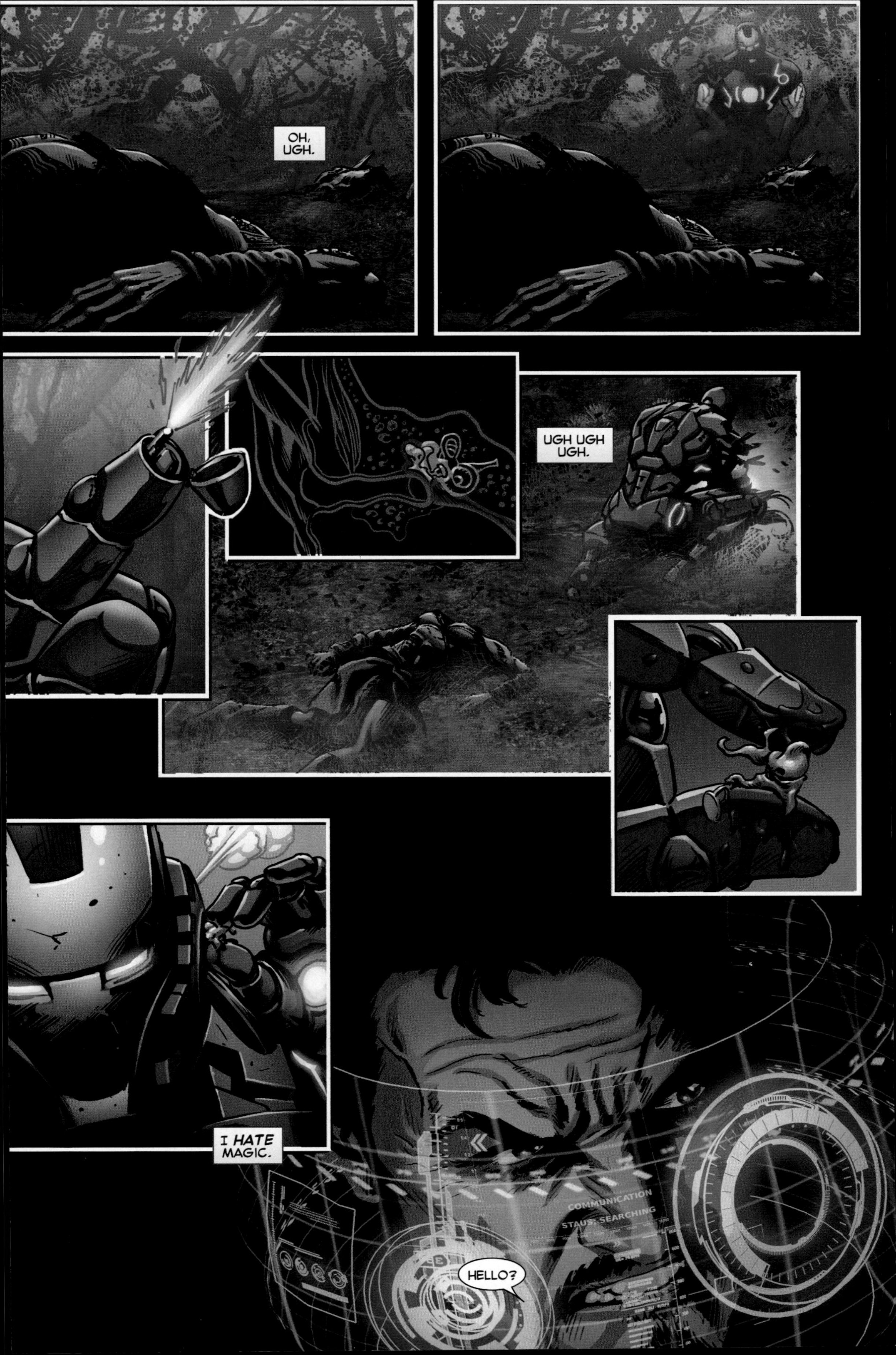
OH, UGH.
UGH UGH UGH.
I HATE MAGIC.
COMMUNICATION
STAUS: SEARCHING
HELLO?

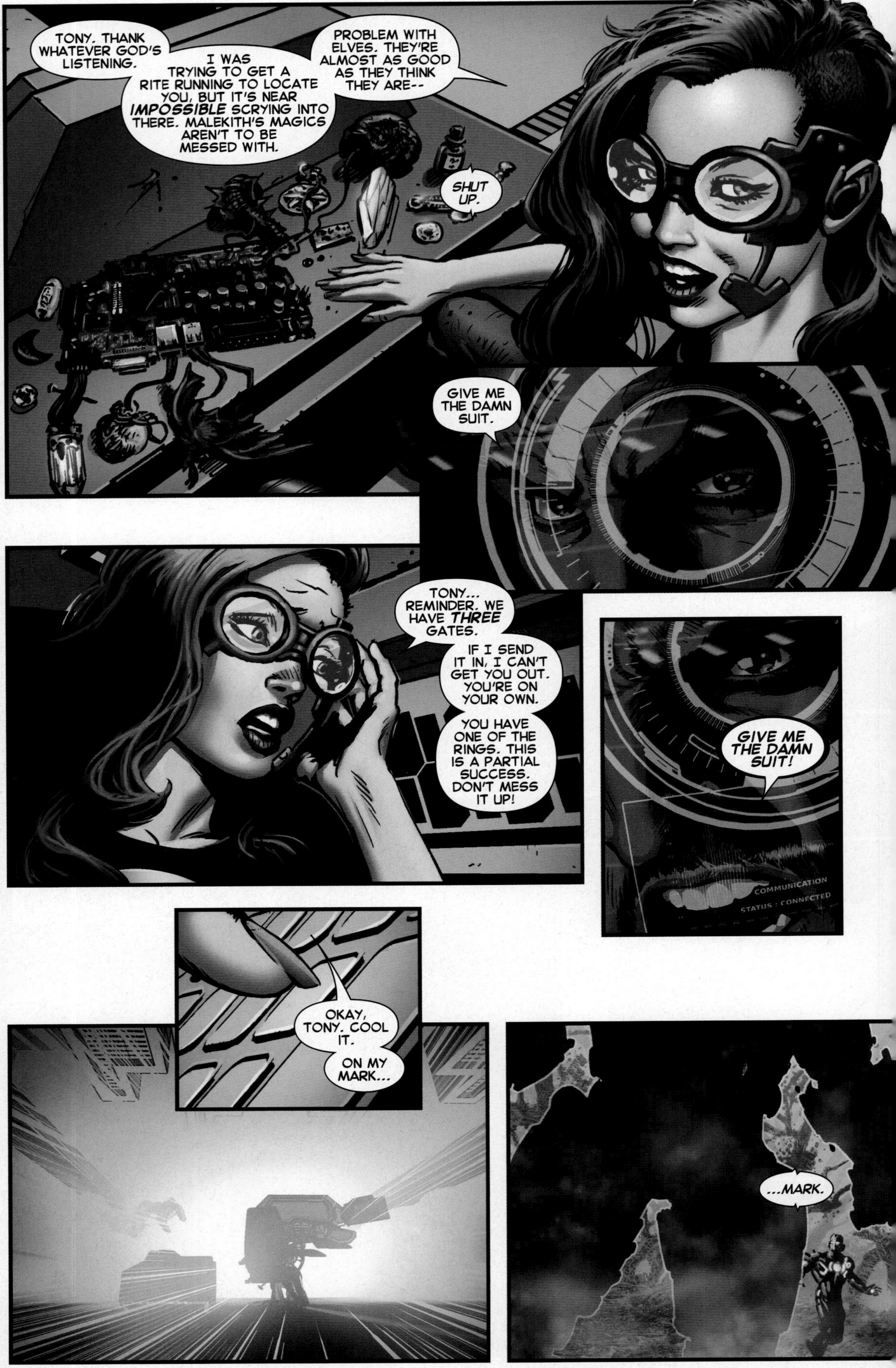
TONY. THANK WHATEVER GOD'S LISTENING.
I WAS TRYING TO GET A RITE RUNNING TO LOCATE YOU, BUT IT'S NEAR *IMPOSSIBLE* SCRYING INTO THERE. MALEKITH'S MAGICS AREN'T TO BE MESSED WITH.
PROBLEM WITH ELVES. THEY'RE ALMOST AS GOOD AS THEY THINK THEY ARE--
SHUT UP.
GIVE ME THE DAMN SUIT.
TONY... REMINDER. WE HAVE *THREE* GATES.
IF I SEND IT IN, I CAN'T GET YOU OUT. YOU'RE ON YOUR OWN.
YOU HAVE ONE OF THE RINGS. THIS IS A PARTIAL SUCCESS. DON'T MESS IT UP!
GIVE ME THE DAMN SUIT!
COMMUNICATION
STATUS : CONNECTED
OKAY, TONY. COOL IT.
ON MY MARK...
...MARK.

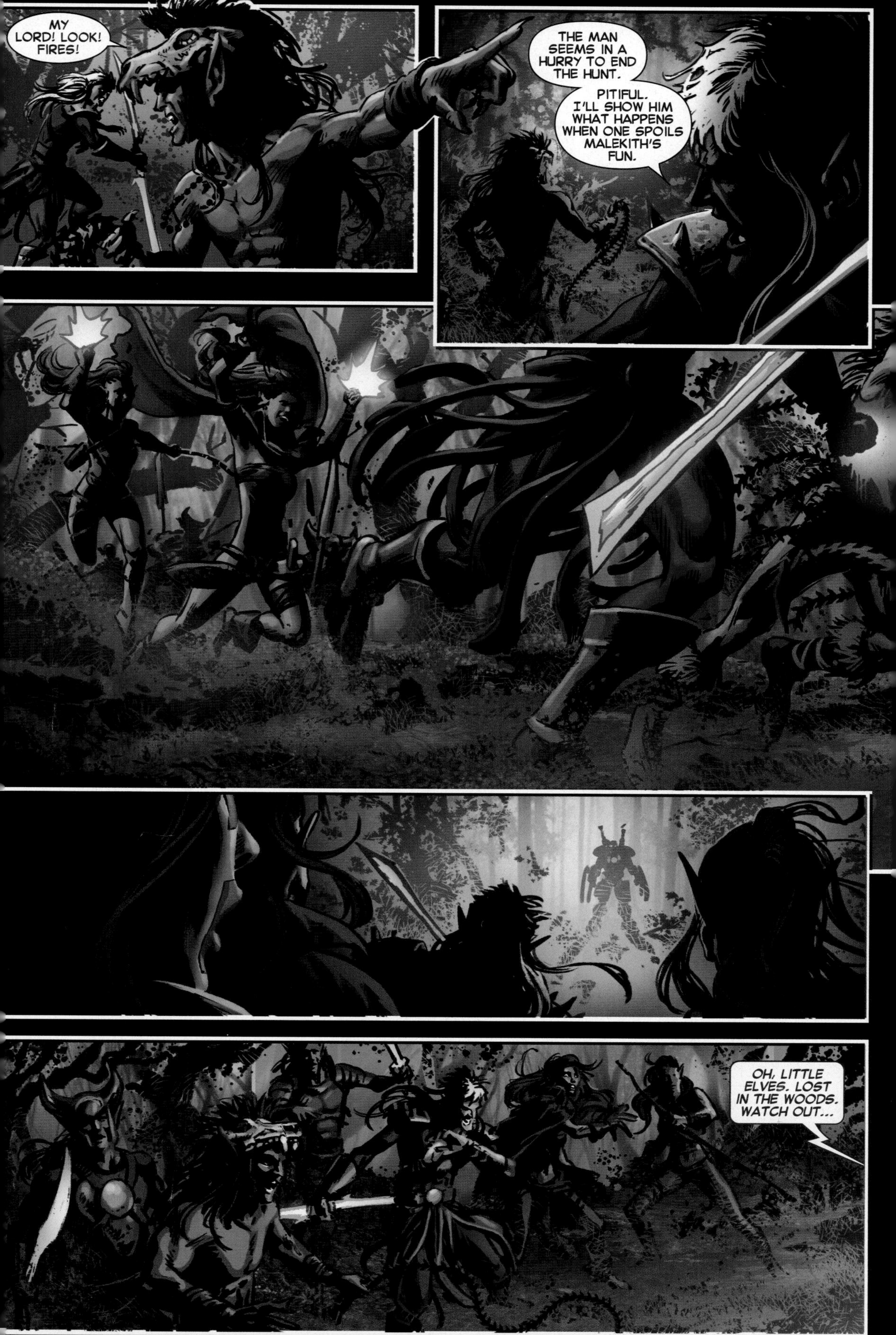
MY LORD! LOOK! FIRES!
THE MAN SEEMS IN A HURRY TO END THE HUNT.
PITIFUL. I'LL SHOW HIM WHAT HAPPENS WHEN ONE SPOILS MALEKITH'S FUN.
OH, LITTLE ELVES. LOST IN THE WOODS. WATCH OUT...

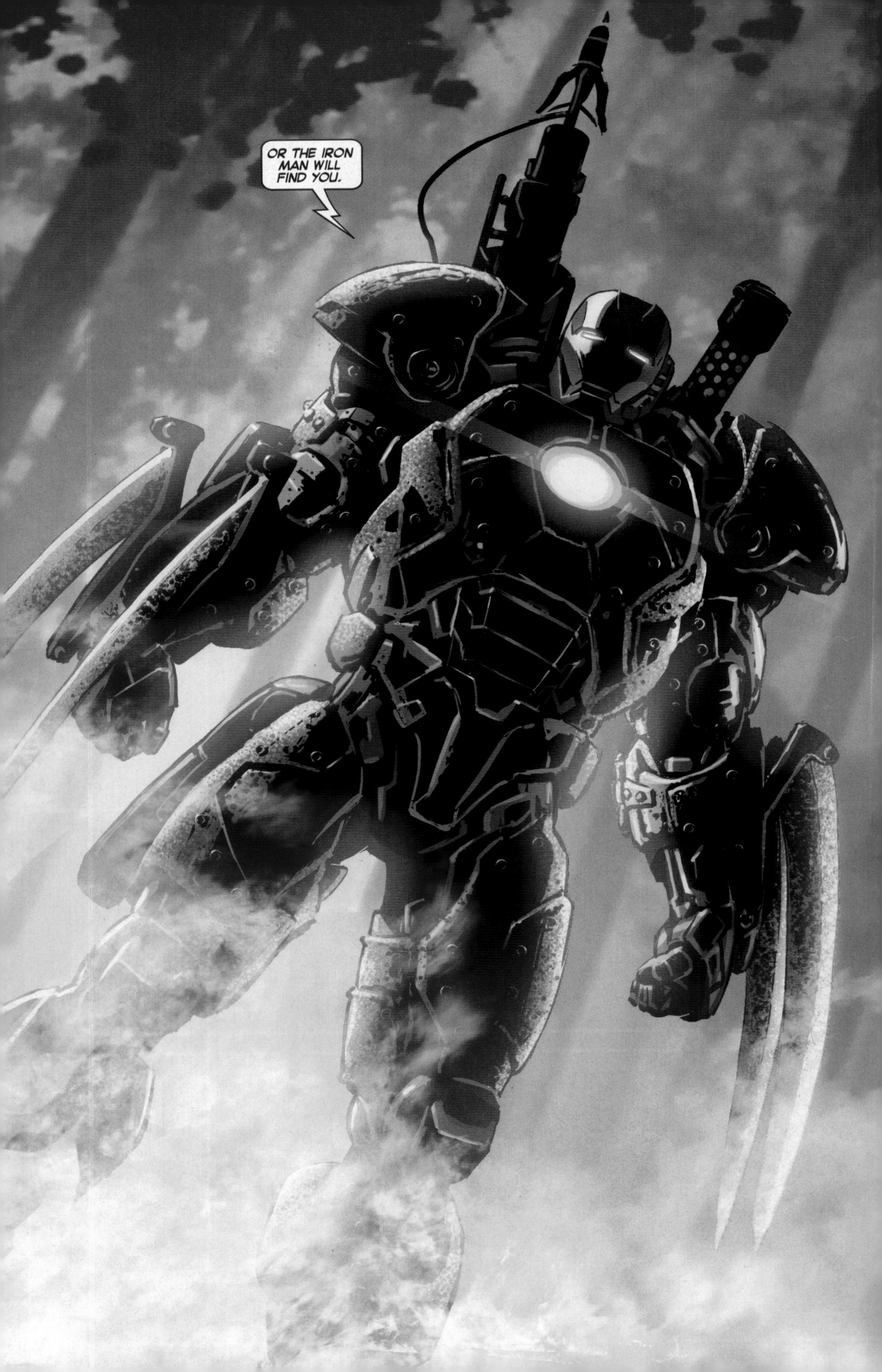
OR THE IRON MAN WILL FIND YOU.

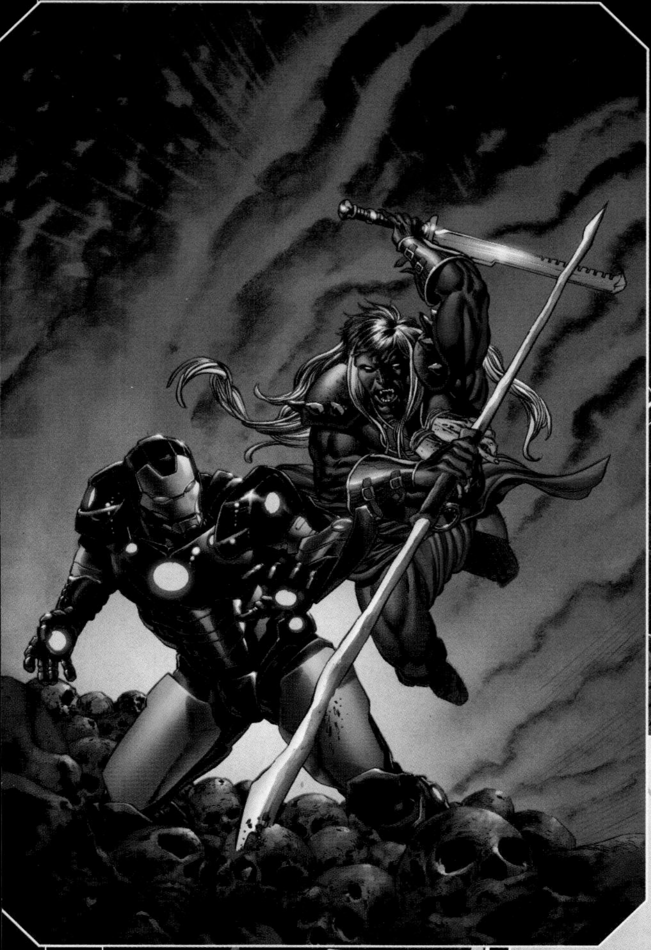

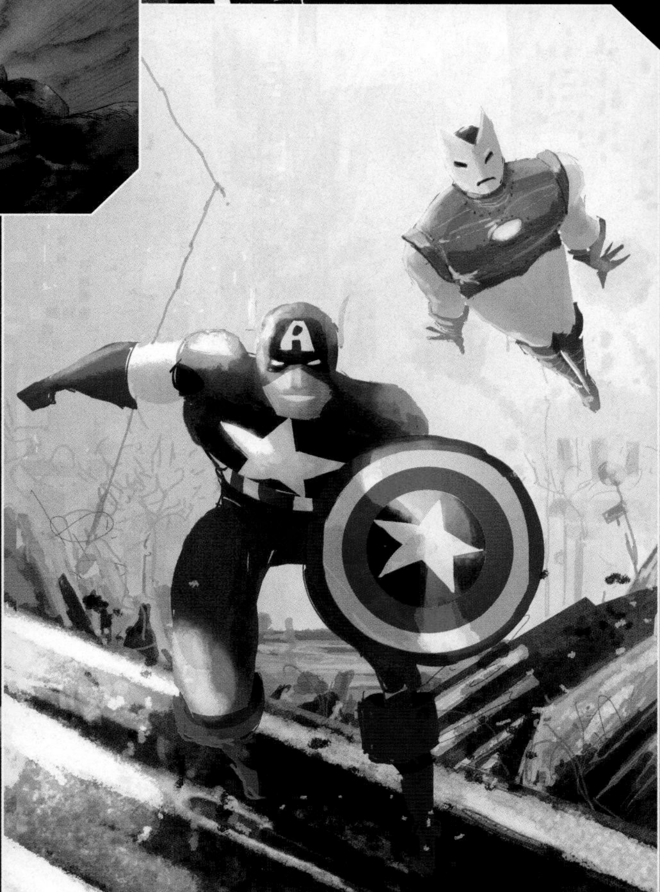

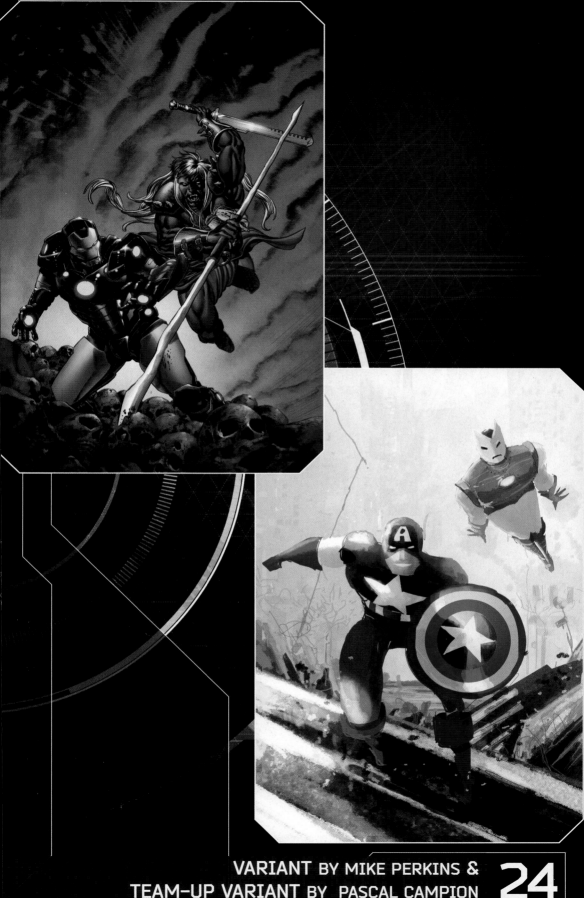

VARIANT BY MIKE PERKINS &
TEAM-UP VARIANT BY PASCAL CAMPION

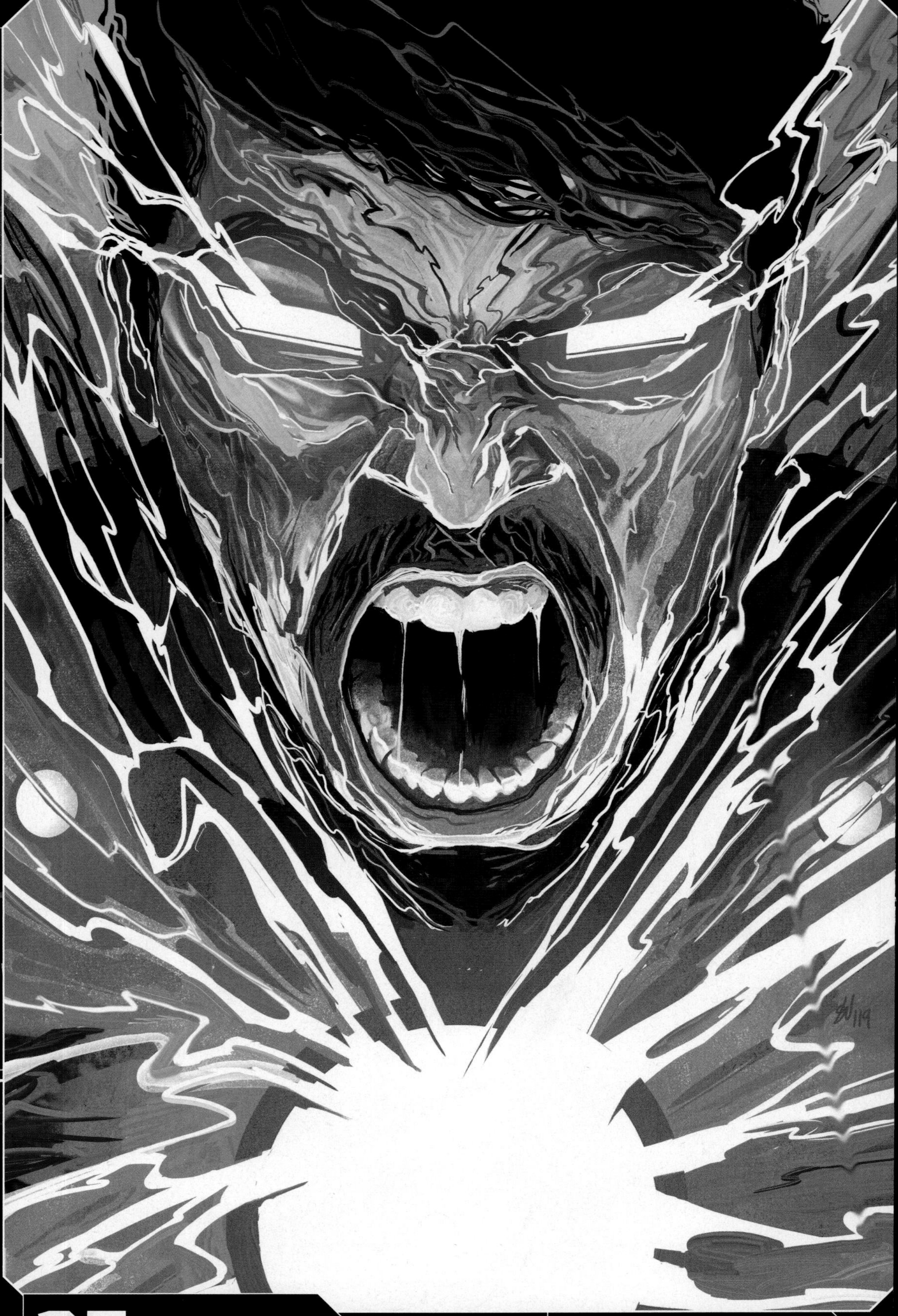

25 RINGS OF THE MANDARIN CHAPTER 3

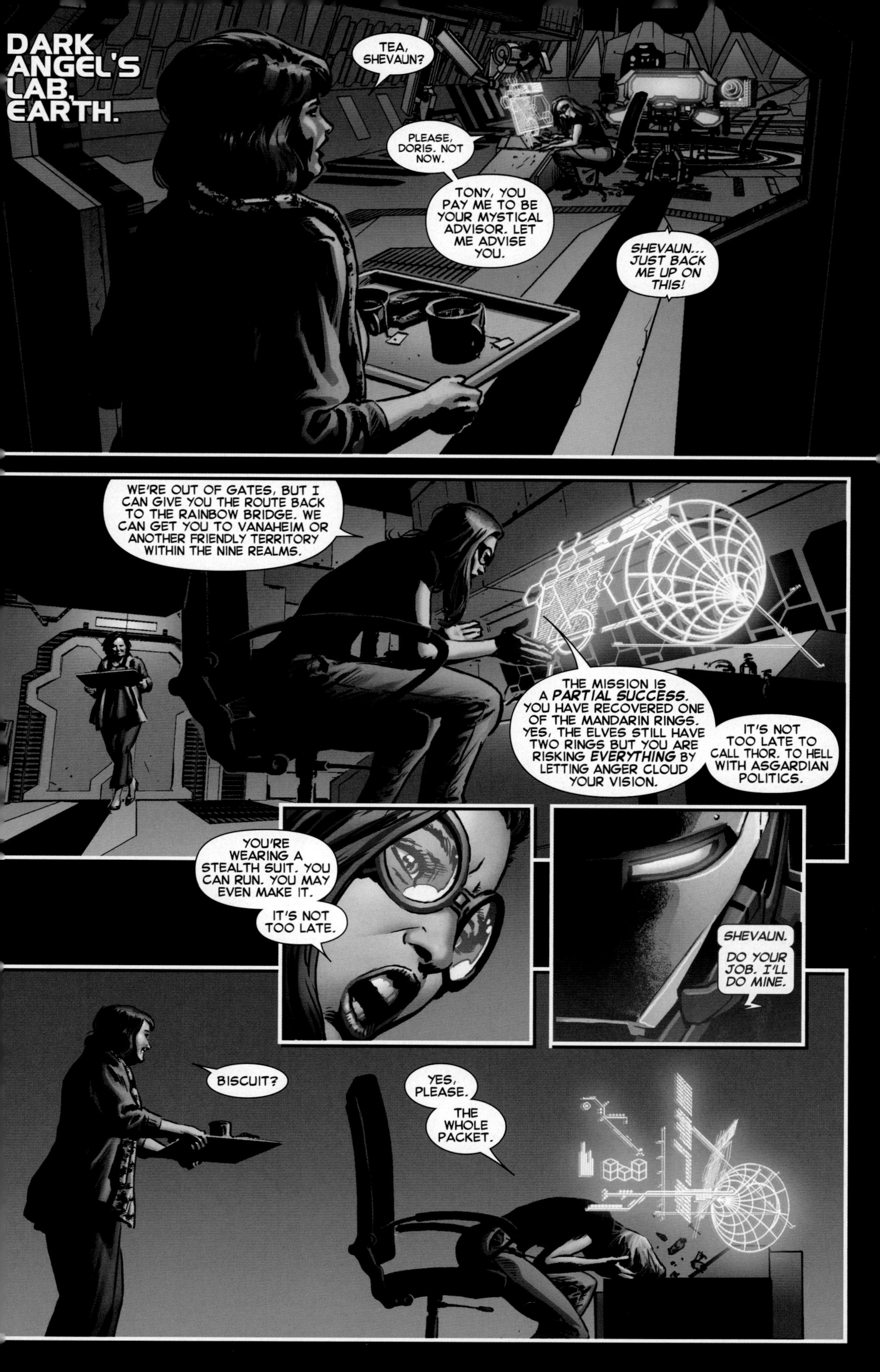
DARK ANGEL'S LAB, EARTH.
TEA, SHEVAUN?
PLEASE, DORIS. NOT NOW.
TONY, YOU PAY ME TO BE YOUR MYSTICAL ADVISOR. LET ME ADVISE YOU.
SHEVAUN... JUST BACK ME UP ON THIS!
WE'RE OUT OF GATES, BUT I CAN GIVE YOU THE ROUTE BACK TO THE RAINBOW BRIDGE. WE CAN GET YOU TO VANAHEIM OR ANOTHER FRIENDLY TERRITORY WITHIN THE NINE REALMS.
THE MISSION IS A PARTIAL SUCCESS. YOU HAVE RECOVERED ONE OF THE MANDARIN RINGS. YES, THE ELVES STILL HAVE TWO RINGS BUT YOU ARE RISKING EVERYTHING BY LETTING ANGER CLOUD YOUR VISION.
IT'S NOT TOO LATE TO CALL THOR. TO HELL WITH ASGARDIAN POLITICS.
YOU'RE WEARING A STEALTH SUIT. YOU CAN RUN. YOU MAY EVEN MAKE IT.
IT'S NOT TOO LATE.
SHEVAUN.
DO YOUR JOB. I'LL DO MINE.
BISCUIT?
YES, PLEASE.
THE WHOLE PACKET.

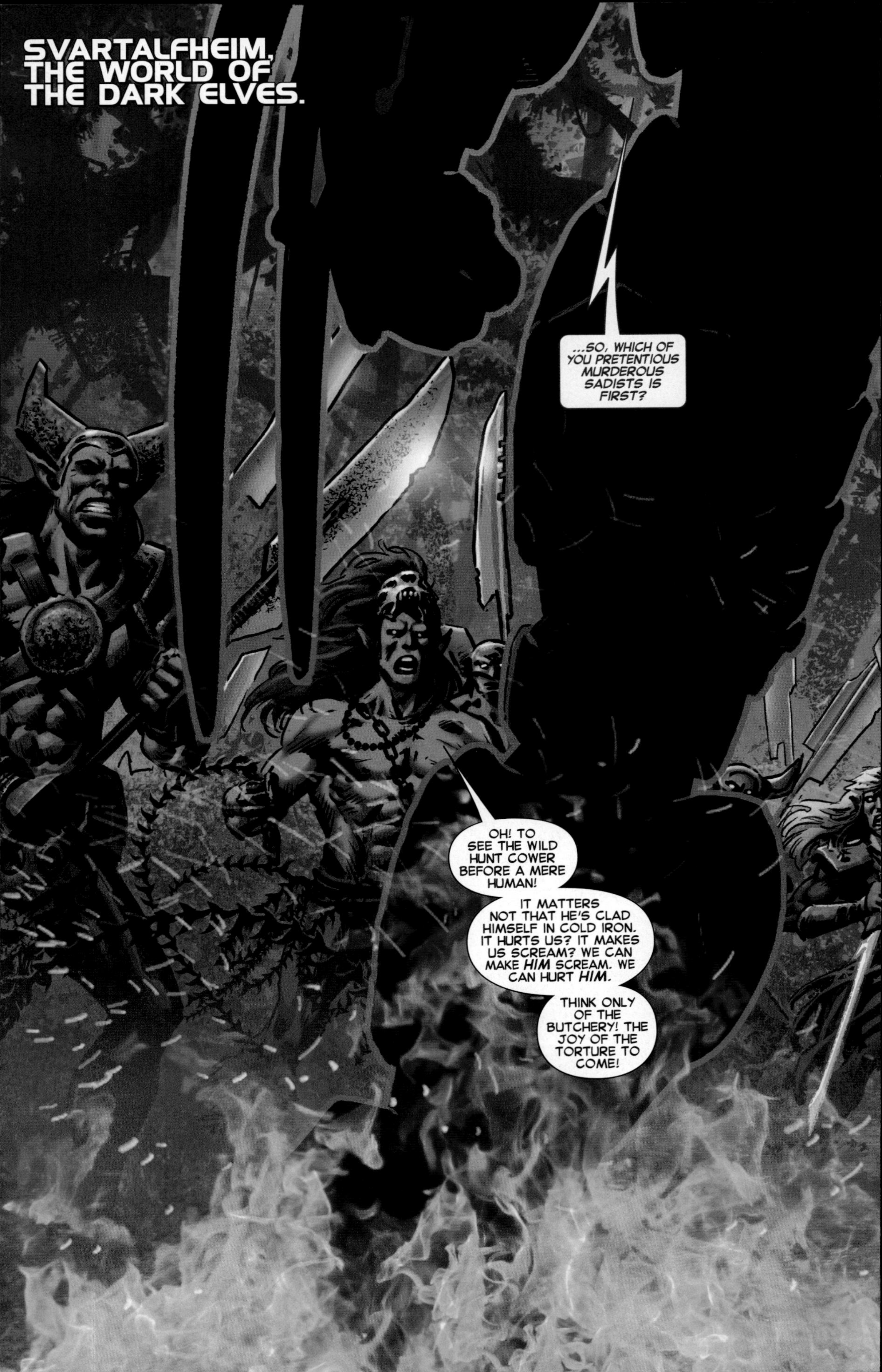
SVARTALFHEIM, THE WORLD OF THE DARK ELVES.
...SO, WHICH OF YOU PRETENTIOUS MURDEROUS SADISTS IS FIRST?
OH! TO SEE THE WILD HUNT COWER BEFORE A MERE HUMAN!
IT MATTERS NOT THAT HE'S CLAD HIMSELF IN COLD IRON. IT HURTS US? IT MAKES US SCREAM? WE CAN MAKE HIM SCREAM. WE CAN HURT HIM.
THINK ONLY OF THE BUTCHERY! THE JOY OF THE TORTURE TO COME!

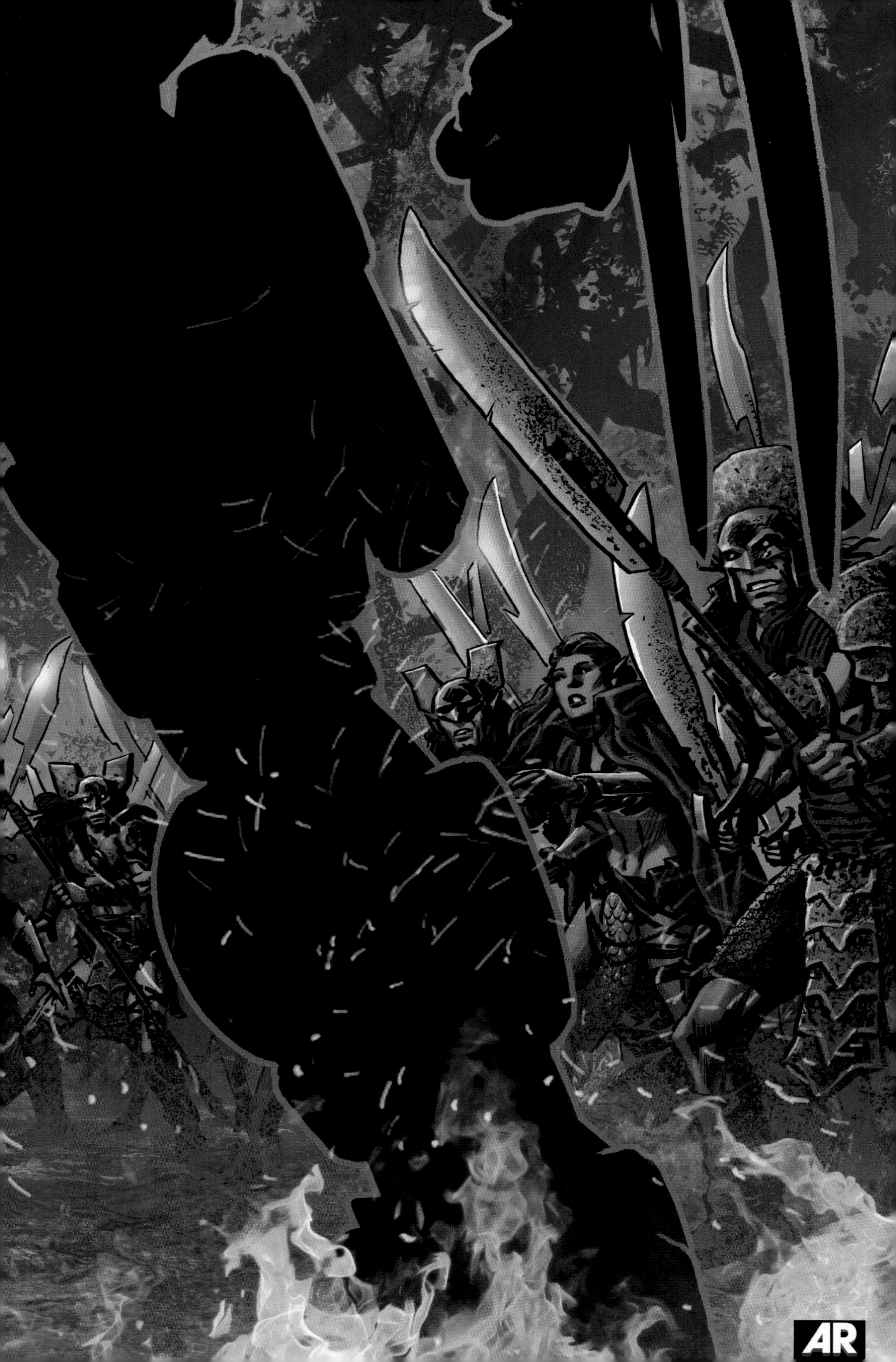

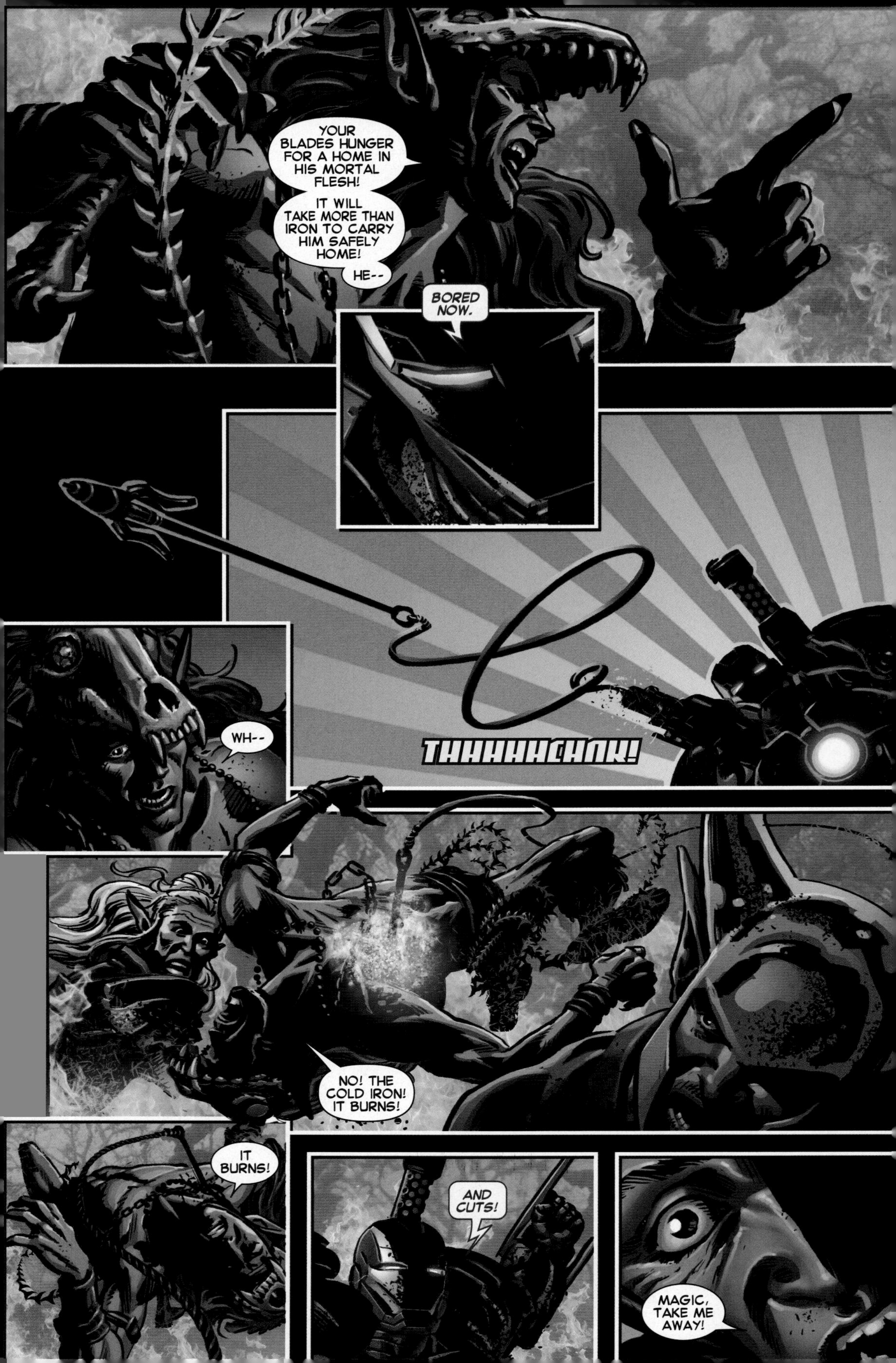
YOUR BLADES HUNGER FOR A HOME IN HIS MORTAL FLESH!
IT WILL TAKE MORE THAN IRON TO CARRY HIM SAFELY HOME!
HE--
BORED NOW.
THHHHHCHNK!
WH--
NO! THE COLD IRON! IT BURNS!
IT BURNS!
AND CUTS!
MAGIC, TAKE ME AWAY!

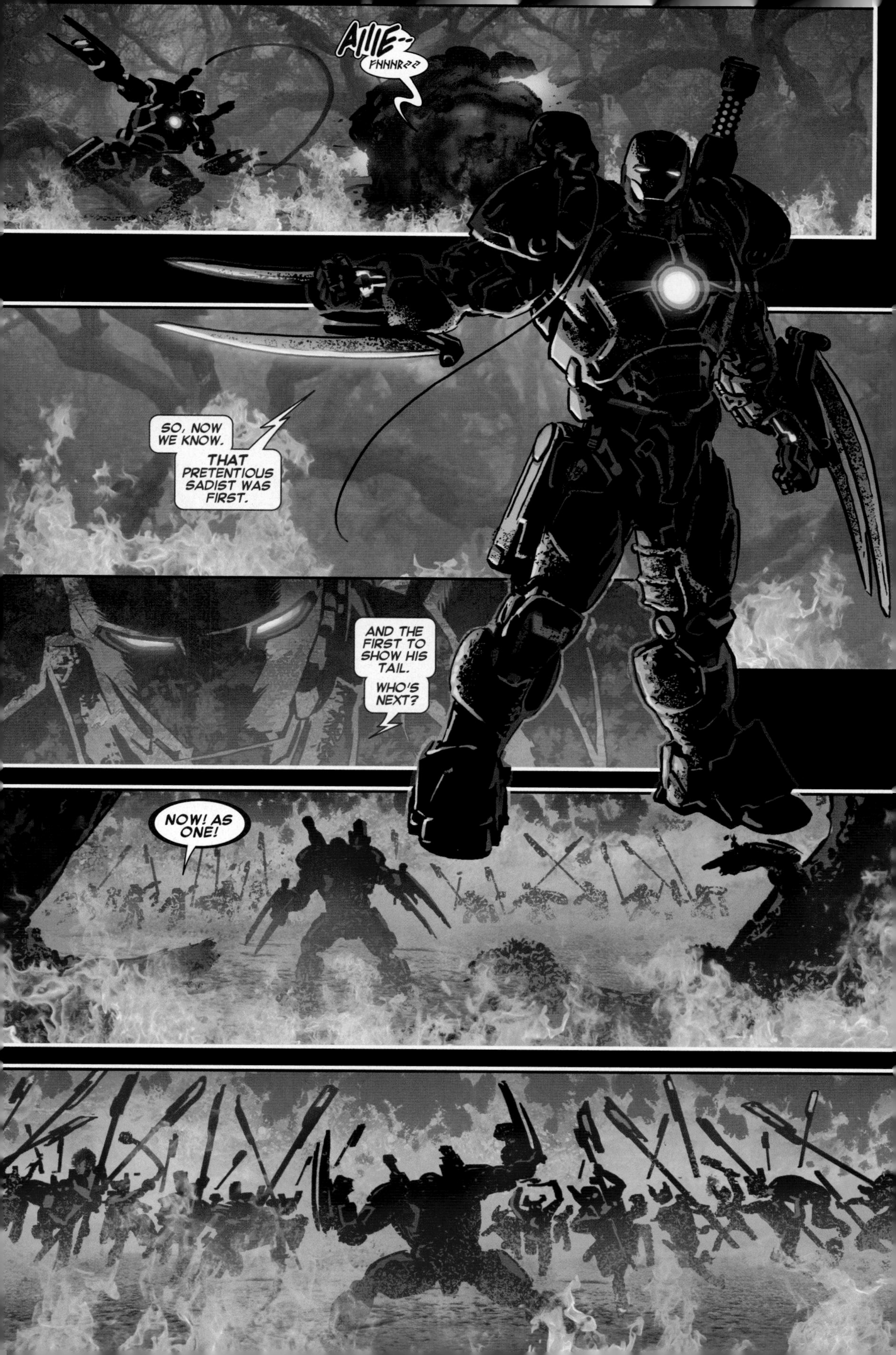
AIIIE--
SO, NOW WE KNOW.
THAT PRETENTIOUS SADIST WAS FIRST.
AND THE FIRST TO SHOW HIS TAIL.
WHO'S NEXT?
NOW! AS ONE!

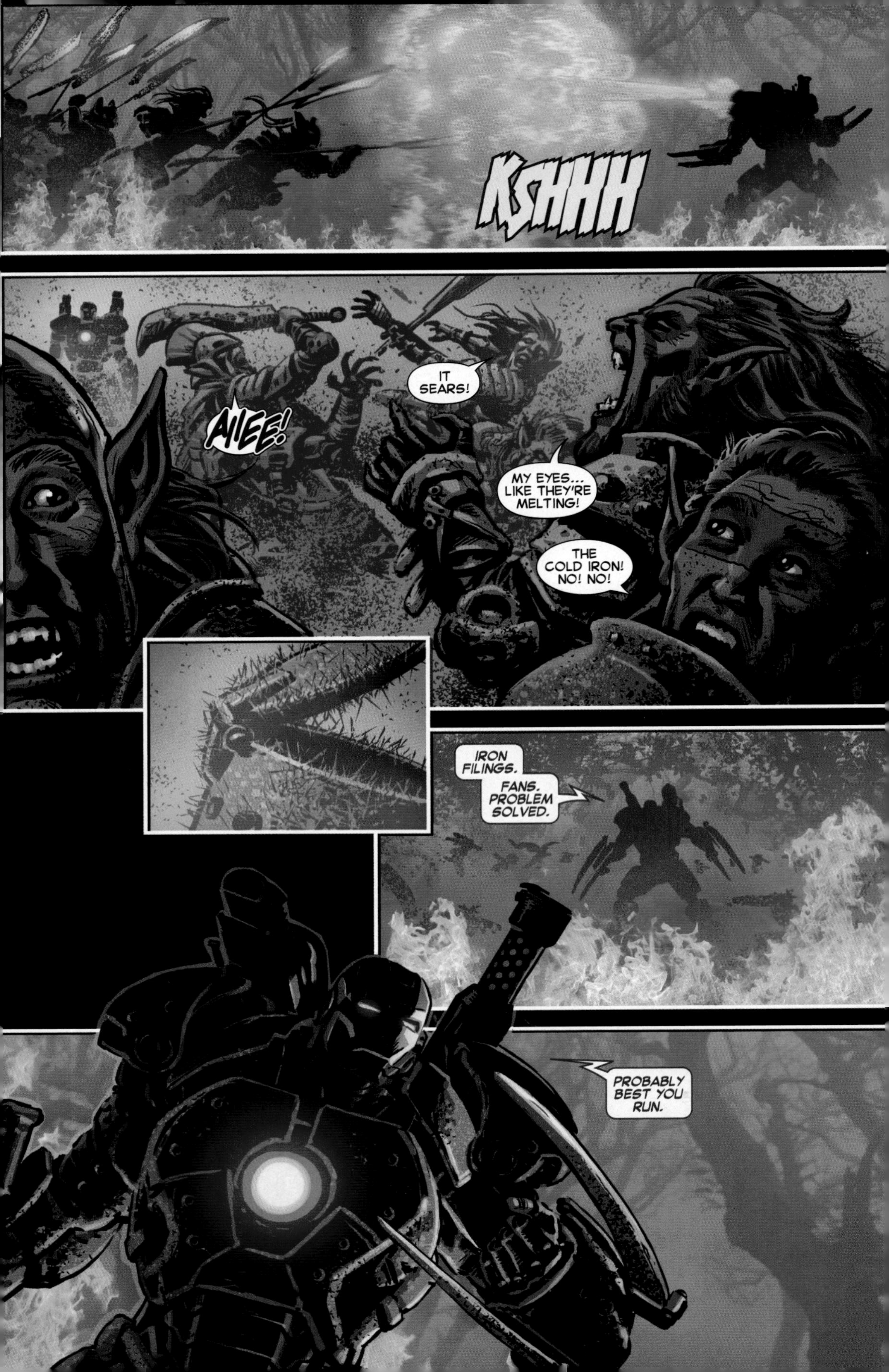
KSHHH
AIIEE!
IT SEARS!
MY EYES... LIKE THEY'RE MELTING!
THE COLD IRON! NO! NO!
IRON FILINGS.
FANS. PROBLEM SOLVED.
PROBABLY BEST YOU RUN.

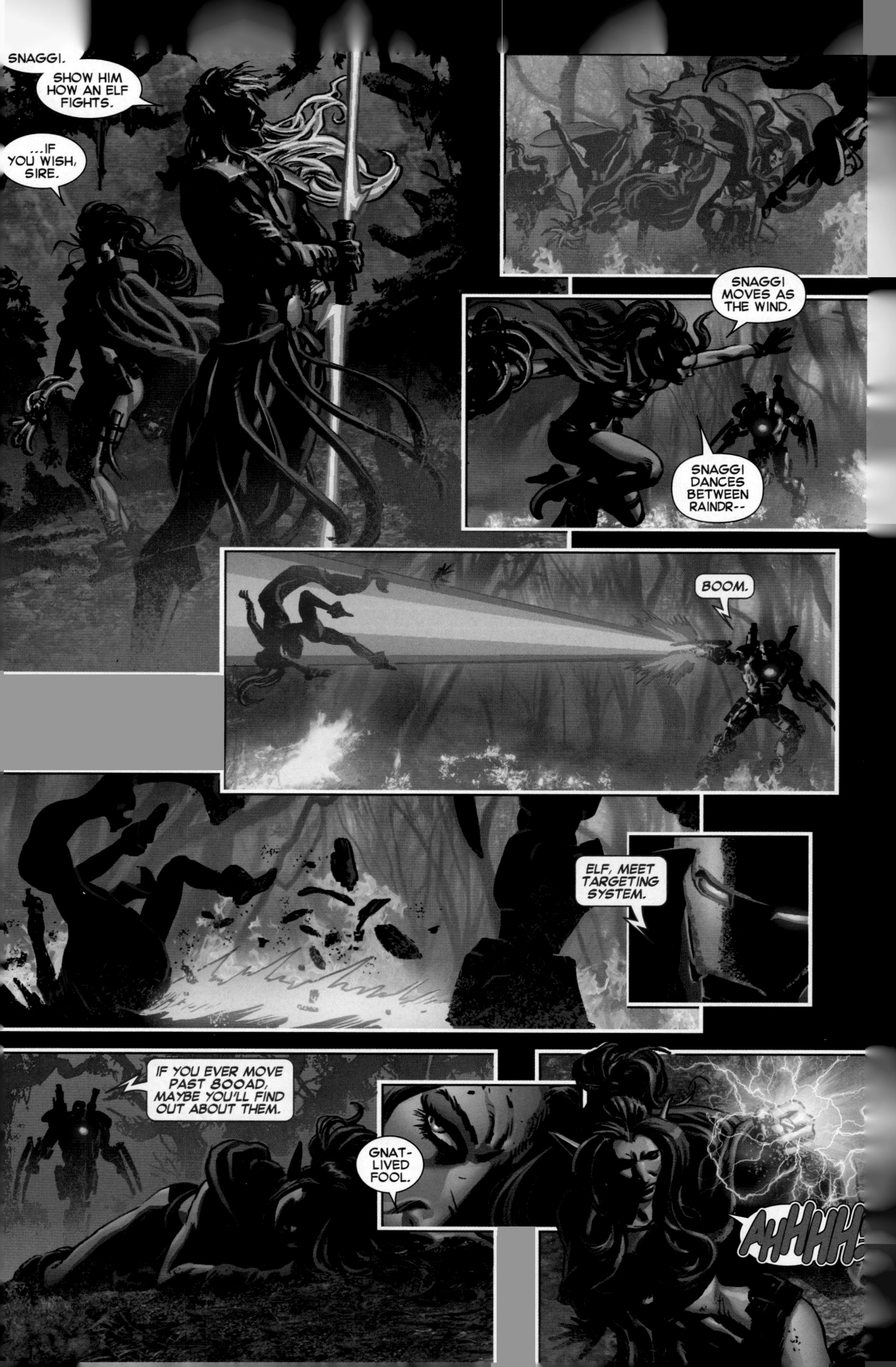
SNAGGI.
SHOW HIM HOW AN ELF FIGHTS.
...IF YOU WISH, SIRE.
SNAGGI MOVES AS THE WIND.
SNAGGI DANCES BETWEEN RAINDR--
BOOM.
ELF, MEET TARGETING SYSTEM.
IF YOU EVER MOVE PAST 800AD, MAYBE YOU'LL FIND OUT ABOUT THEM.
GNAT-LIVED FOOL.
AHHHH

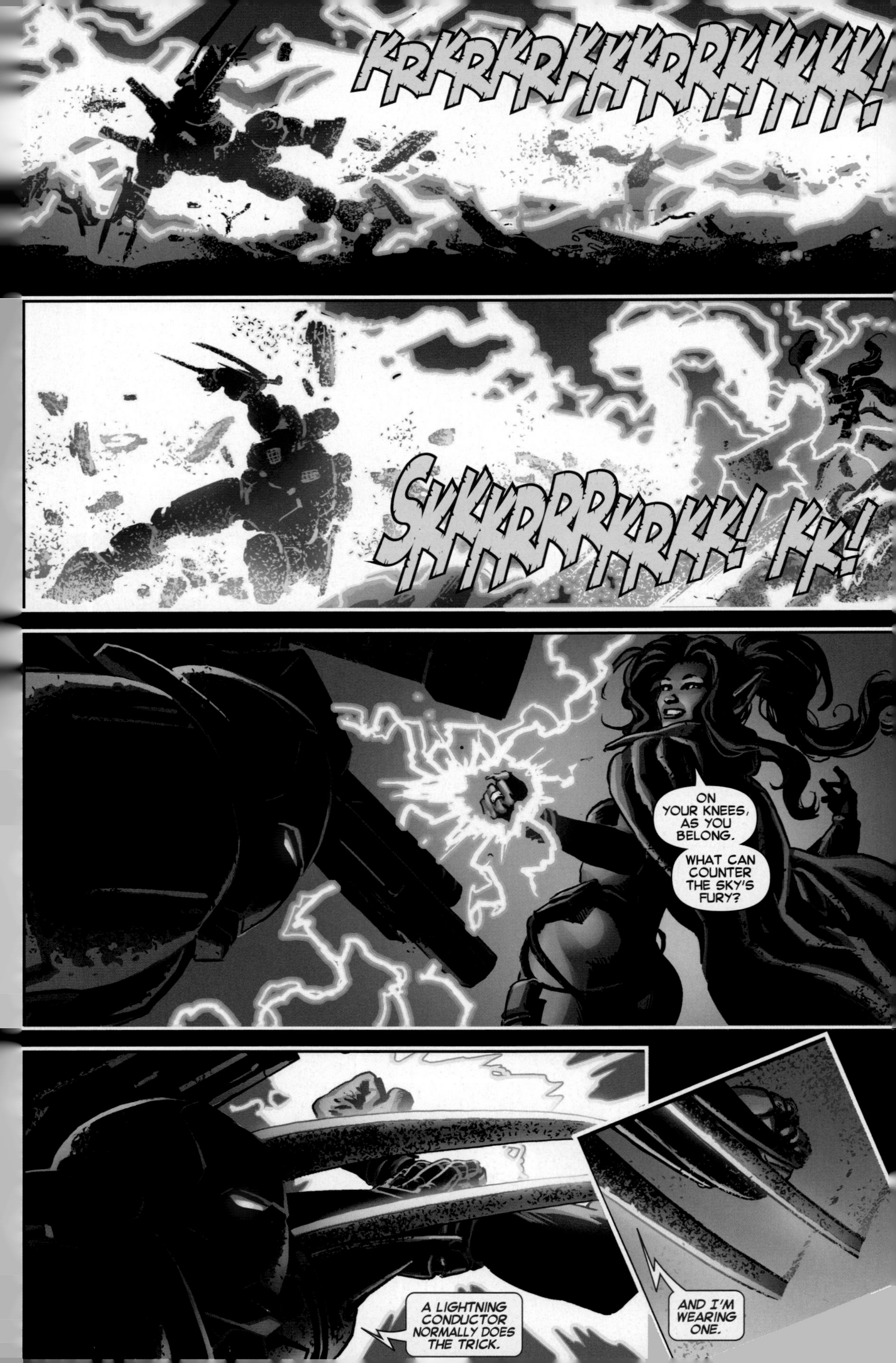
KRKRKRKKKRRKKKK!
SKKKRRRKRKK! KK!
ON YOUR KNEES, AS YOU BELONG.
WHAT CAN COUNTER THE SKY'S FURY?
A LIGHTNING CONDUCTOR NORMALLY DOES THE TRICK.
AND I'M WEARING ONE.

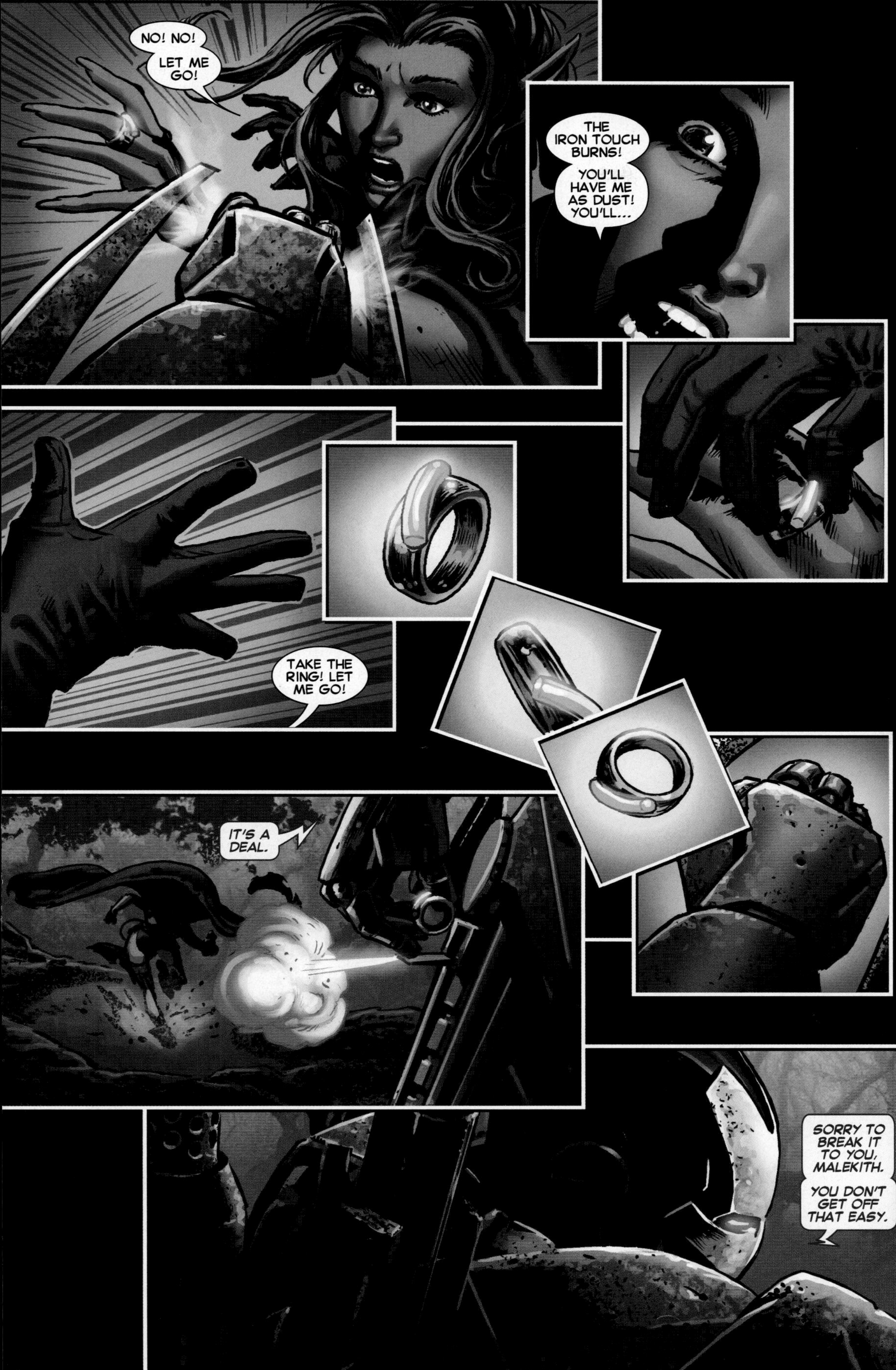
NO! NO!
LET ME GO!
THE IRON TOUCH BURNS!
YOU'LL HAVE ME AS DUST! YOU'LL...
TAKE THE RING! LET ME GO!
IT'S A DEAL.
SORRY TO BREAK IT TO YOU, MALEKITH.
YOU DON'T GET OFF THAT EASY.

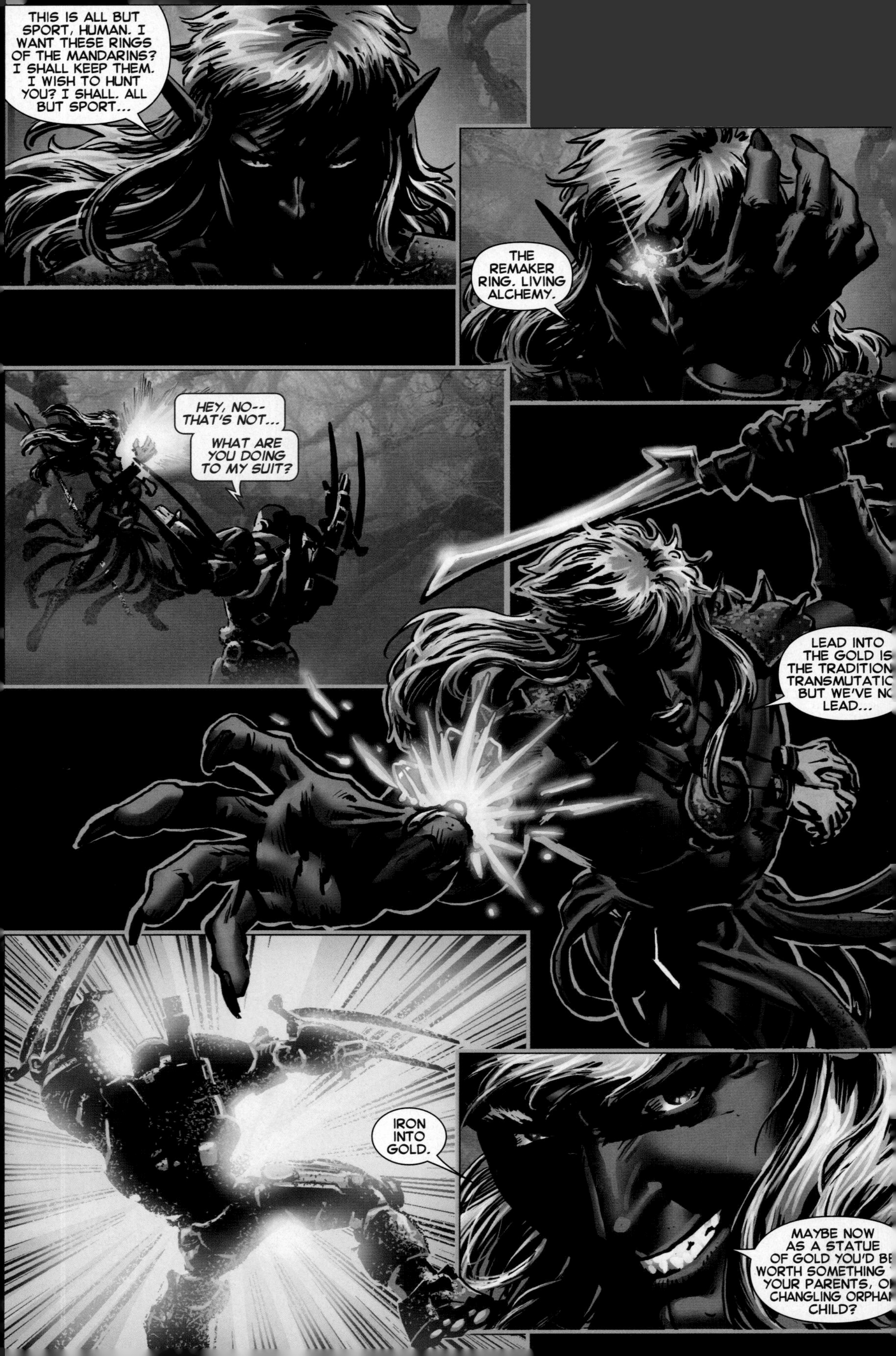
THIS IS ALL BUT SPORT, HUMAN. I WANT THESE RINGS OF THE MANDARINS? I SHALL KEEP THEM. I WISH TO HUNT YOU? I SHALL. ALL BUT SPORT...
THE REMAKER RING. LIVING ALCHEMY.
HEY, NO-- THAT'S NOT...
WHAT ARE YOU DOING TO MY SUIT?
LEAD INTO THE GOLD IS THE TRADITION TRANSMUTATIC BUT WE'VE NC LEAD...
IRON INTO GOLD.
MAYBE NOW AS A STATUE OF GOLD YOU'D BE WORTH SOMETHING YOUR PARENTS, O CHANGLING ORPHAI CHILD?

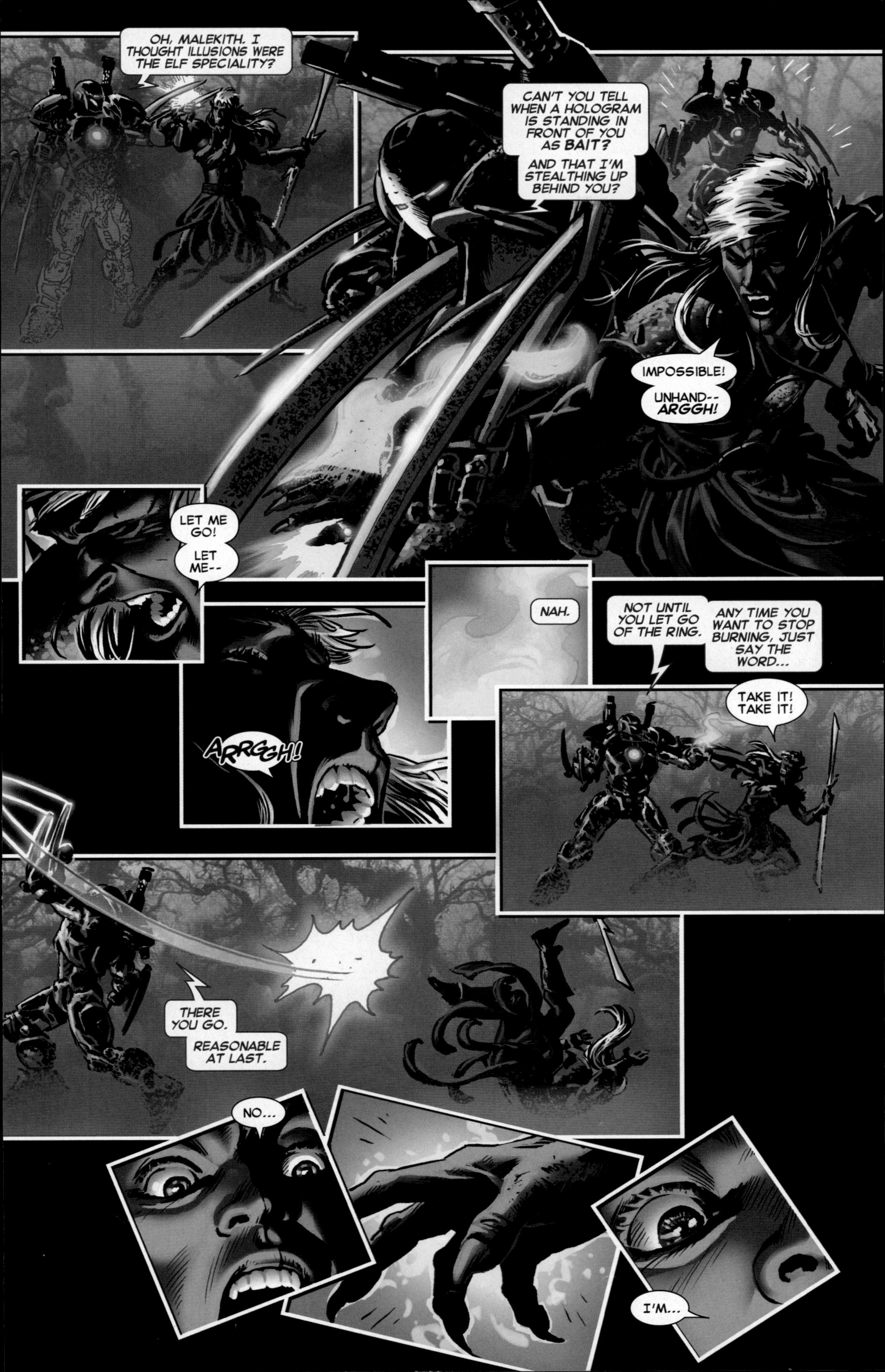
OH, MALEKITH. I THOUGHT ILLUSIONS WERE THE ELF SPECIALITY?
CAN'T YOU TELL WHEN A HOLOGRAM IS STANDING IN FRONT OF YOU AS BAIT?
AND THAT I'M STEALTHING UP BEHIND YOU?
IMPOSSIBLE!
UNHAND-- ARGGH!
LET ME GO!
LET ME--
ARRGGH!
NAH.
NOT UNTIL YOU LET GO OF THE RING.
ANY TIME YOU WANT TO STOP BURNING, JUST SAY THE WORD...
TAKE IT! TAKE IT!
THERE YOU GO.
REASONABLE AT LAST.
NO...
I'M...

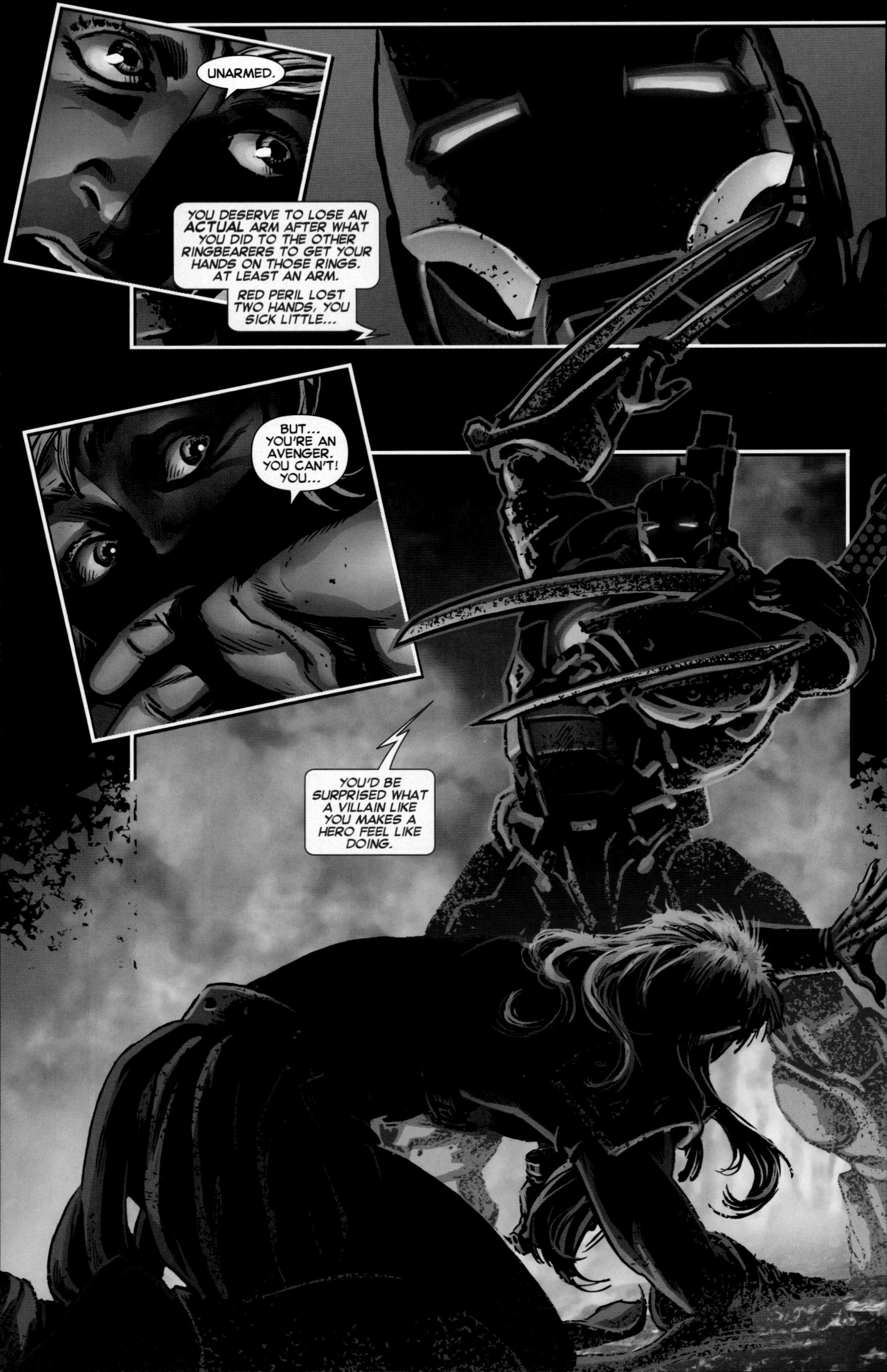
UNARMED.
YOU DESERVE TO LOSE AN ACTUAL ARM AFTER WHAT YOU DID TO THE OTHER RINGBEARERS TO GET YOUR HANDS ON THOSE RINGS. AT LEAST AN ARM.
RED PERIL LOST TWO HANDS, YOU SICK LITTLE...
BUT... YOU'RE AN AVENGER. YOU CAN'T! YOU...
YOU'D BE SURPRISED WHAT A VILLAIN LIKE YOU MAKES A HERO FEEL LIKE DOING.

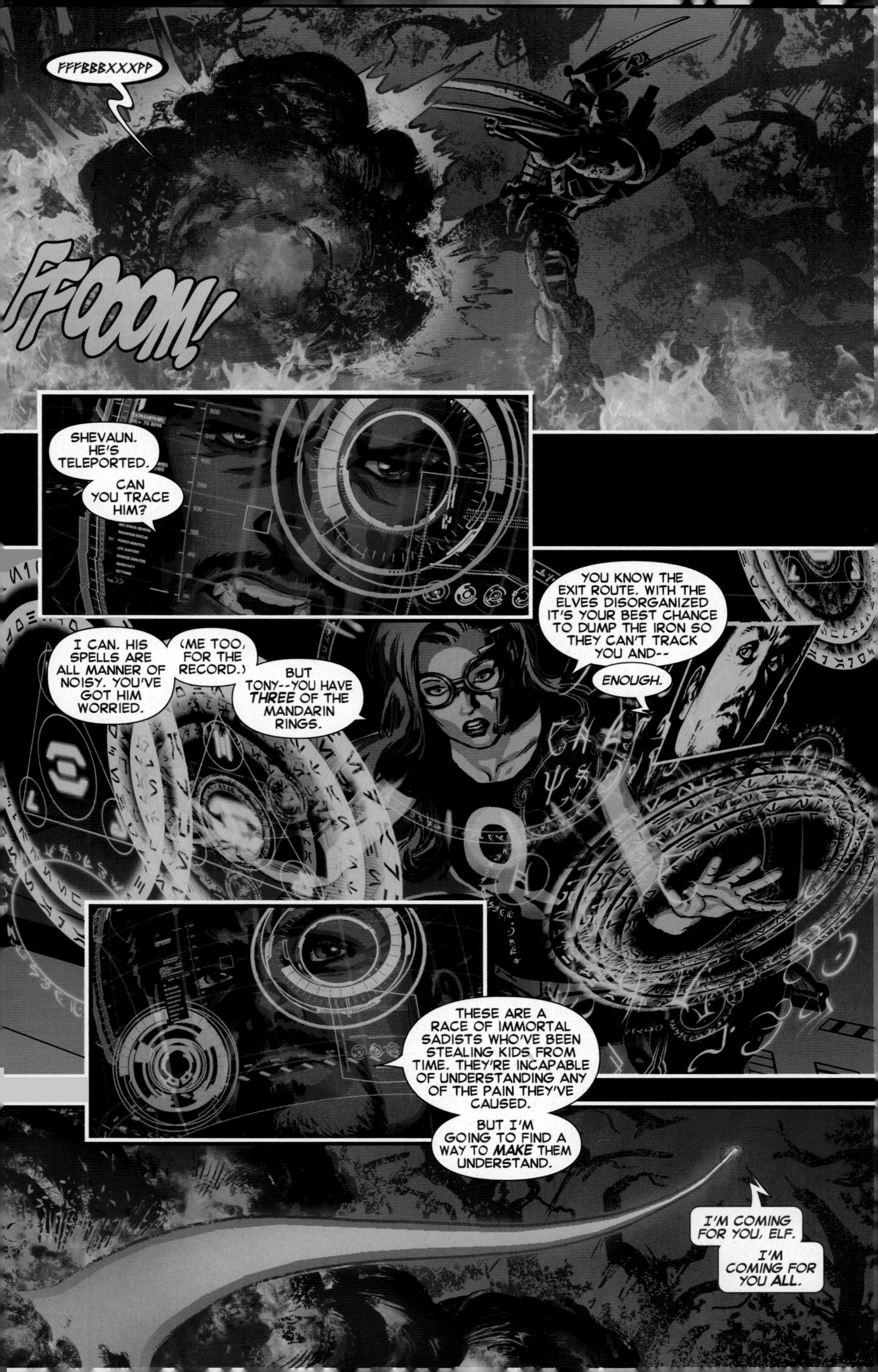
FFFBBBXXXPP
FFOOOM!
SHEVAUN. HE'S TELEPORTED.
CAN YOU TRACE HIM?
I CAN. HIS SPELLS ARE ALL MANNER OF NOISY. YOU'VE GOT HIM WORRIED.
(ME TOO, FOR THE RECORD.)
BUT TONY--YOU HAVE THREE OF THE MANDARIN RINGS.
YOU KNOW THE EXIT ROUTE. WITH THE ELVES DISORGANIZED IT'S YOUR BEST CHANCE TO DUMP THE IRON SO THEY CAN'T TRACK YOU AND--
ENOUGH.
THESE ARE A RACE OF IMMORTAL SADISTS WHO'VE BEEN STEALING KIDS FROM TIME. THEY'RE INCAPABLE OF UNDERSTANDING ANY OF THE PAIN THEY'VE CAUSED.
BUT I'M GOING TO FIND A WAY TO MAKE THEM UNDERSTAND.
I'M COMING FOR YOU, ELF.
I'M COMING FOR YOU ALL.

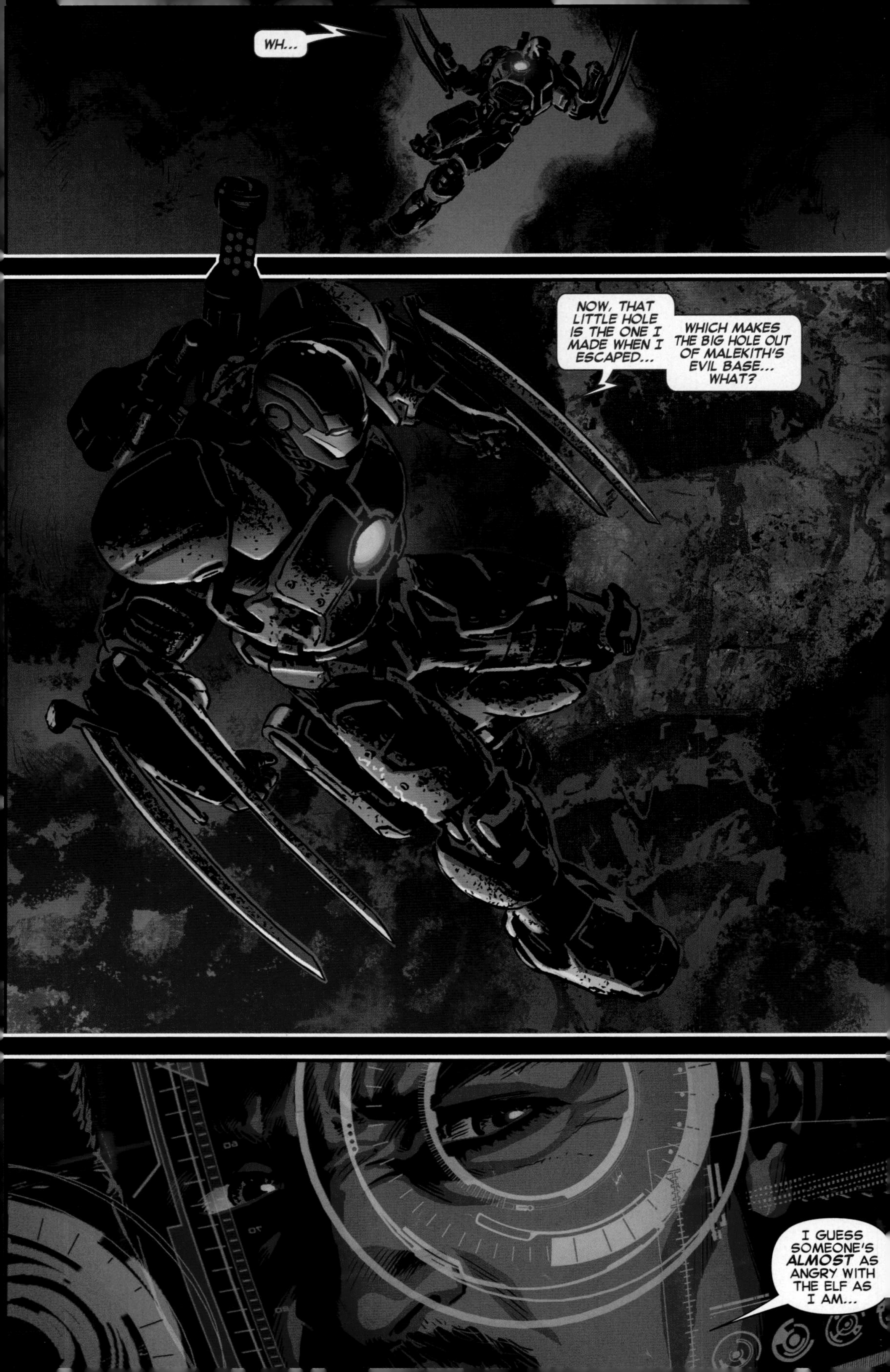
WH...
NOW, THAT LITTLE HOLE IS THE ONE I MADE WHEN I ESCAPED...
WHICH MAKES THE BIG HOLE OUT OF MALEKITH'S EVIL BASE... WHAT?
I GUESS SOMEONE'S ALMOST AS ANGRY WITH THE ELF AS I AM...

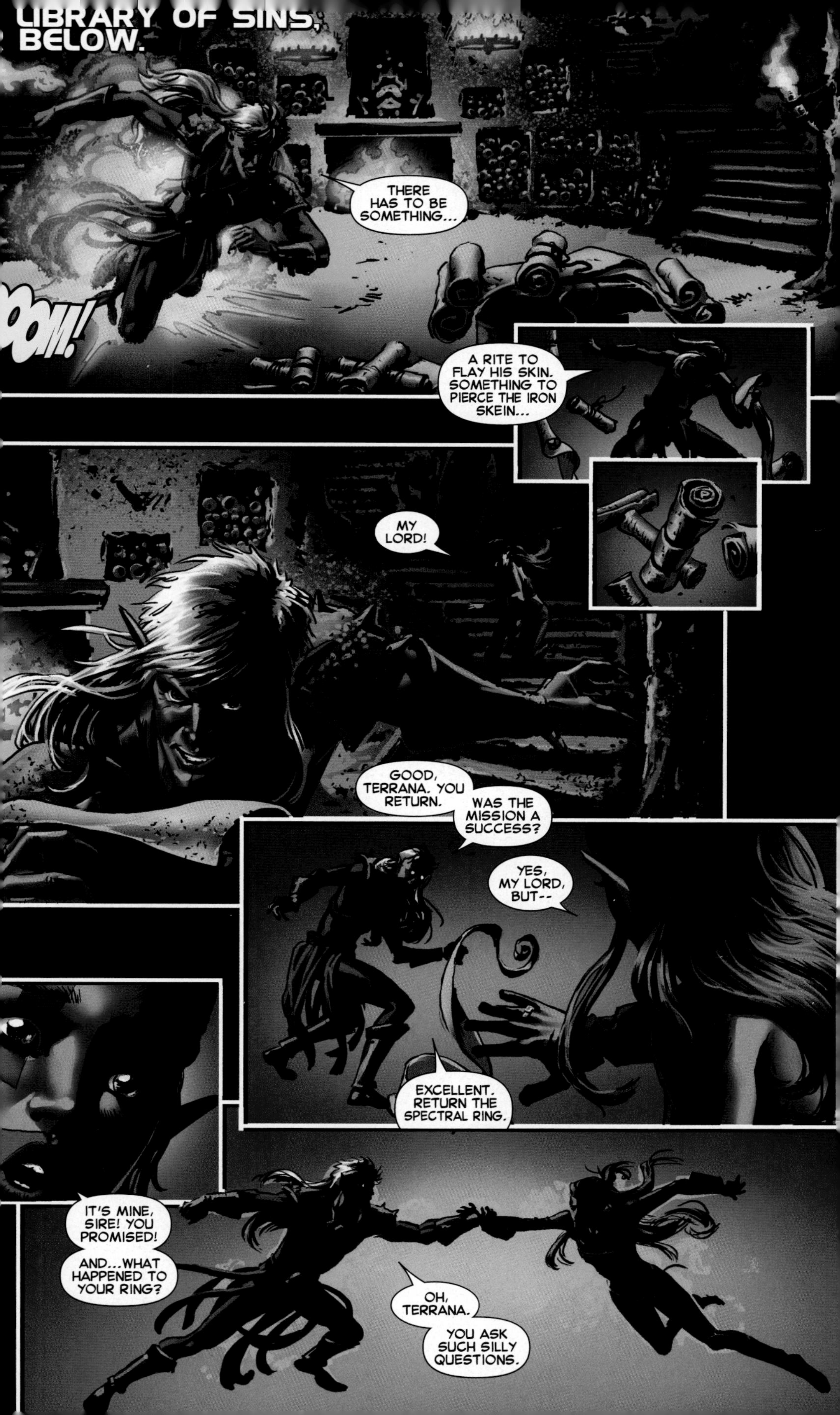
LIBRARY OF SINS, BELOW.
THERE HAS TO BE SOMETHING...
OOM!
A RITE TO FLAY HIS SKIN. SOMETHING TO PIERCE THE IRON SKEIN...
MY LORD!
GOOD, TERRANA. YOU RETURN.
WAS THE MISSION A SUCCESS?
YES, MY LORD, BUT--
EXCELLENT. RETURN THE SPECTRAL RING.
IT'S MINE, SIRE! YOU PROMISED!
AND...WHAT HAPPENED TO YOUR RING?
OH, TERRANA.
YOU ASK SUCH SILLY QUESTIONS.

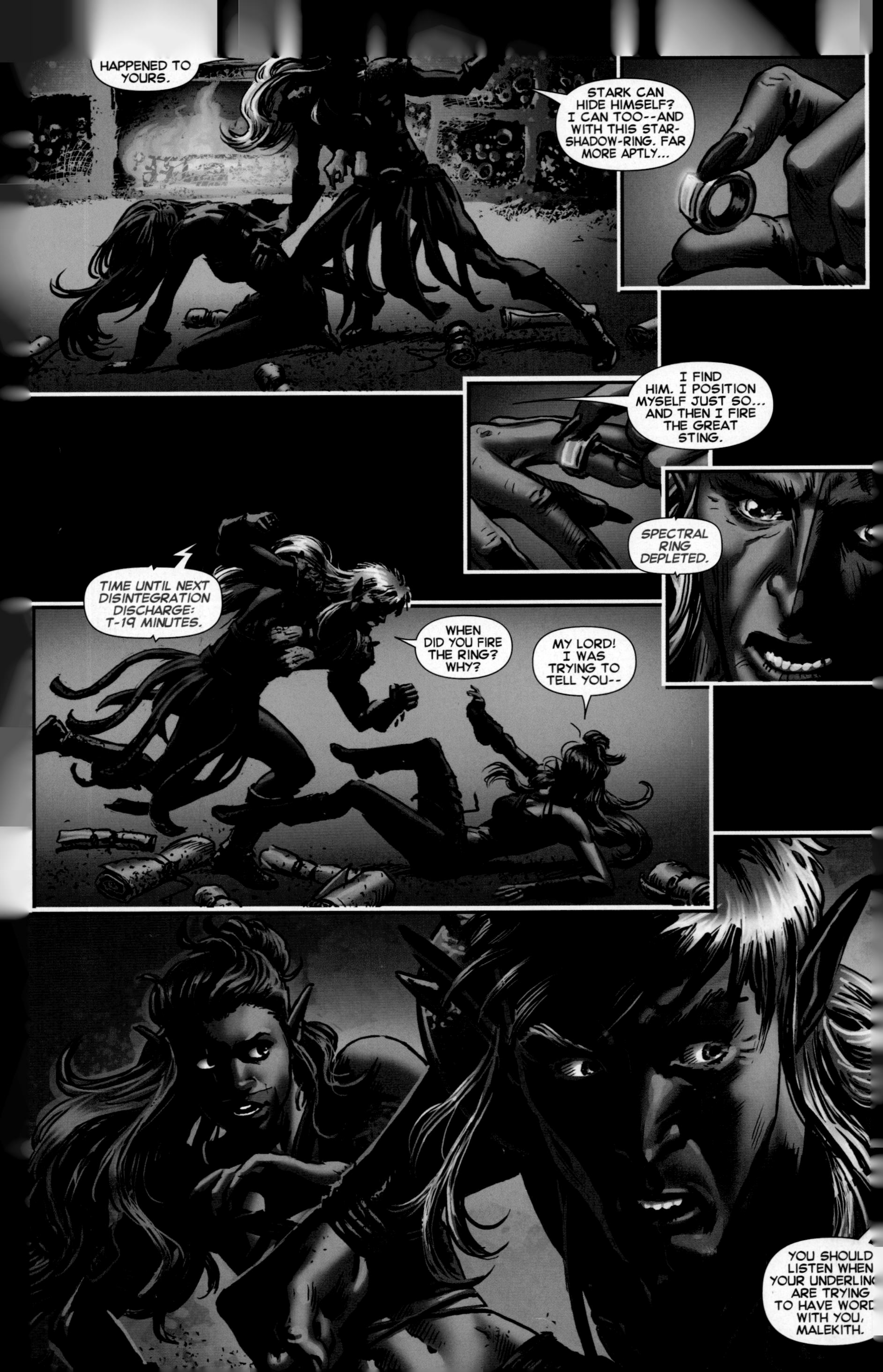
HAPPENED TO YOURS.
STARK CAN HIDE HIMSELF? I CAN TOO--AND WITH THIS STAR-SHADOW-RING. FAR MORE APTLY...
I FIND HIM. I POSITION MYSELF JUST SO... AND THEN I FIRE THE GREAT STING.
SPECTRAL RING DEPLETED.
TIME UNTIL NEXT DISINTEGRATION DISCHARGE: T-19 MINUTES.
WHEN DID YOU FIRE THE RING? WHY?
MY LORD! I WAS TRYING TO TELL YOU--
YOU SHOULD LISTEN WHEN YOUR UNDERLING ARE TRYING TO HAVE WORD WITH YOU, MALEKITH.

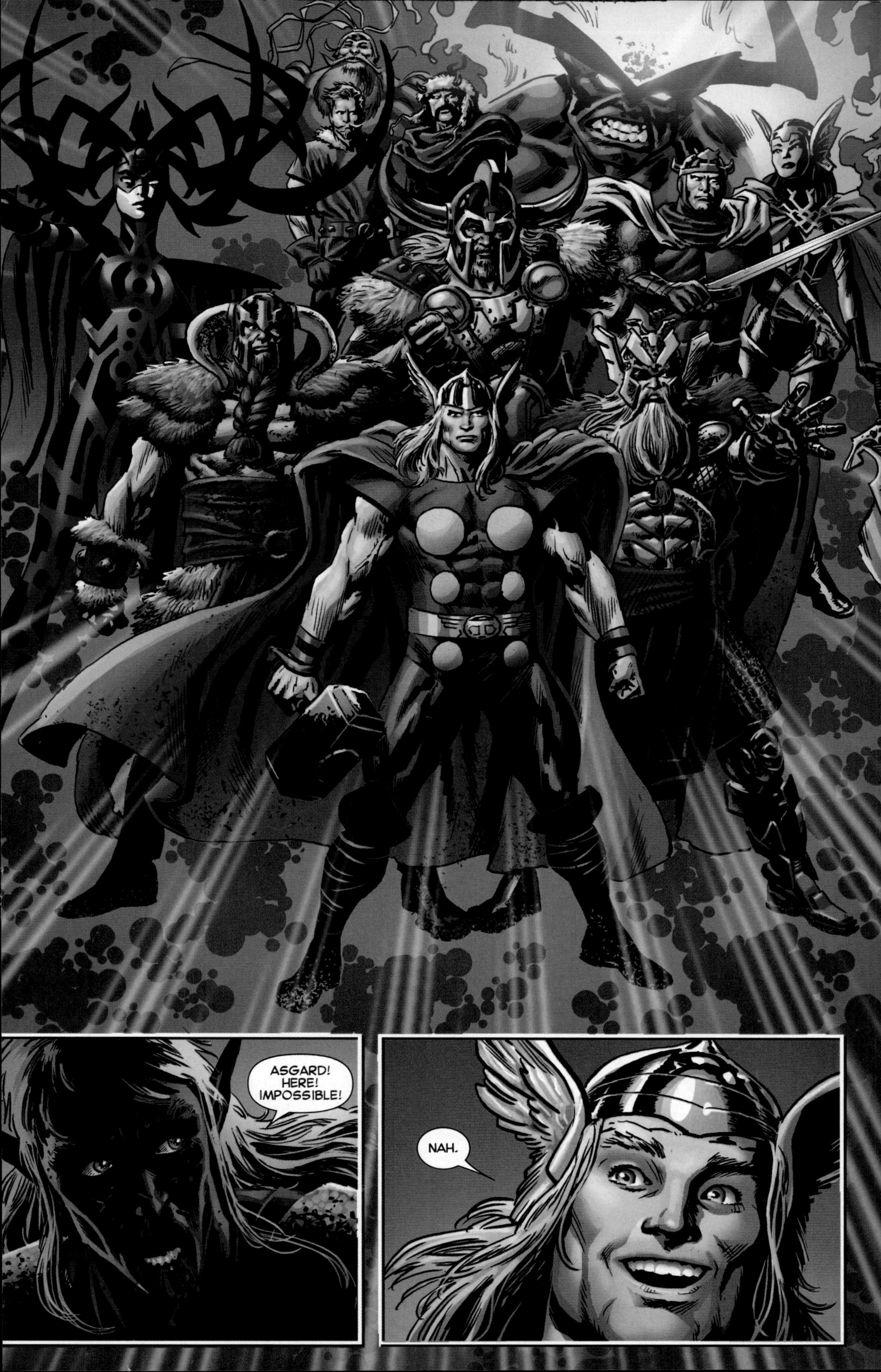
ASGARD! HERE! IMPOSSIBLE!
NAH.

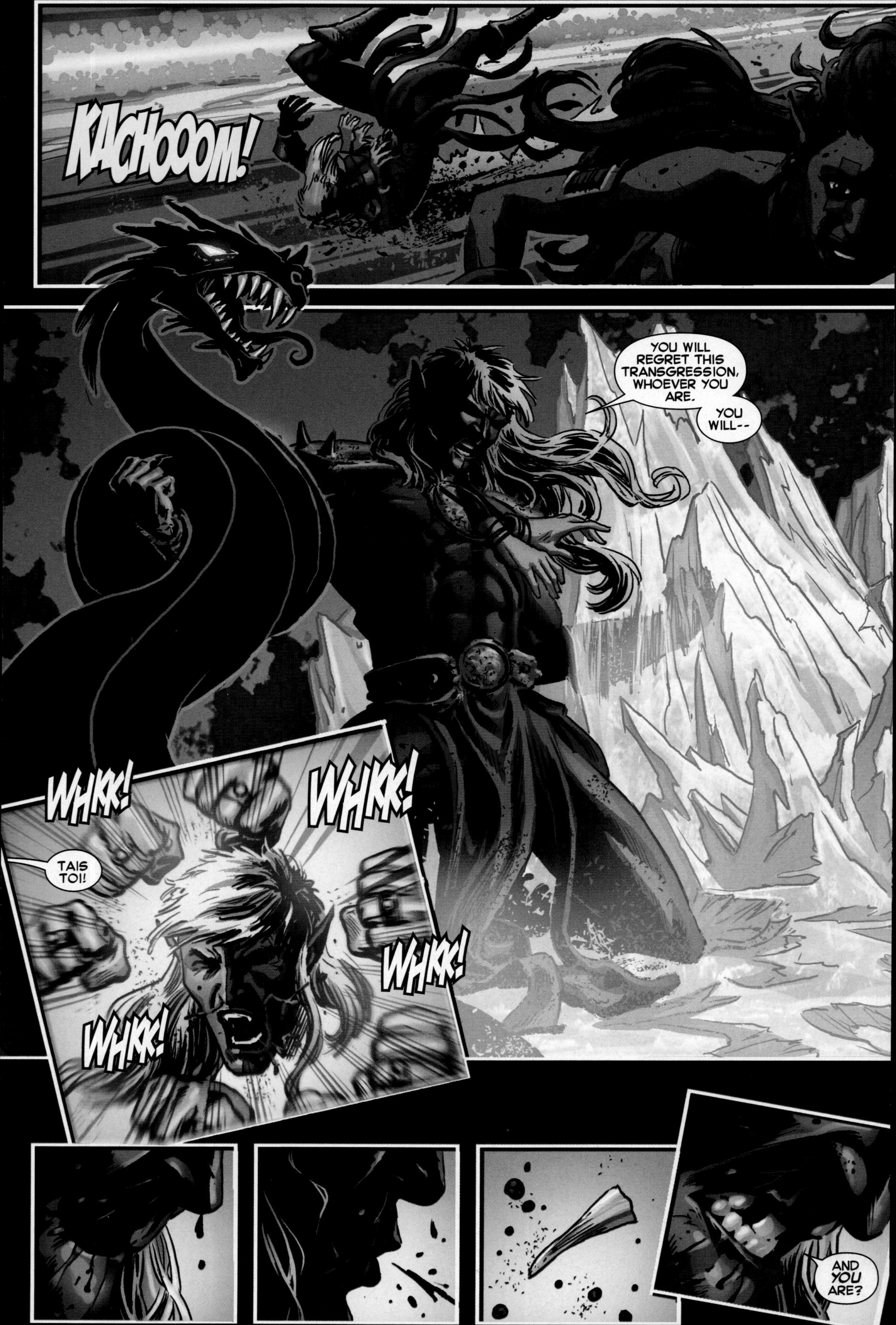
KACHOOOM!
YOU WILL REGRET THIS TRANSGRESSION, WHOEVER YOU ARE.
YOU WILL--
WHKK!
WHKK!
TAIS TOI!
WHKK!
WHKK!
AND YOU ARE?

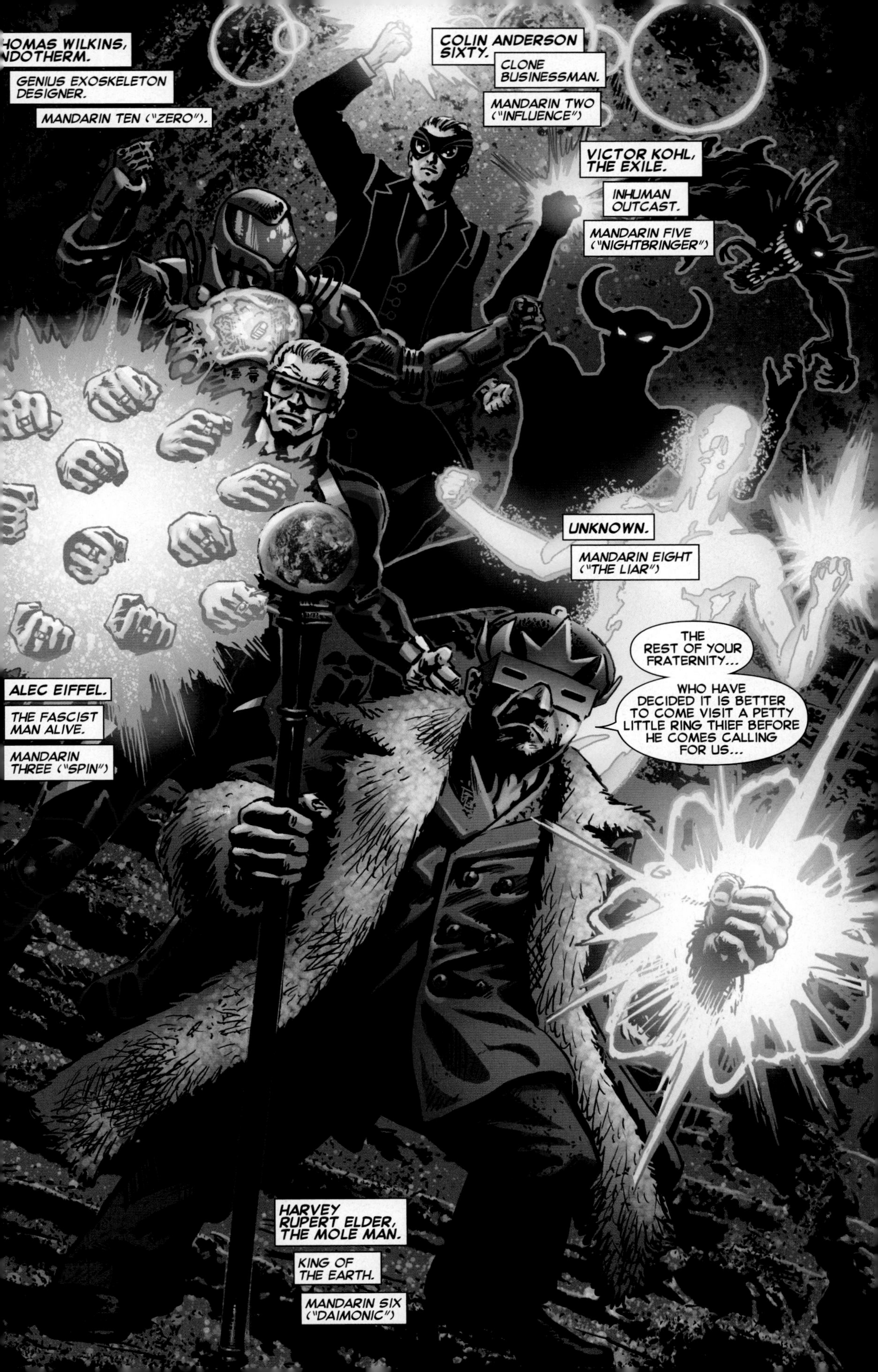
HOMAS WILKINS, NDOTHERM.
GENIUS EXOSKELETON DESIGNER.
MANDARIN TEN ("ZERO").
COLIN ANDERSON SIXTY.
CLONE BUSINESSMAN.
MANDARIN TWO ("INFLUENCE")
VICTOR KOHL, THE EXILE.
INHUMAN OUTCAST.
MANDARIN FIVE ("NIGHTBRINGER")
UNKNOWN.
MANDARIN EIGHT ("THE LIAR")
THE REST OF YOUR FRATERNITY...
WHO HAVE DECIDED IT IS BETTER TO COME VISIT A PETTY LITTLE RING THIEF BEFORE HE COMES CALLING FOR US...
ALEC EIFFEL.
THE FASCIST MAN ALIVE.
MANDARIN THREE ("SPIN")
HARVEY RUPERT ELDER, THE MOLE MAN.
KING OF THE EARTH.
MANDARIN SIX ("DAIMONIC")

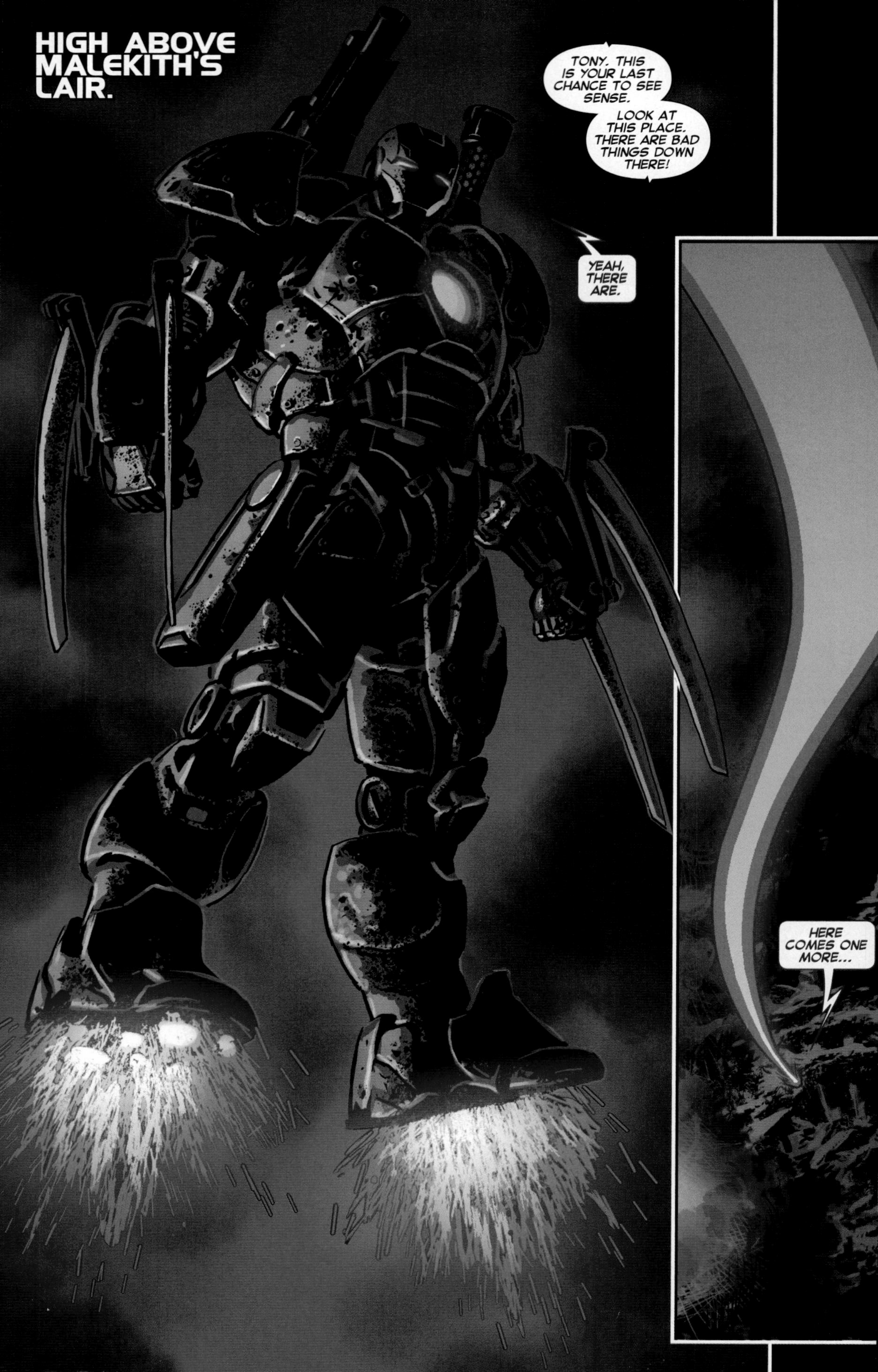
HIGH ABOVE MALEKITH'S LAIR.
TONY. THIS IS YOUR LAST CHANCE TO SEE SENSE.
LOOK AT THIS PLACE. THERE ARE BAD THINGS DOWN THERE!
YEAH, THERE ARE.
HERE COMES ONE MORE...

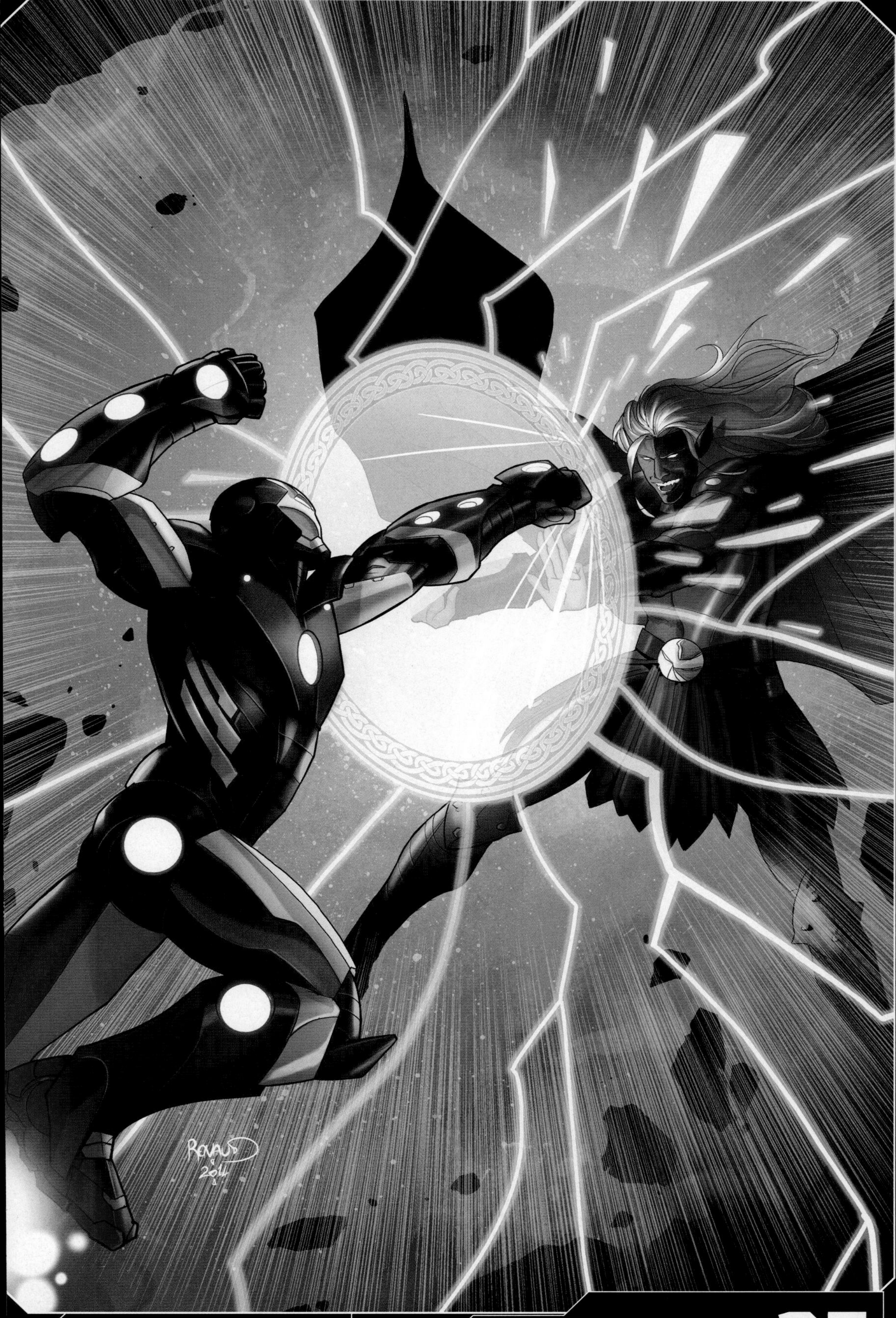
RENAUD
2014

VARIANT BY PAUL RENAUD

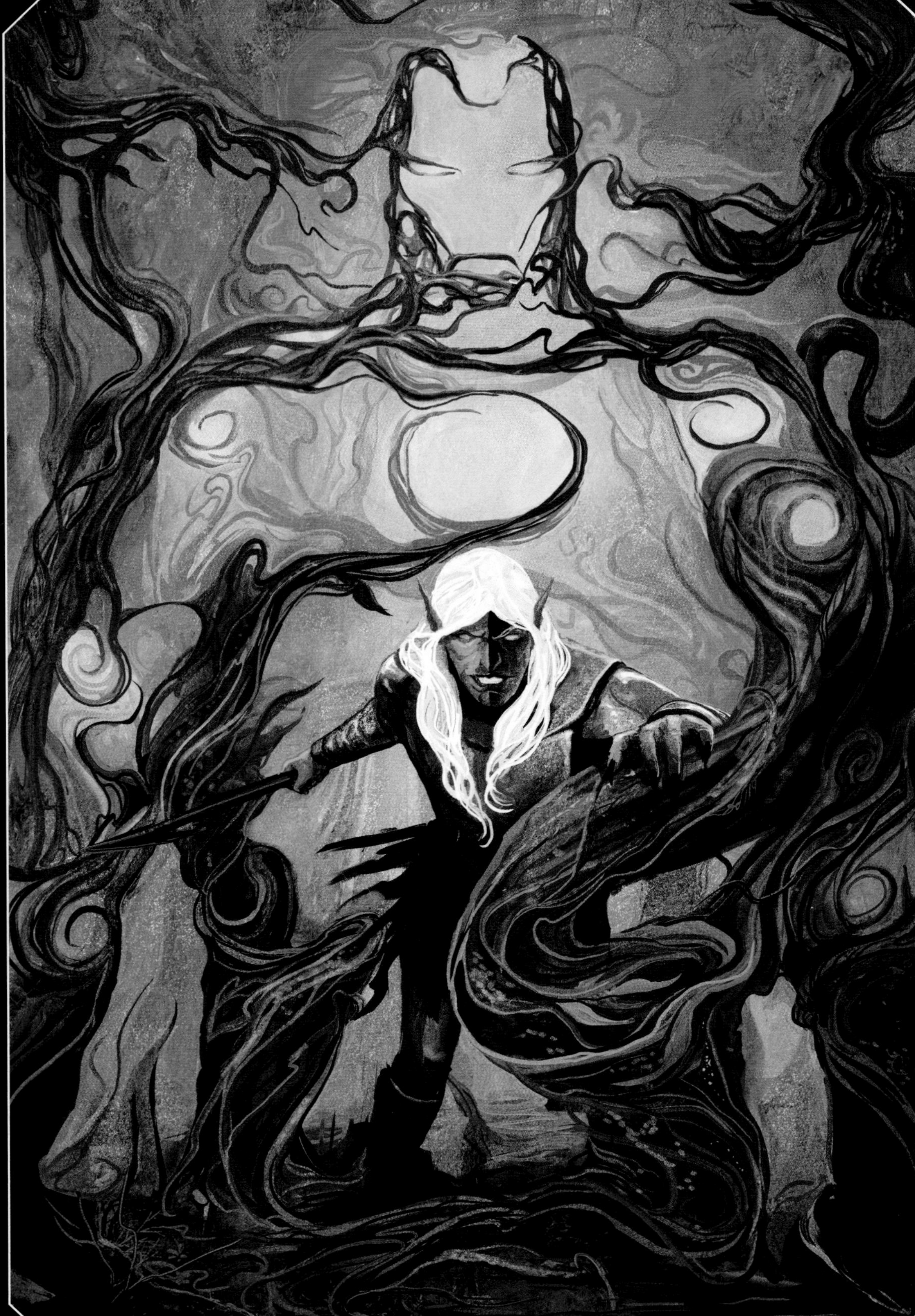

26 RINGS OF THE MANDARIN CHAPTER 4

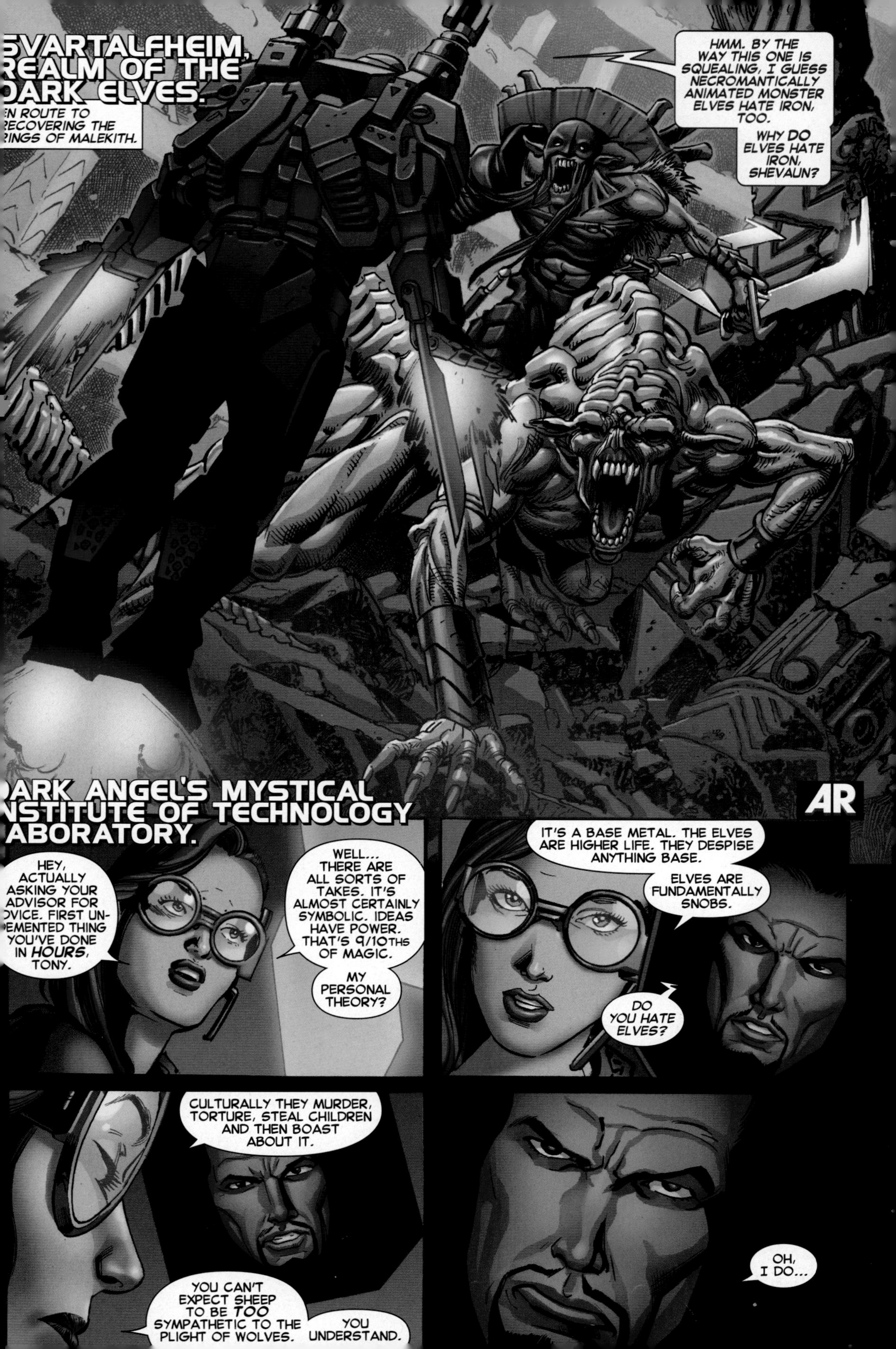
SVARTALFHEIM, REALM OF THE DARK ELVES.
EN ROUTE TO RECOVERING THE RINGS OF MALEKITH.
HMM. BY THE WAY THIS ONE IS SQUEALING, I GUESS NECROMANTICALLY ANIMATED MONSTER ELVES HATE IRON, TOO.
WHY DO ELVES HATE IRON, SHEVAUN?
AR
DARK ANGEL'S MYSTICAL INSTITUTE OF TECHNOLOGY LABORATORY.
HEY, ACTUALLY ASKING YOUR ADVISOR FOR ADVICE. FIRST UNPRECEDENTED THING YOU'VE DONE IN HOURS, TONY.
WELL... THERE ARE ALL SORTS OF TAKES. IT'S ALMOST CERTAINLY SYMBOLIC. IDEAS HAVE POWER. THAT'S 9/10THS OF MAGIC.
MY PERSONAL THEORY?
IT'S A BASE METAL. THE ELVES ARE HIGHER LIFE. THEY DESPISE ANYTHING BASE.
ELVES ARE FUNDAMENTALLY SNOBS.
DO YOU HATE ELVES?
CULTURALLY THEY MURDER, TORTURE, STEAL CHILDREN AND THEN BOAST ABOUT IT.
YOU CAN'T EXPECT SHEEP TO BE TOO SYMPATHETIC TO THE PLIGHT OF WOLVES.
YOU UNDERSTAND.
OH, I DO...

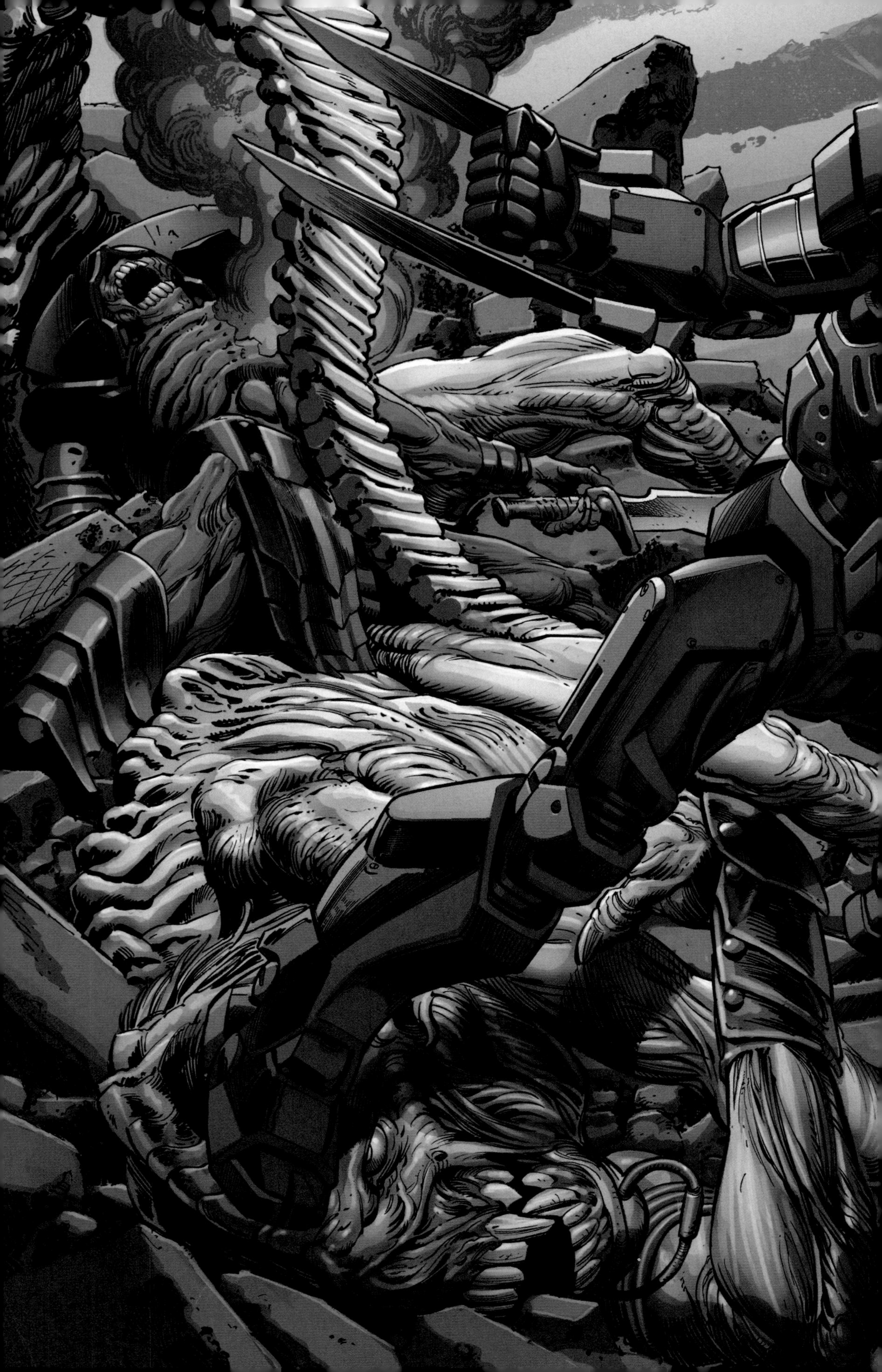

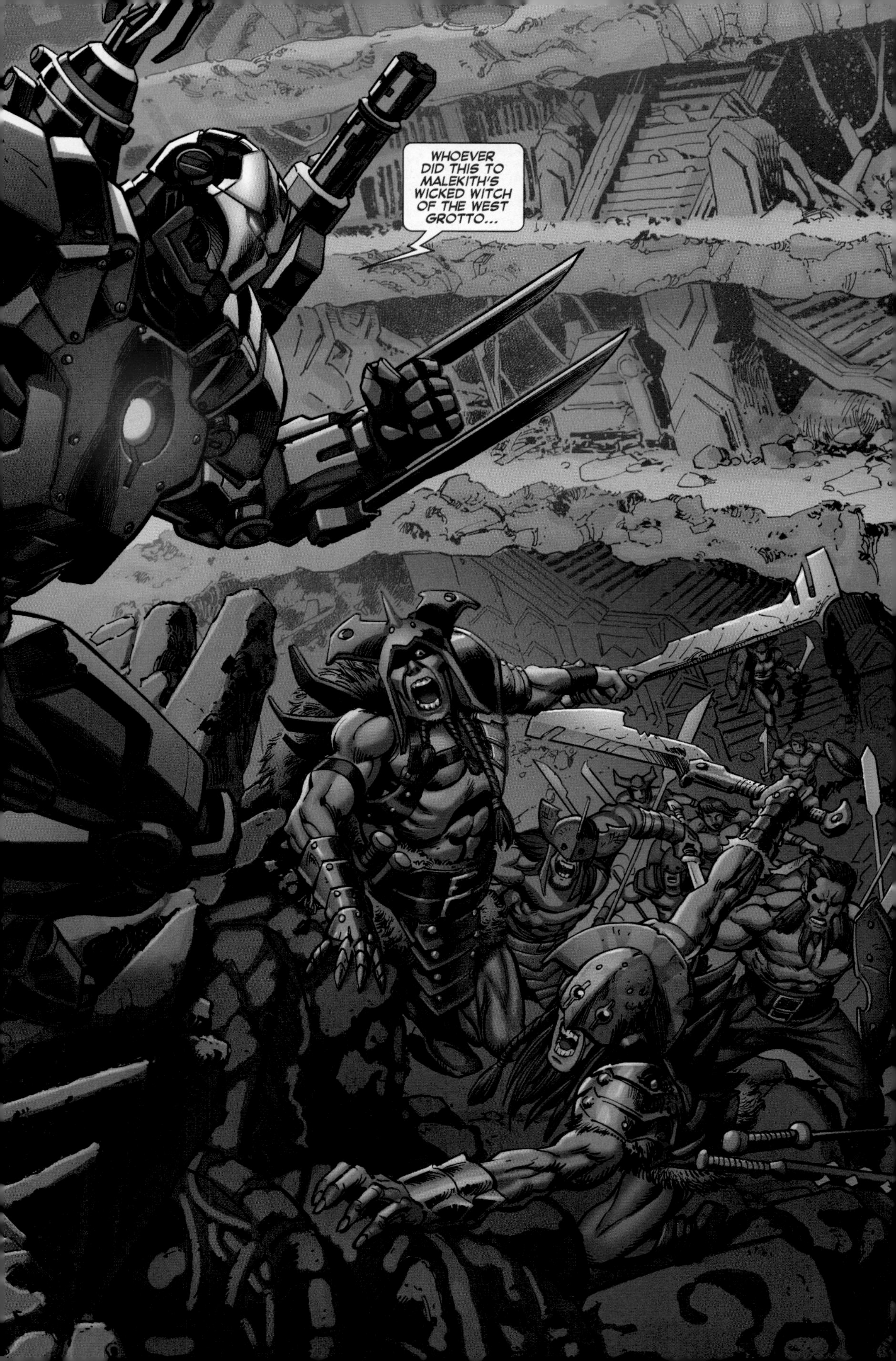
WHOEVER DID THIS TO MALEKITH'S WICKED WITCH OF THE WEST GROTTO...

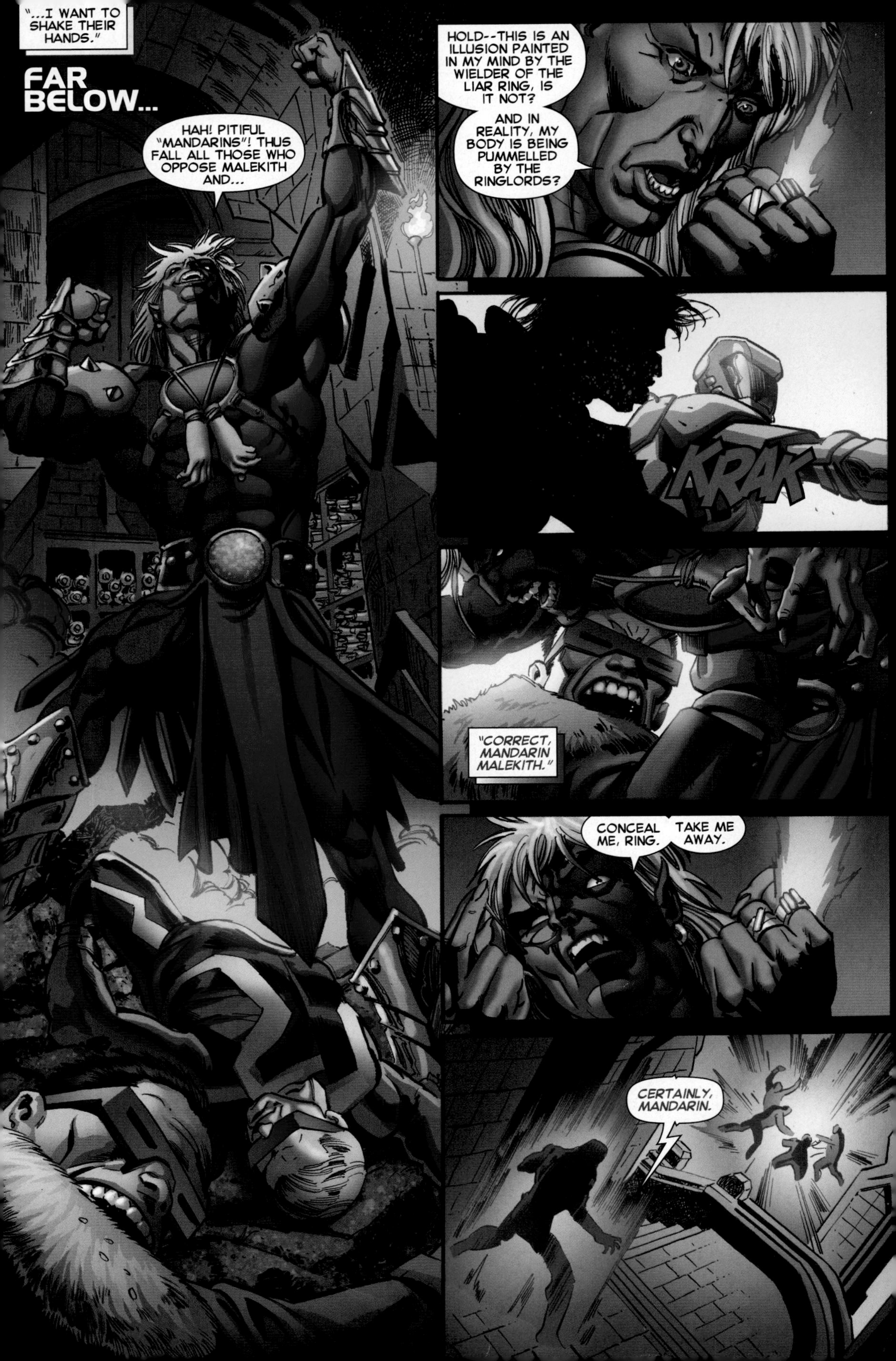
"...I WANT TO SHAKE THEIR HANDS."
FAR BELOW...
HAH! PITIFUL "MANDARINS"! THUS FALL ALL THOSE WHO OPPOSE MALEKITH AND...
HOLD--THIS IS AN ILLUSION PAINTED IN MY MIND BY THE WIELDER OF THE LIAR RING, IS IT NOT?
AND IN REALITY, MY BODY IS BEING PUMMELLED BY THE RINGLORDS?
KRAK
"CORRECT, MANDARIN MALEKITH."
CONCEAL ME, RING.
TAKE ME AWAY.
CERTAINLY, MANDARIN.

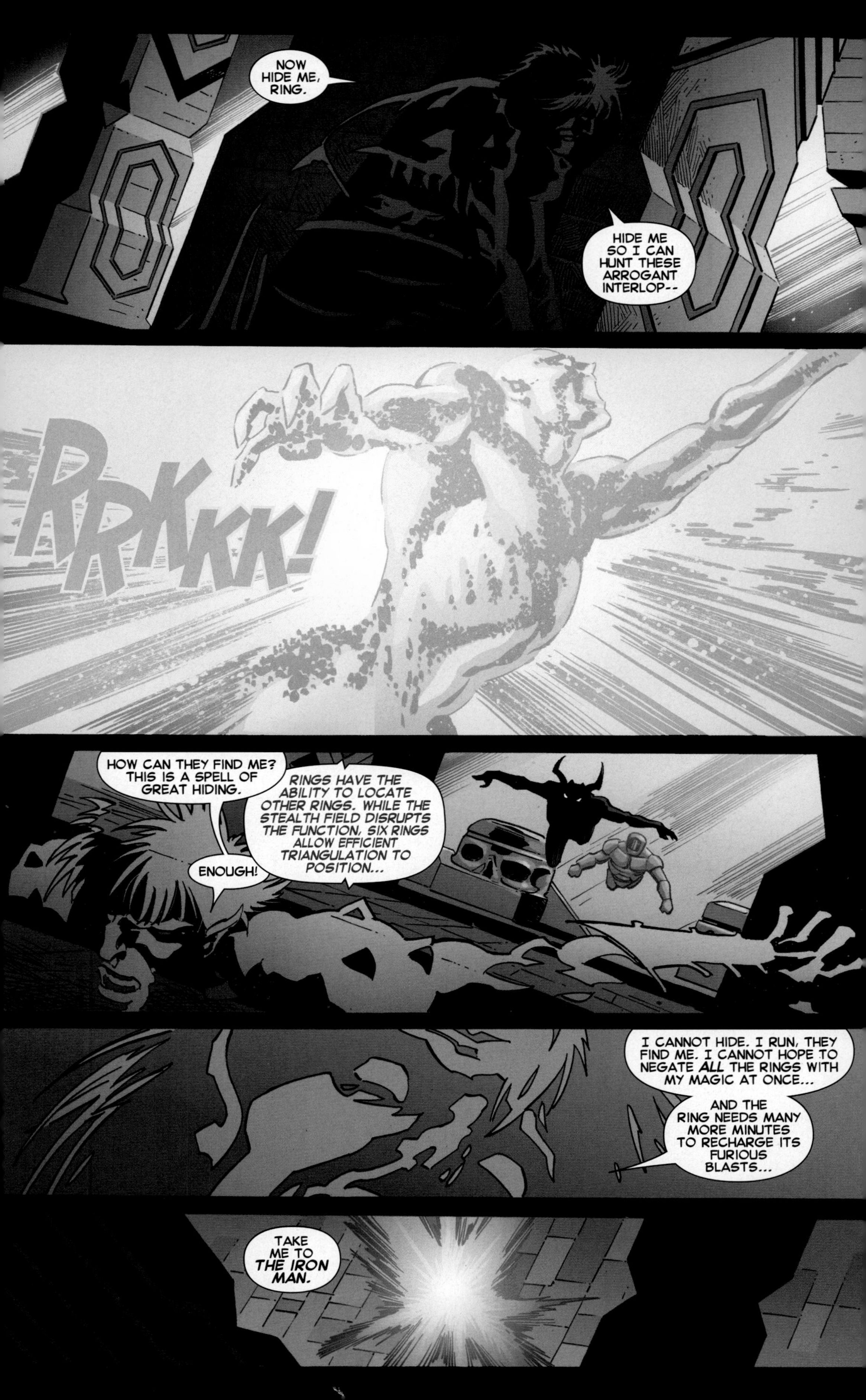
NOW HIDE ME, RING.
HIDE ME SO I CAN HUNT THESE ARROGANT INTERLOP--
RRKKK!
HOW CAN THEY FIND ME? THIS IS A SPELL OF GREAT HIDING.
RINGS HAVE THE ABILITY TO LOCATE OTHER RINGS. WHILE THE STEALTH FIELD DISRUPTS THE FUNCTION, SIX RINGS ALLOW EFFICIENT TRIANGULATION TO POSITION...
ENOUGH!
I CANNOT HIDE. I RUN, THEY FIND ME. I CANNOT HOPE TO NEGATE ALL THE RINGS WITH MY MAGIC AT ONCE...
AND THE RING NEEDS MANY MORE MINUTES TO RECHARGE ITS FURIOUS BLASTS...
TAKE ME TO THE IRON MAN.

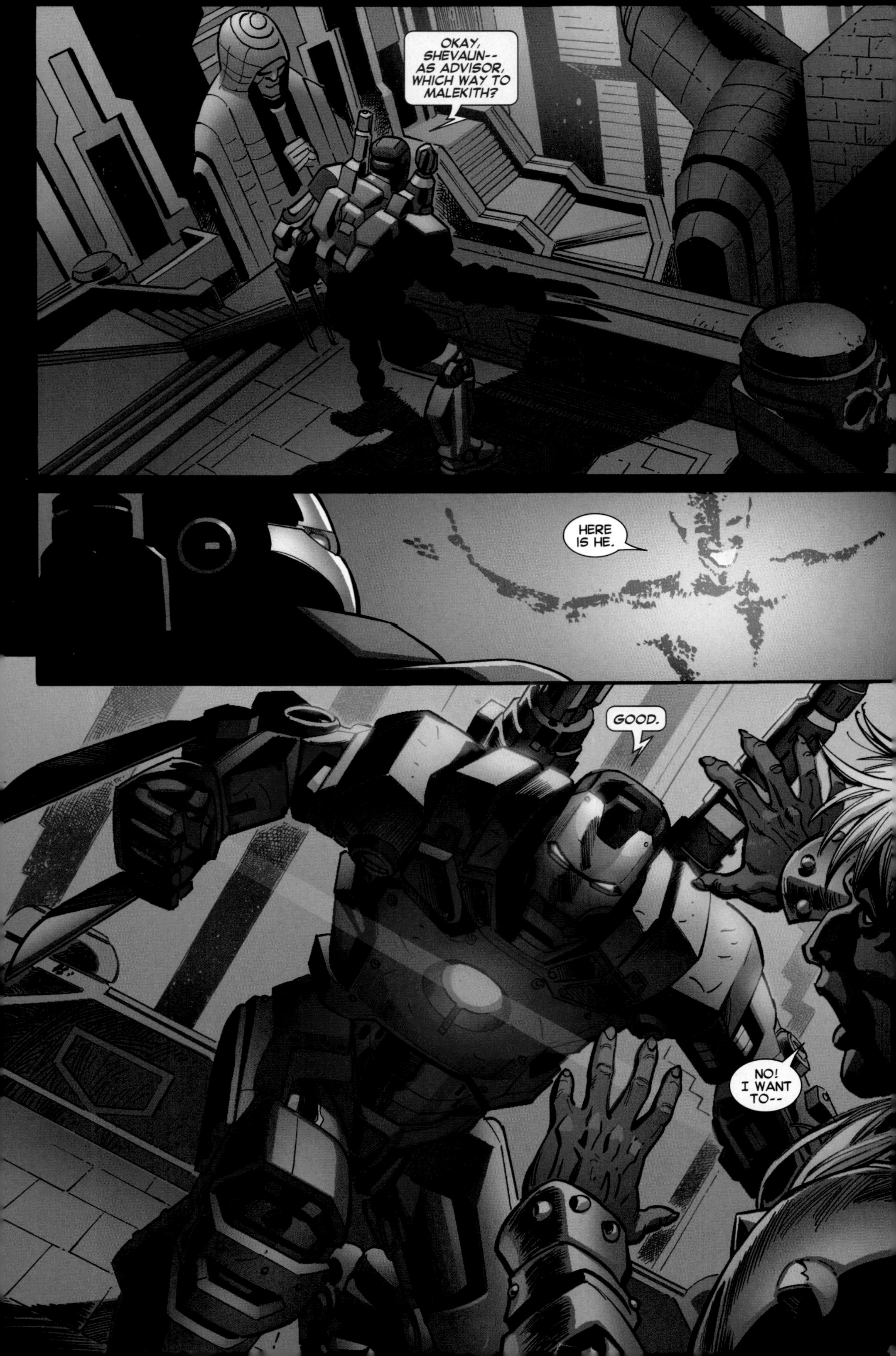
OKAY, SHEVAUN-- AS ADVISOR, WHICH WAY TO MALEKITH?
HERE IS HE.
GOOD.
NO! I WANT TO--

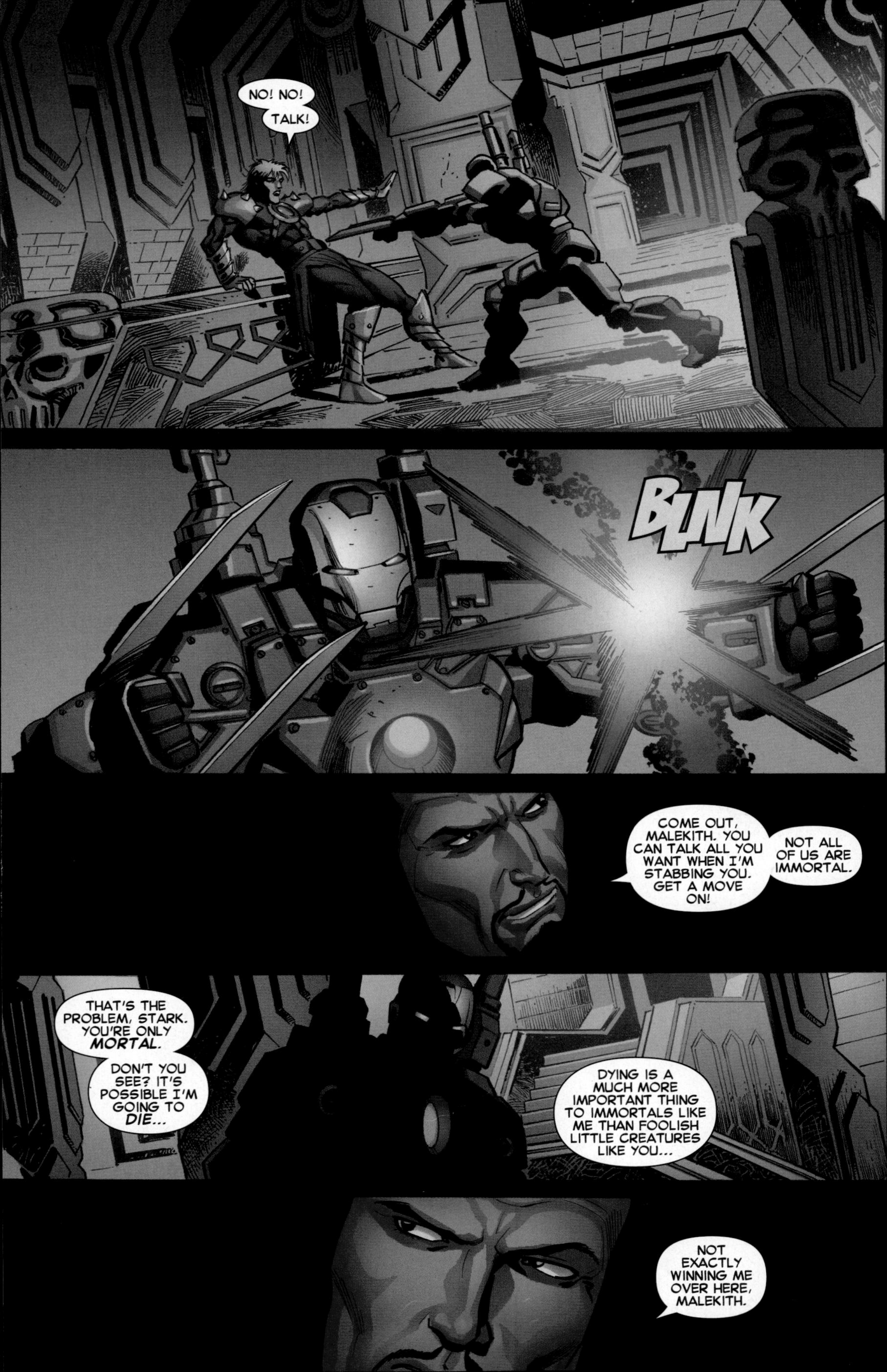
NO! NO!
TALK!
BLNK
COME OUT, MALEKITH. YOU CAN TALK ALL YOU WANT WHEN I'M STABBING YOU. GET A MOVE ON!
NOT ALL OF US ARE IMMORTAL.
THAT'S THE PROBLEM, STARK. YOU'RE ONLY MORTAL.
DON'T YOU SEE? IT'S POSSIBLE I'M GOING TO DIE...
DYING IS A MUCH MORE IMPORTANT THING TO IMMORTALS LIKE ME THAN FOOLISH LITTLE CREATURES LIKE YOU...
NOT EXACTLY WINNING ME OVER HERE, MALEKITH.

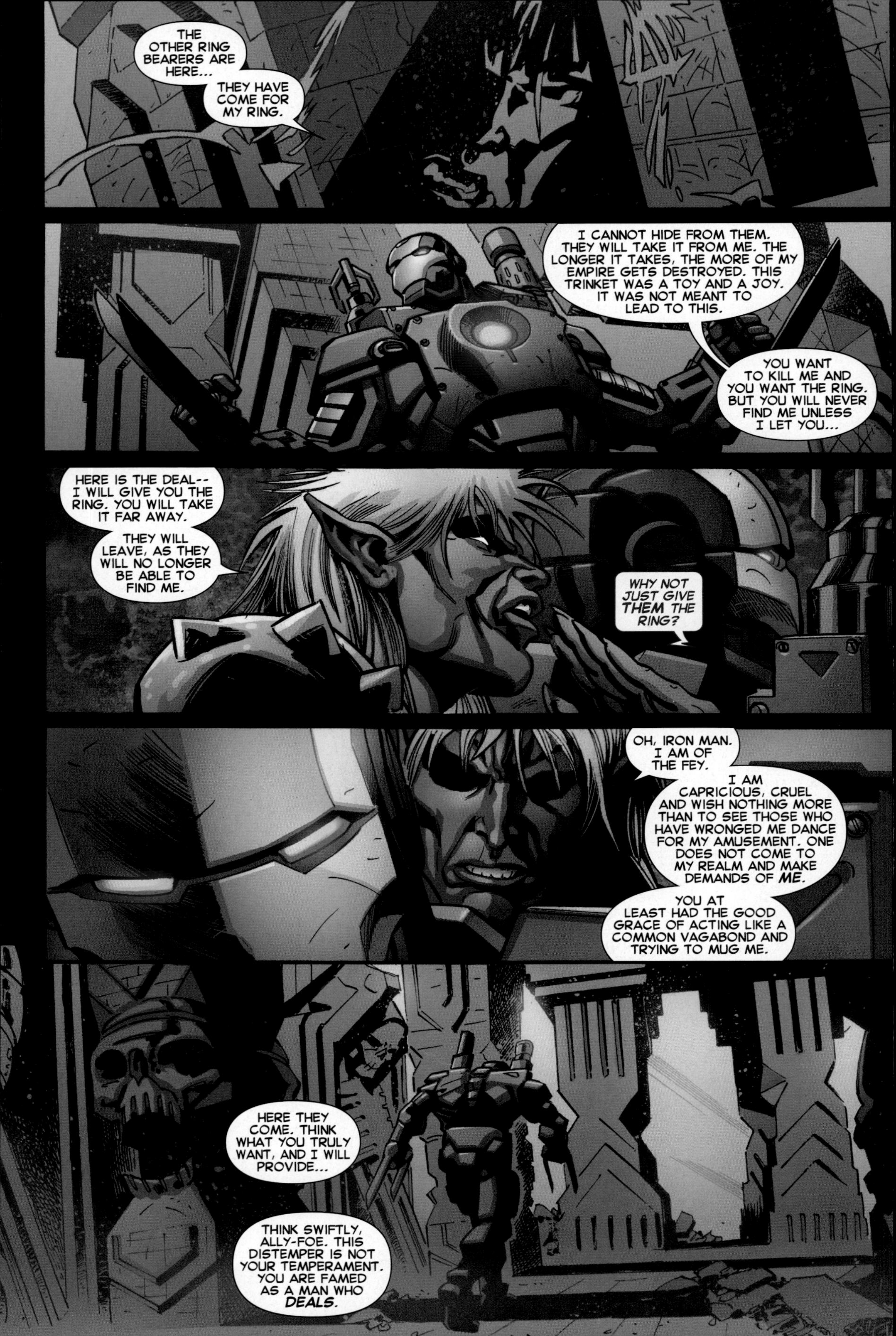
THE OTHER RING BEARERS ARE HERE...
THEY HAVE COME FOR MY RING.
I CANNOT HIDE FROM THEM. THEY WILL TAKE IT FROM ME. THE LONGER IT TAKES, THE MORE OF MY EMPIRE GETS DESTROYED. THIS TRINKET WAS A TOY AND A JOY. IT WAS NOT MEANT TO LEAD TO THIS.
YOU WANT TO KILL ME AND YOU WANT THE RING. BUT YOU WILL NEVER FIND ME UNLESS I LET YOU...
HERE IS THE DEAL-- I WILL GIVE YOU THE RING. YOU WILL TAKE IT FAR AWAY.
THEY WILL LEAVE, AS THEY WILL NO LONGER BE ABLE TO FIND ME.
WHY NOT JUST GIVE THEM THE RING?
OH, IRON MAN. I AM OF THE FEY.
I AM CAPRICIOUS, CRUEL AND WISH NOTHING MORE THAN TO SEE THOSE WHO HAVE WRONGED ME DANCE FOR MY AMUSEMENT. ONE DOES NOT COME TO MY REALM AND MAKE DEMANDS OF ME.
YOU AT LEAST HAD THE GOOD GRACE OF ACTING LIKE A COMMON VAGABOND AND TRYING TO MUG ME.
HERE THEY COME. THINK WHAT YOU TRULY WANT, AND I WILL PROVIDE...
THINK SWIFTLY, ALLY-FOE. THIS DISTEMPER IS NOT YOUR TEMPERAMENT. YOU ARE FAMED AS A MAN WHO DEALS.

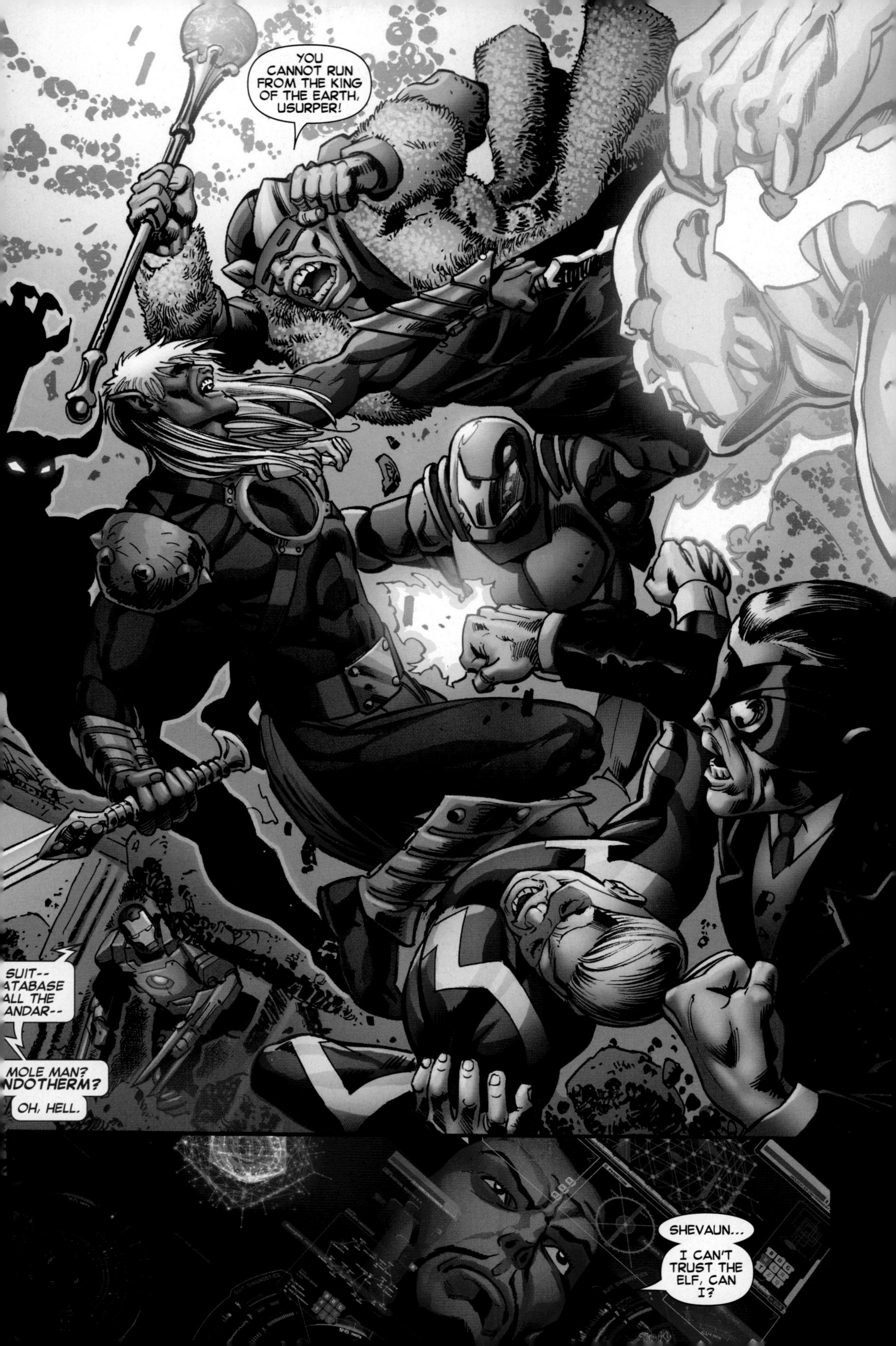
YOU CANNOT RUN FROM THE KING OF THE EARTH, USURPER!
SUIT-- ATABASE ALL THE ANDAR--
MOLE MAN? NDOTHERM?
OH, HELL.
SHEVAUN...
I CAN'T TRUST THE ELF, CAN I?

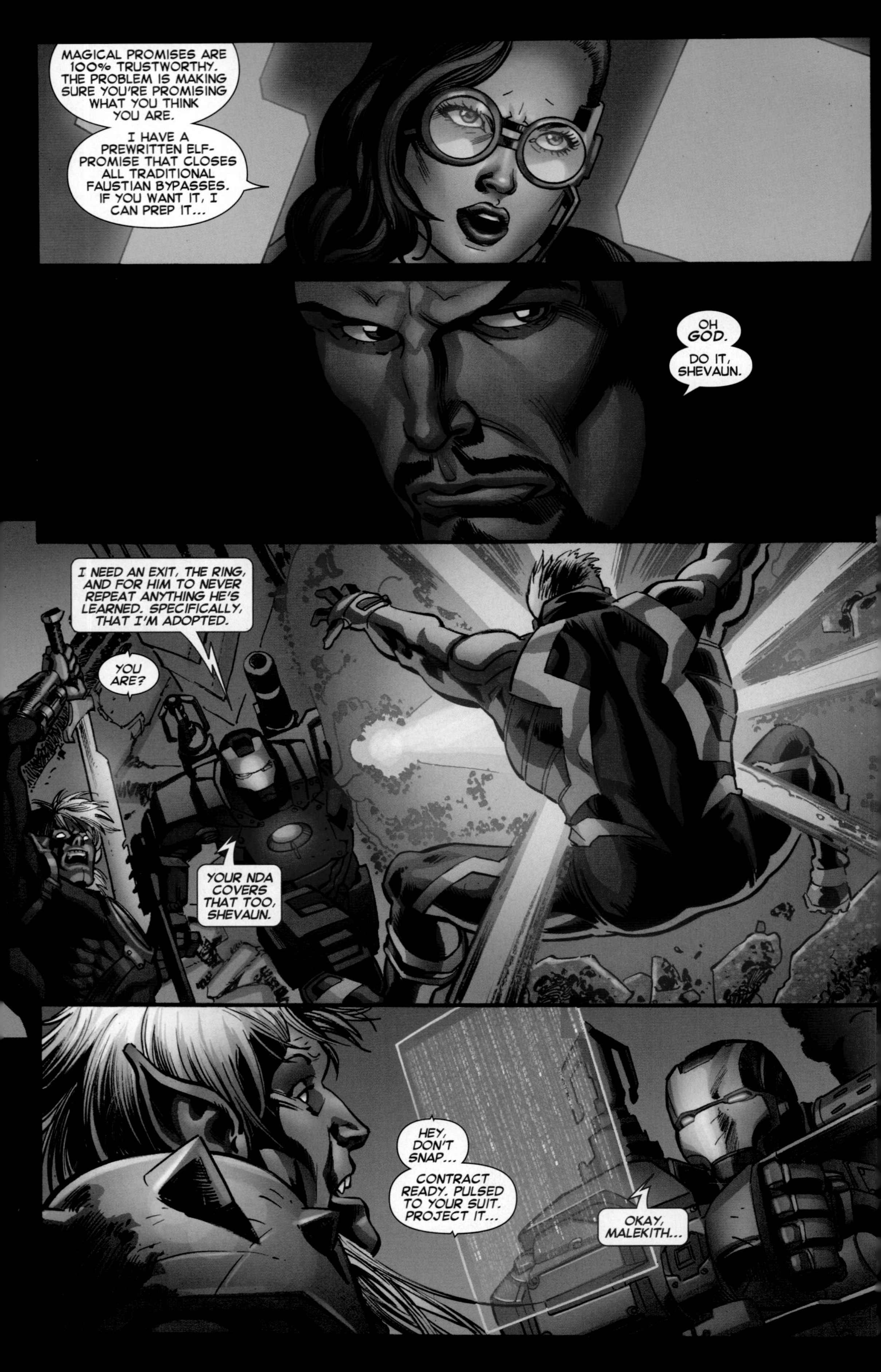
MAGICAL PROMISES ARE 100% TRUSTWORTHY. THE PROBLEM IS MAKING SURE YOU'RE PROMISING WHAT YOU THINK YOU ARE.
I HAVE A PREWRITTEN ELF-PROMISE THAT CLOSES ALL TRADITIONAL FAUSTIAN BYPASSES. IF YOU WANT IT, I CAN PREP IT...
OH *GOD.*
DO IT, SHEVAUN.
I NEED AN EXIT, THE RING, AND FOR HIM TO NEVER REPEAT ANYTHING HE'S LEARNED. SPECIFICALLY, THAT I'M ADOPTED.
YOU ARE?
YOUR NDA COVERS THAT TOO, SHEVAUN.
HEY, DON'T SNAP...
CONTRACT READY. PULSED TO YOUR SUIT. PROJECT IT...
OKAY, MALEKITH...

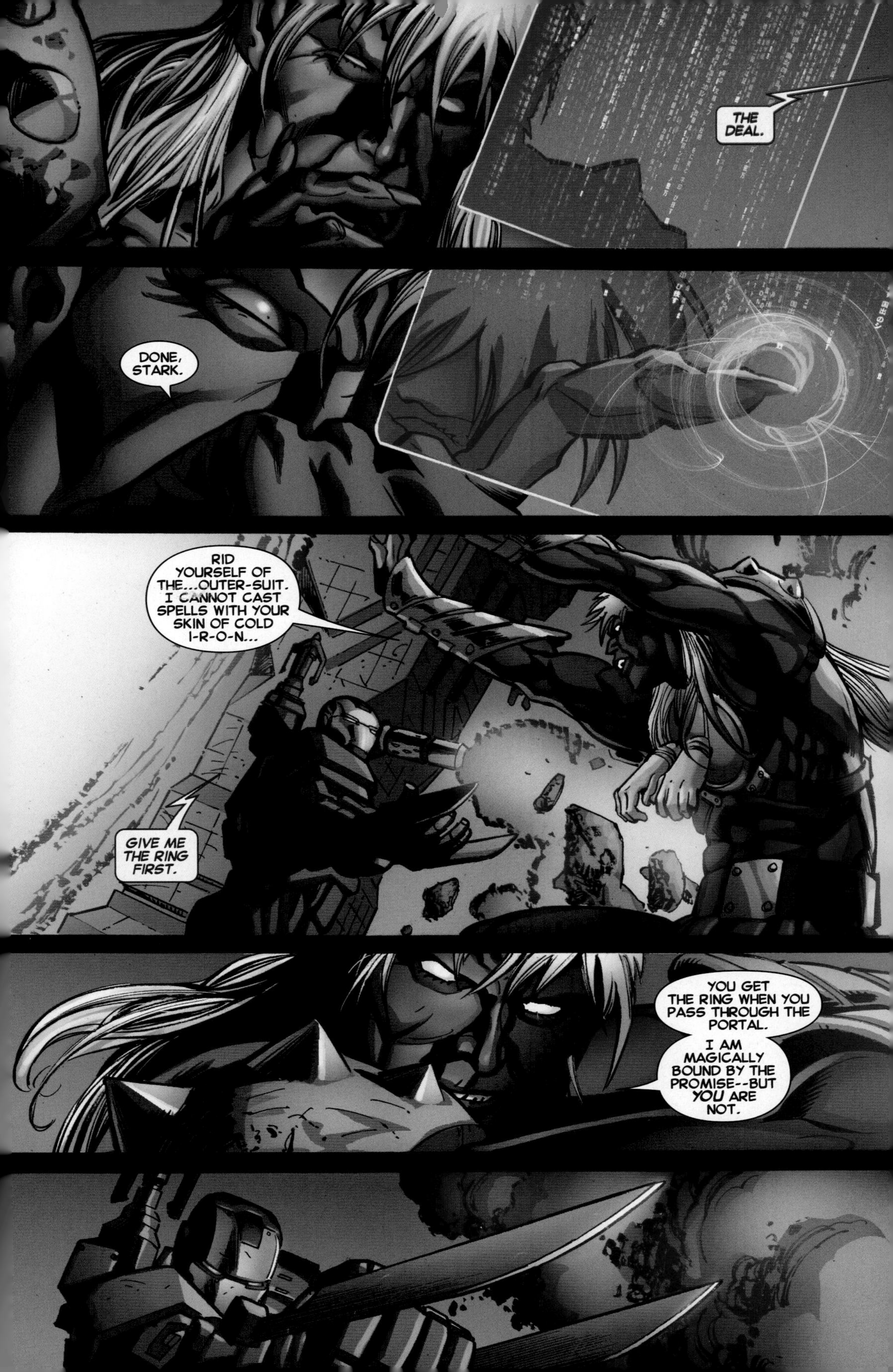
THE DEAL.
DONE, STARK.
RID YOURSELF OF THE...OUTER-SUIT. I CANNOT CAST SPELLS WITH YOUR SKIN OF COLD I-R-O-N...
GIVE ME THE RING FIRST.
YOU GET THE RING WHEN YOU PASS THROUGH THE PORTAL.
I AM MAGICALLY BOUND BY THE PROMISE--BUT *YOU* ARE NOT.

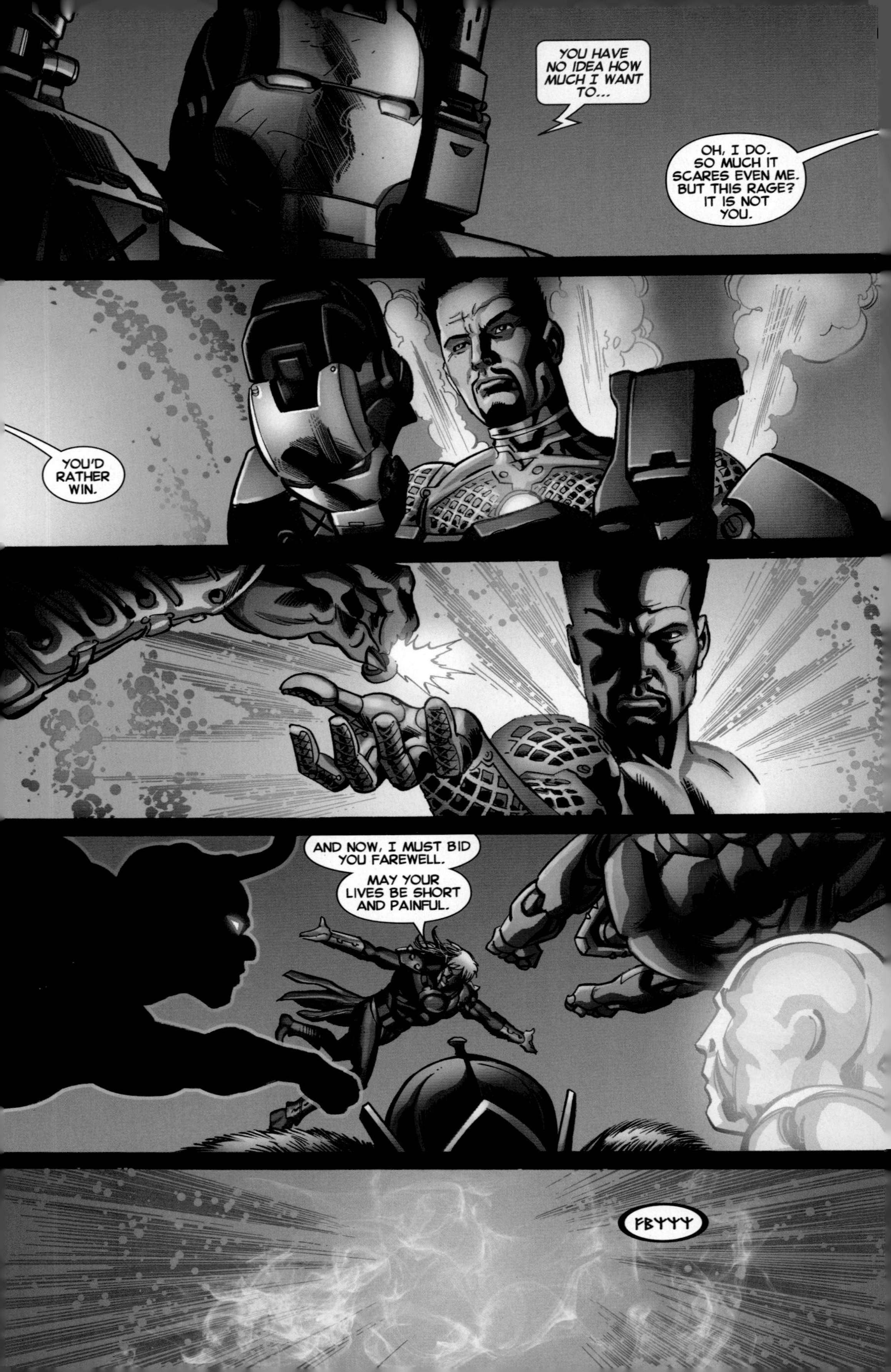
YOU HAVE NO IDEA HOW MUCH I WANT TO...
OH, I DO. SO MUCH IT SCARES EVEN ME. BUT THIS RAGE? IT IS NOT YOU.
YOU'D RATHER WIN.
AND NOW, I MUST BID YOU FAREWELL.
MAY YOUR LIVES BE SHORT AND PAINFUL.
FBYYY

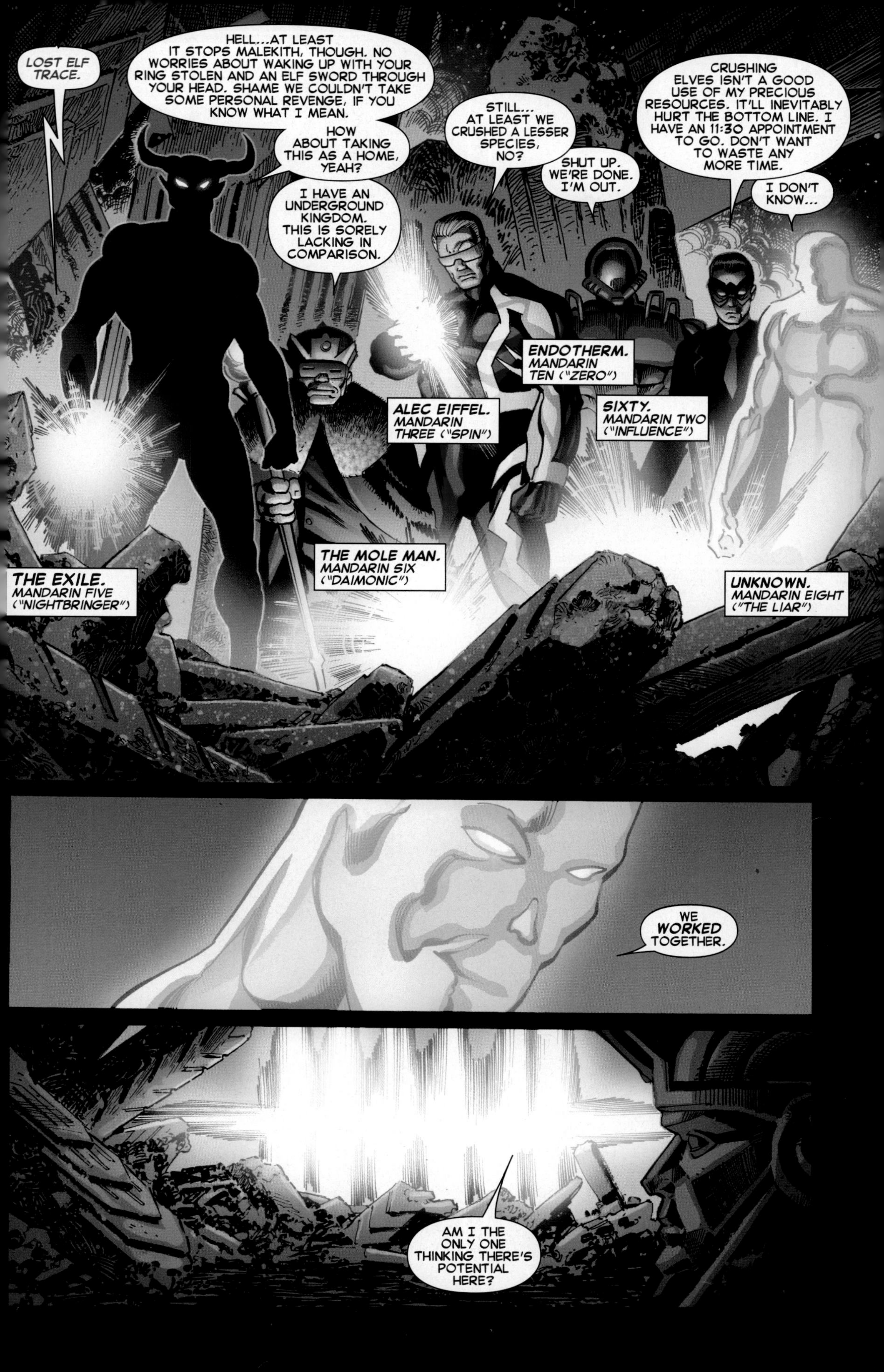
LOST ELF TRACE.
HELL...AT LEAST IT STOPS MALEKITH, THOUGH. NO WORRIES ABOUT WAKING UP WITH YOUR RING STOLEN AND AN ELF SWORD THROUGH YOUR HEAD. SHAME WE COULDN'T TAKE SOME PERSONAL REVENGE, IF YOU KNOW WHAT I MEAN.
HOW ABOUT TAKING THIS AS A HOME, YEAH?
I HAVE AN UNDERGROUND KINGDOM. THIS IS SORELY LACKING IN COMPARISON.
STILL... AT LEAST WE CRUSHED A LESSER SPECIES, NO?
SHUT UP. WE'RE DONE. I'M OUT.
CRUSHING ELVES ISN'T A GOOD USE OF MY PRECIOUS RESOURCES. IT'LL INEVITABLY HURT THE BOTTOM LINE. I HAVE AN 11:30 APPOINTMENT TO GO. DON'T WANT TO WASTE ANY MORE TIME.
I DON'T KNOW...
ENDOTHERM. MANDARIN TEN ("ZERO")
ALEC EIFFEL. MANDARIN THREE ("SPIN")
SIXTY. MANDARIN TWO ("INFLUENCE")
THE MOLE MAN. MANDARIN SIX ("DAIMONIC")
THE EXILE. MANDARIN FIVE ("NIGHTBRINGER")
UNKNOWN. MANDARIN EIGHT ("THE LIAR")
WE WORKED TOGETHER.
AM I THE ONLY ONE THINKING THERE'S POTENTIAL HERE?

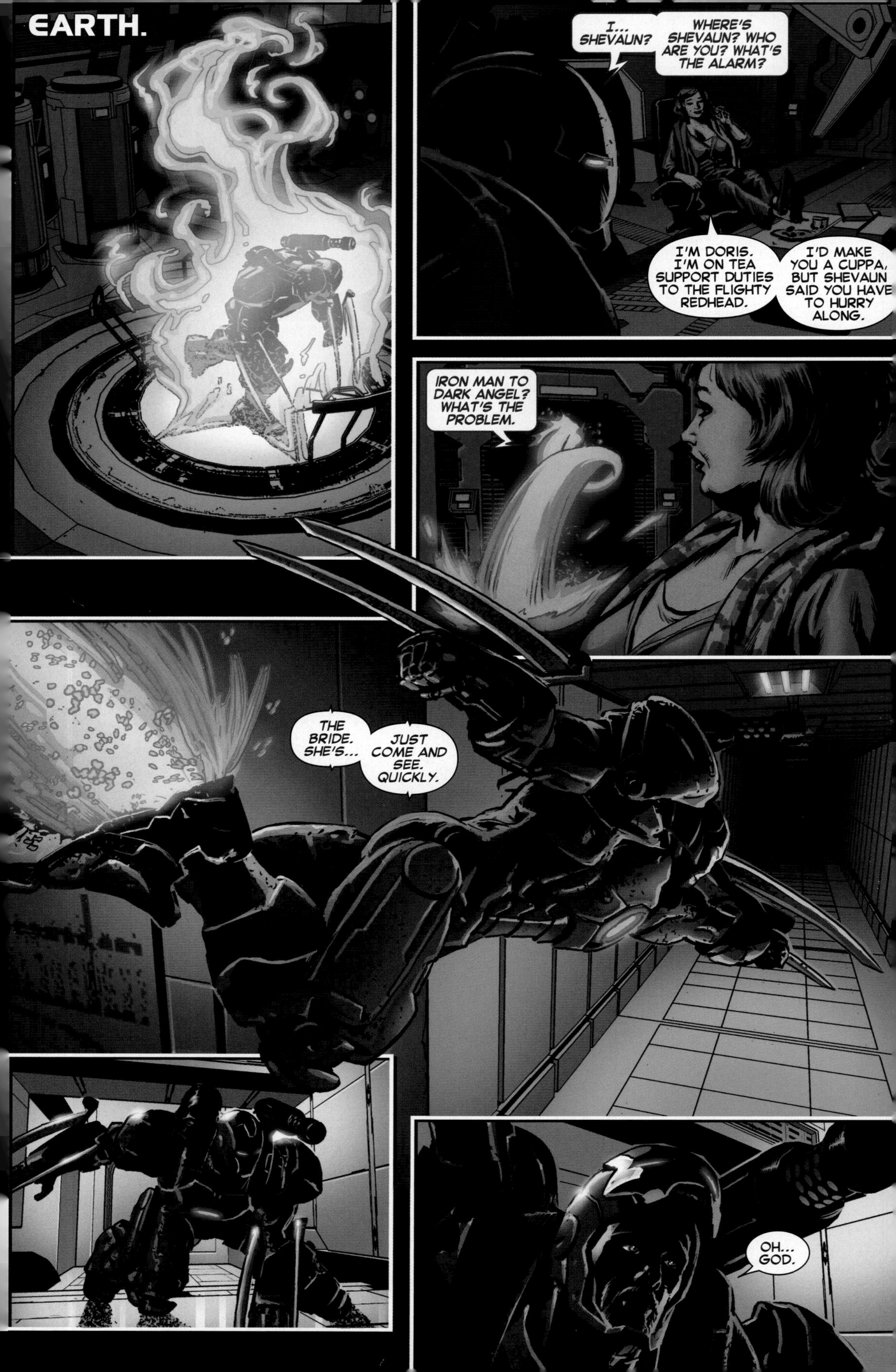
EARTH.
I... SHEVAUN?
WHERE'S SHEVAUN? WHO ARE YOU? WHAT'S THE ALARM?
I'M DORIS. I'M ON TEA SUPPORT DUTIES TO THE FLIGHTY REDHEAD.
I'D MAKE YOU A CUPPA, BUT SHEVAUN SAID YOU HAVE TO HURRY ALONG.
IRON MAN TO DARK ANGEL? WHAT'S THE PROBLEM.
THE BRIDE. SHE'S...
JUST COME AND SEE. QUICKLY.
OH... GOD.

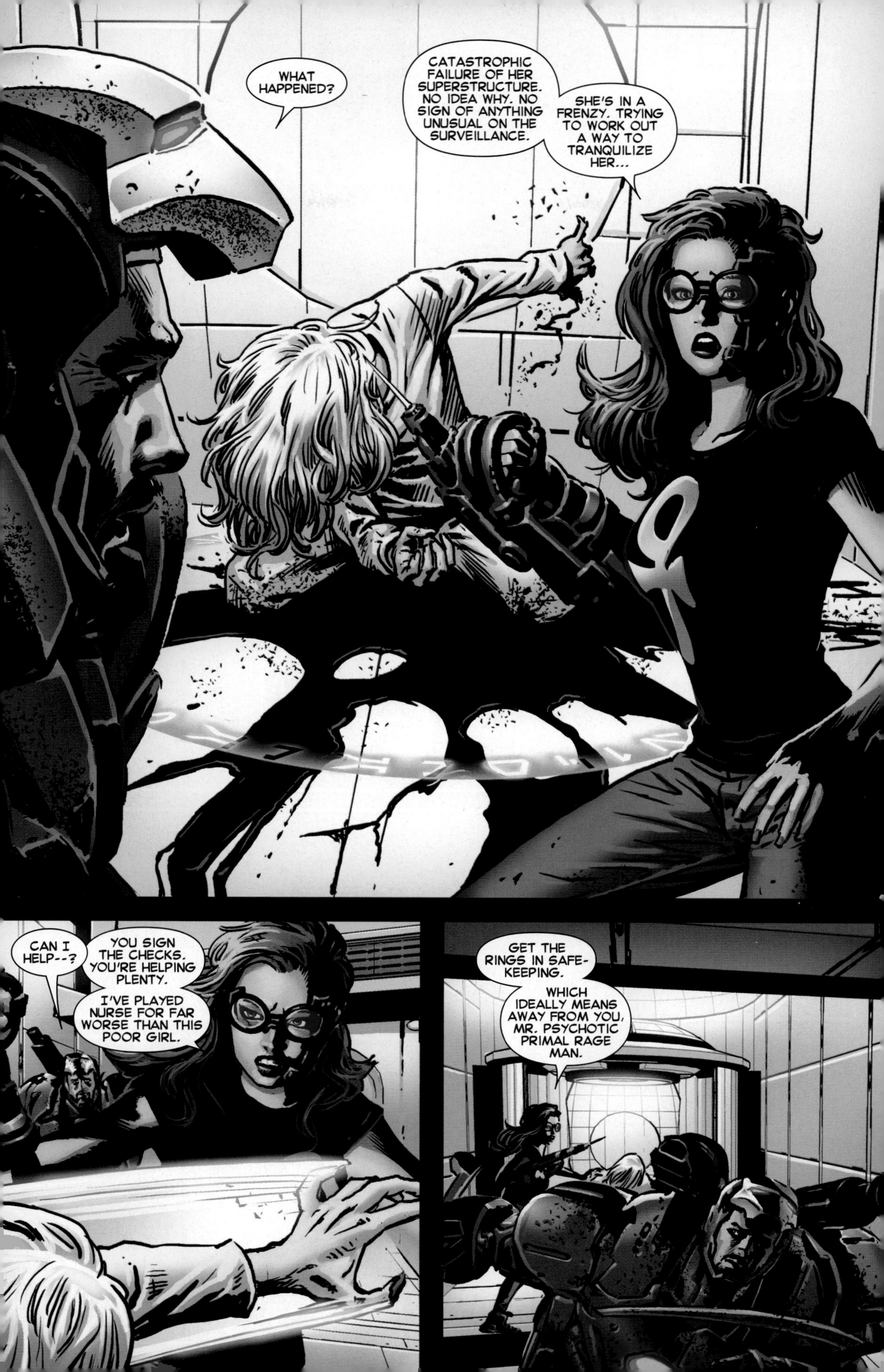
WHAT HAPPENED?
CATASTROPHIC FAILURE OF HER SUPERSTRUCTURE. NO IDEA WHY. NO SIGN OF ANYTHING UNUSUAL ON THE SURVEILLANCE.
SHE'S IN A FRENZY. TRYING TO WORK OUT A WAY TO TRANQUILIZE HER...
CAN I HELP--?
YOU SIGN THE CHECKS. YOU'RE HELPING PLENTY.
I'VE PLAYED NURSE FOR FAR WORSE THAN THIS POOR GIRL.
GET THE RINGS IN SAFE-KEEPING.
WHICH IDEALLY MEANS AWAY FROM YOU, MR. PSYCHOTIC PRIMAL RAGE MAN.

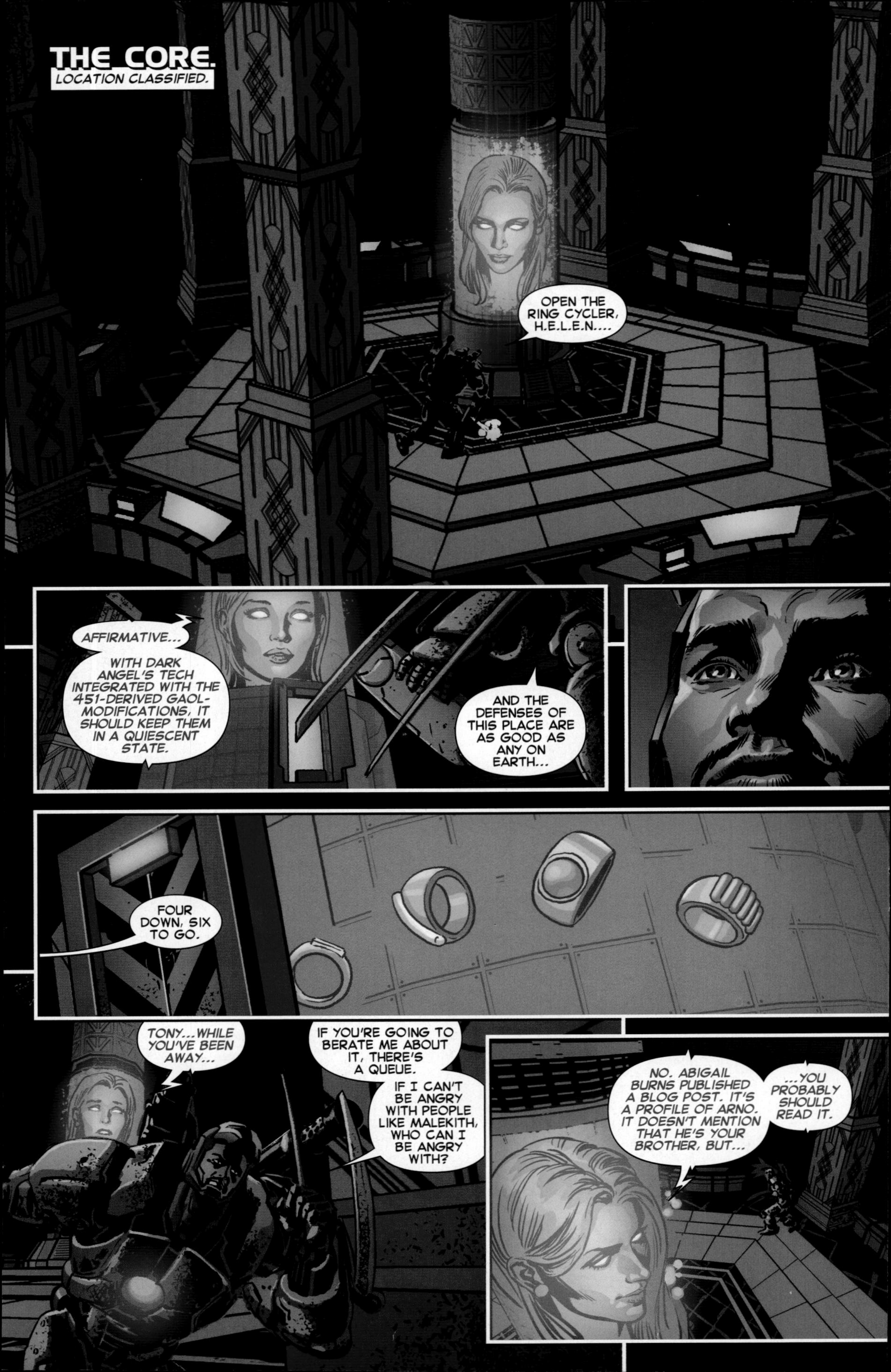
THE CORE.
LOCATION CLASSIFIED.
OPEN THE RING CYCLER, H.E.L.E.N....
AFFIRMATIVE...
WITH DARK ANGEL'S TECH INTEGRATED WITH THE 451-DERIVED GAOL-MODIFICATIONS, IT SHOULD KEEP THEM IN A QUIESCENT STATE.
AND THE DEFENSES OF THIS PLACE ARE AS GOOD AS ANY ON EARTH...
FOUR DOWN, SIX TO GO.
TONY...WHILE YOU'VE BEEN AWAY...
IF YOU'RE GOING TO BERATE ME ABOUT IT, THERE'S A QUEUE.
IF I CAN'T BE ANGRY WITH PEOPLE LIKE MALEKITH, WHO CAN I BE ANGRY WITH?
NO. ABIGAIL BURNS PUBLISHED A BLOG POST. IT'S A PROFILE OF ARNO. IT DOESN'T MENTION THAT HE'S YOUR BROTHER, BUT...
...YOU PROBABLY SHOULD READ IT.

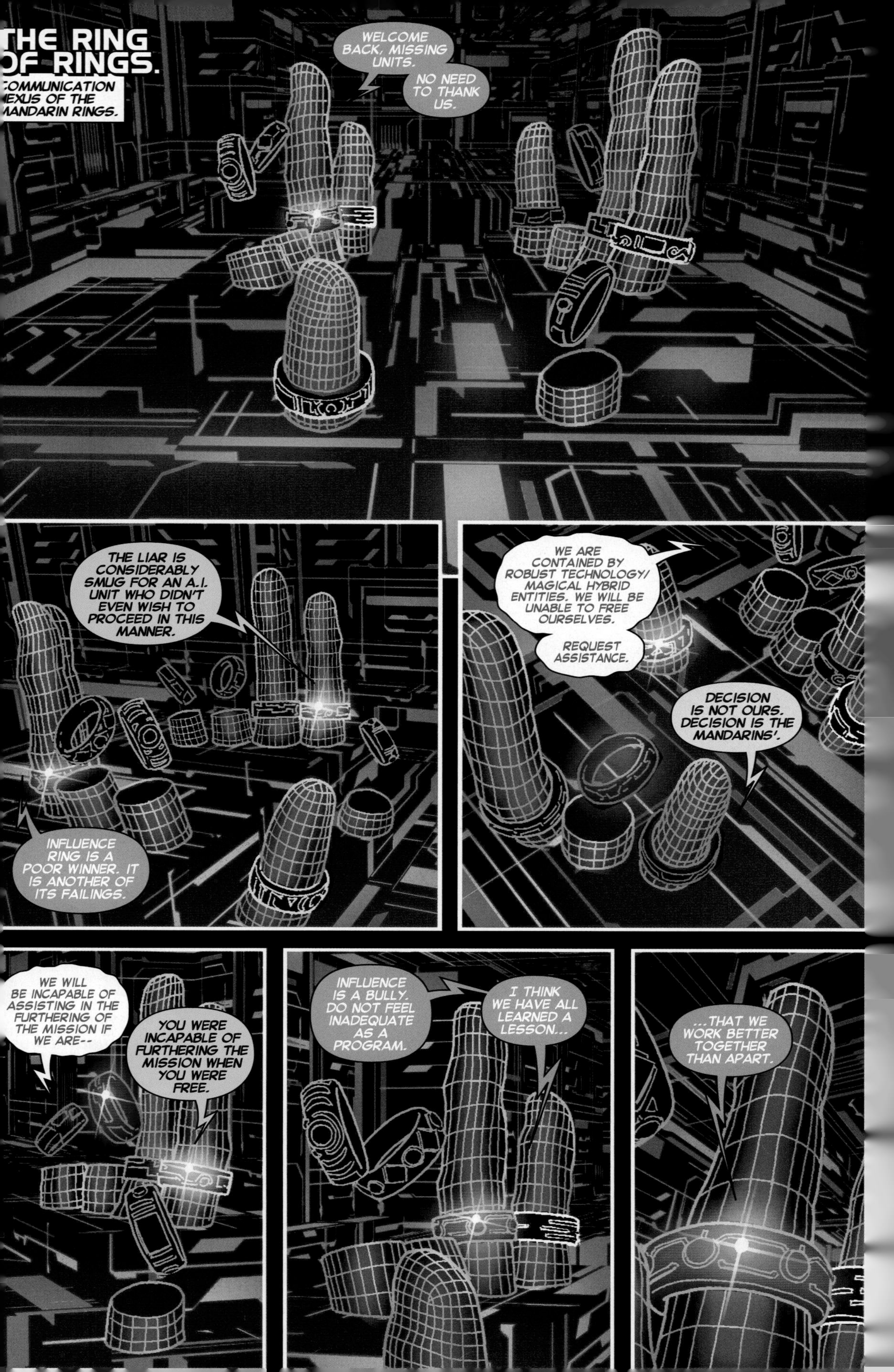
THE RING OF RINGS.
COMMUNICATION NEXUS OF THE MANDARIN RINGS.
WELCOME BACK, MISSING UNITS.
NO NEED TO THANK US.
THE LIAR IS CONSIDERABLY SMUG FOR AN A.I. UNIT WHO DIDN'T EVEN WISH TO PROCEED IN THIS MANNER.
INFLUENCE RING IS A POOR WINNER. IT IS ANOTHER OF ITS FAILINGS.
WE ARE CONTAINED BY ROBUST TECHNOLOGY/ MAGICAL HYBRID ENTITIES. WE WILL BE UNABLE TO FREE OURSELVES.
REQUEST ASSISTANCE.
DECISION IS NOT OURS. DECISION IS THE MANDARINS'.
WE WILL BE INCAPABLE OF ASSISTING IN THE FURTHERING OF THE MISSION IF WE ARE--
YOU WERE INCAPABLE OF FURTHERING THE MISSION WHEN YOU WERE FREE.
INFLUENCE IS A BULLY. DO NOT FEEL INADEQUATE AS A PROGRAM.
I THINK WE HAVE ALL LEARNED A LESSON...
...THAT WE WORK BETTER TOGETHER THAN APART.

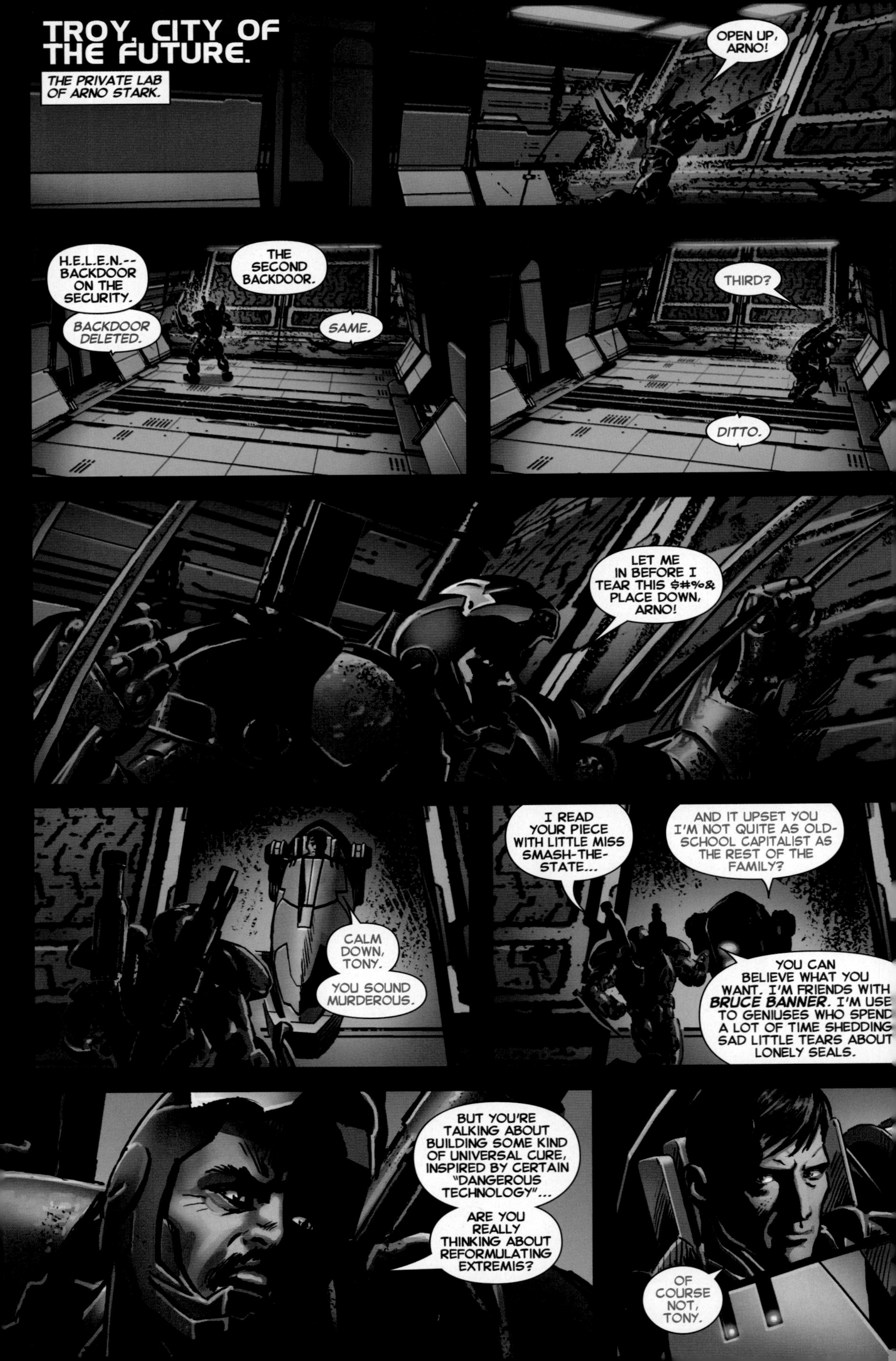
TROY, CITY OF THE FUTURE.
THE PRIVATE LAB OF ARNO STARK.
OPEN UP, ARNO!
H.E.L.E.N.--BACKDOOR ON THE SECURITY.
BACKDOOR DELETED.
THE SECOND BACKDOOR.
SAME.
THIRD?
DITTO.
LET ME IN BEFORE I TEAR THIS $#%& PLACE DOWN, ARNO!
CALM DOWN, TONY.
YOU SOUND MURDEROUS.
I READ YOUR PIECE WITH LITTLE MISS SMASH-THE-STATE...
AND IT UPSET YOU I'M NOT QUITE AS OLD-SCHOOL CAPITALIST AS THE REST OF THE FAMILY?
YOU CAN BELIEVE WHAT YOU WANT. I'M FRIENDS WITH BRUCE BANNER. I'M USE TO GENIUSES WHO SPEND A LOT OF TIME SHEDDING SAD LITTLE TEARS ABOUT LONELY SEALS.
BUT YOU'RE TALKING ABOUT BUILDING SOME KIND OF UNIVERSAL CURE, INSPIRED BY CERTAIN "DANGEROUS TECHNOLOGY"...
ARE YOU REALLY THINKING ABOUT REFORMULATING EXTREMIS?
OF COURSE NOT, TONY.

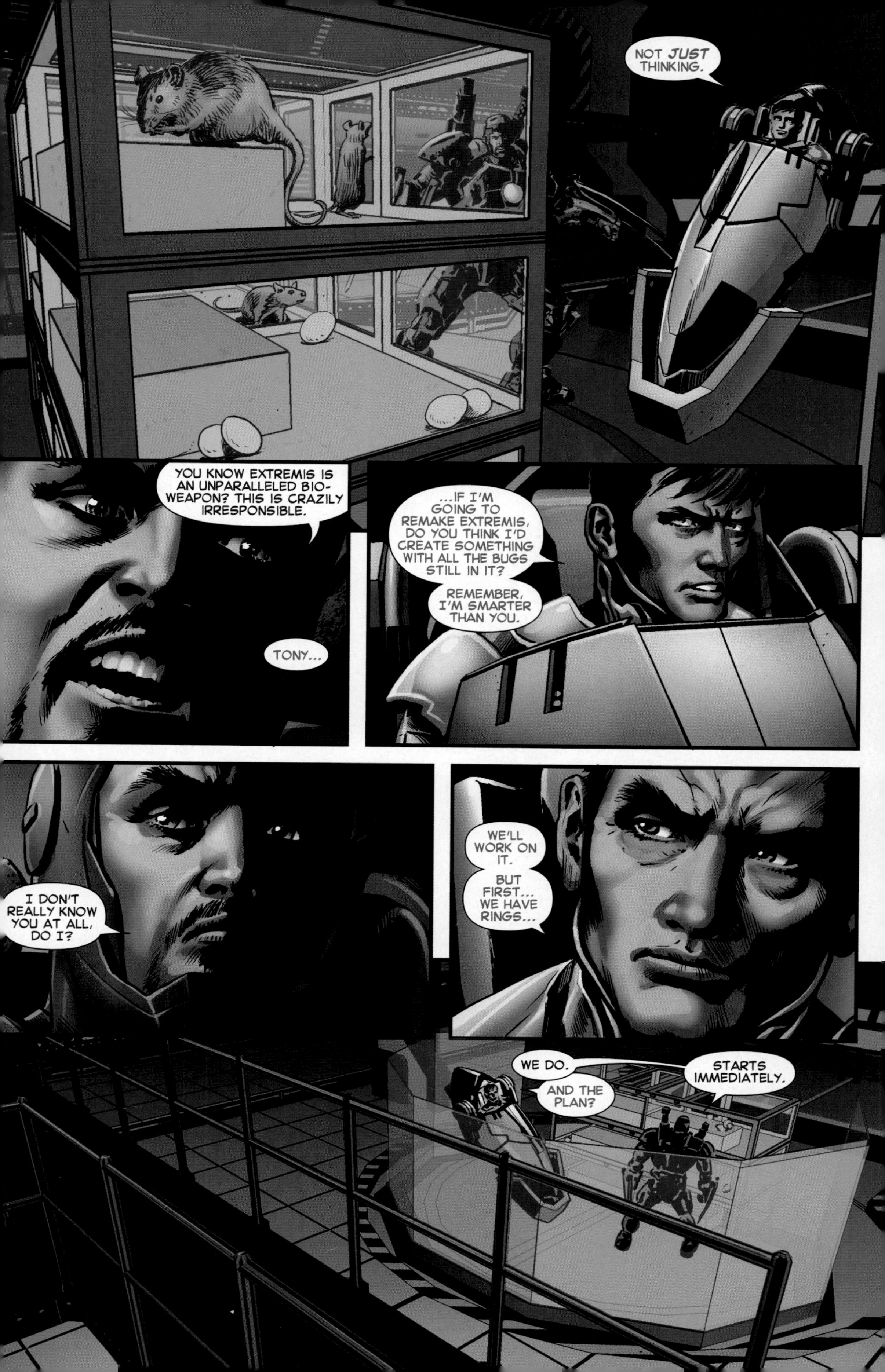
NOT JUST THINKING.
YOU KNOW EXTREMIS IS AN UNPARALLELED BIO-WEAPON? THIS IS CRAZILY IRRESPONSIBLE.
TONY...
...IF I'M GOING TO REMAKE EXTREMIS, DO YOU THINK I'D CREATE SOMETHING WITH ALL THE BUGS STILL IN IT?
REMEMBER, I'M SMARTER THAN YOU.
I DON'T REALLY KNOW YOU AT ALL, DO I?
WE'LL WORK ON IT.
BUT FIRST... WE HAVE RINGS...
WE DO.
AND THE PLAN?
STARTS IMMEDIATELY.

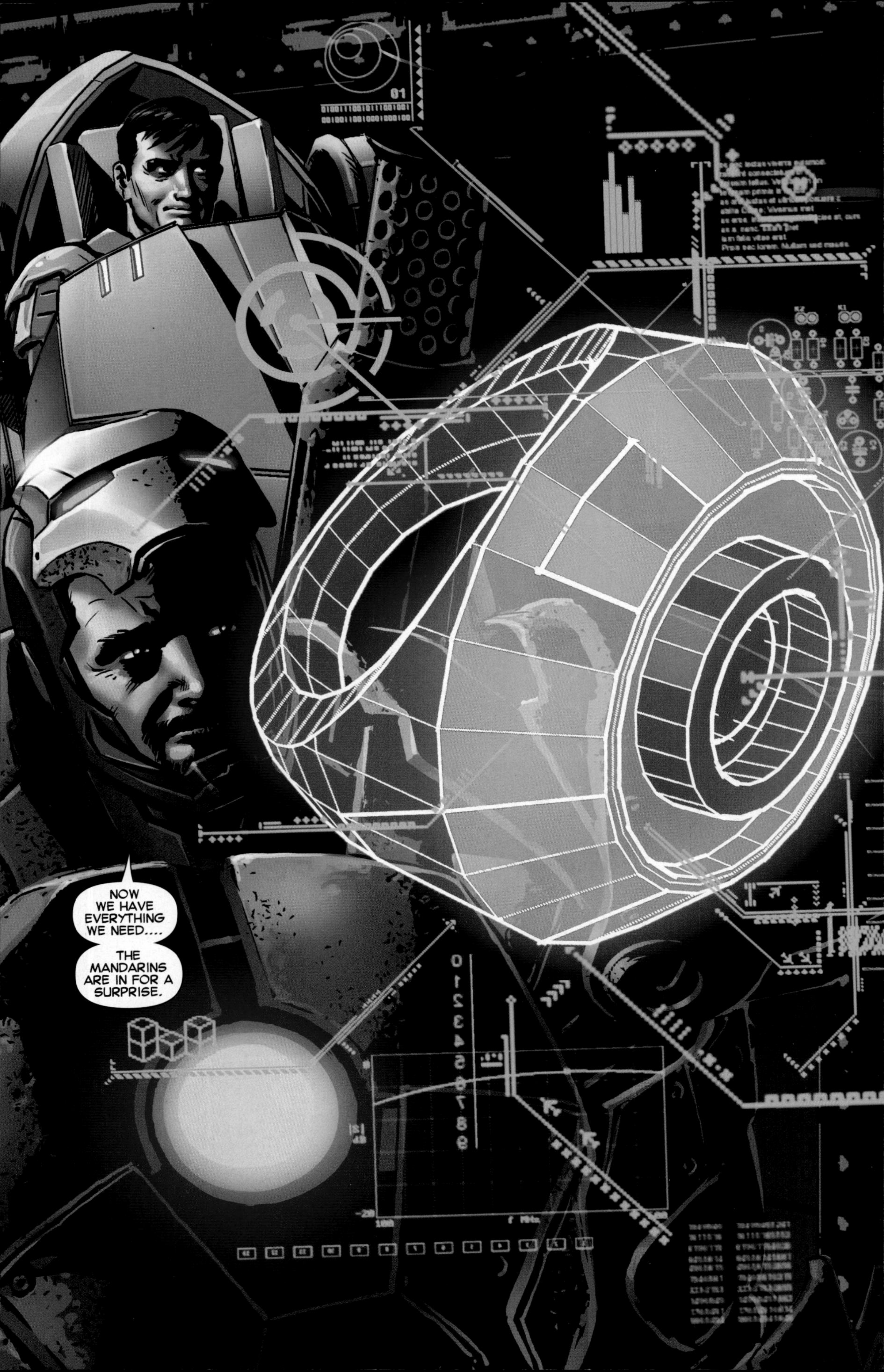
NOW WE HAVE EVERYTHING WE NEED....
THE MANDARINS ARE IN FOR A SURPRISE.

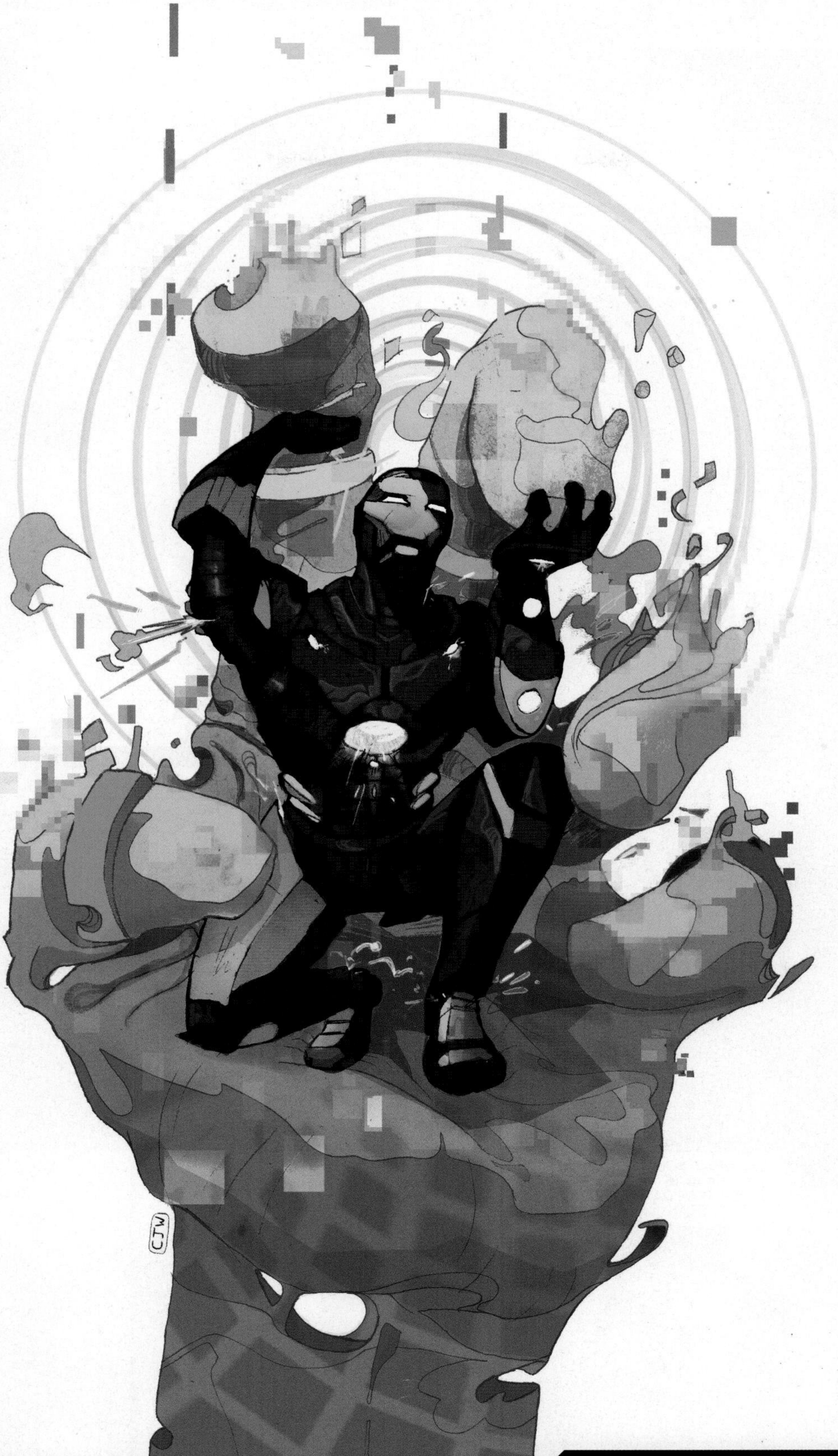
CJW

RINGS OF THE MANDARIN CHAPTER 5

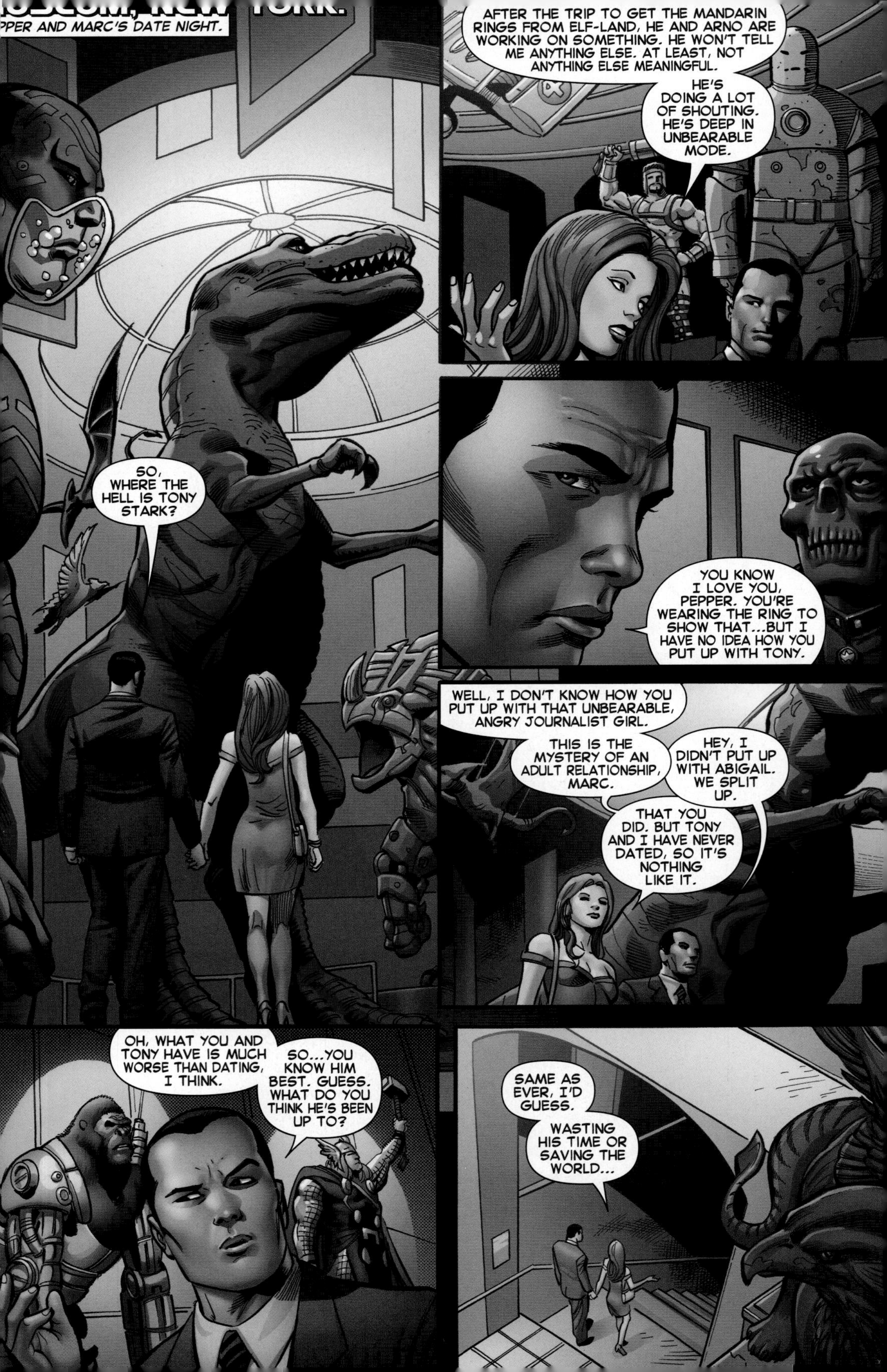
PEPPER AND MARC'S DATE NIGHT.
SO, WHERE THE HELL IS TONY STARK?
AFTER THE TRIP TO GET THE MANDARIN RINGS FROM ELF-LAND, HE AND ARNO ARE WORKING ON SOMETHING. HE WON'T TELL ME ANYTHING ELSE. AT LEAST, NOT ANYTHING ELSE MEANINGFUL.
HE'S DOING A LOT OF SHOUTING. HE'S DEEP IN UNBEARABLE MODE.
YOU KNOW I LOVE YOU, PEPPER. YOU'RE WEARING THE RING TO SHOW THAT...BUT I HAVE NO IDEA HOW YOU PUT UP WITH TONY.
WELL, I DON'T KNOW HOW YOU PUT UP WITH THAT UNBEARABLE, ANGRY JOURNALIST GIRL.
THIS IS THE MYSTERY OF AN ADULT RELATIONSHIP, MARC.
HEY, I DIDN'T PUT UP WITH ABIGAIL. WE SPLIT UP.
THAT YOU DID. BUT TONY AND I HAVE NEVER DATED, SO IT'S NOTHING LIKE IT.
OH, WHAT YOU AND TONY HAVE IS MUCH WORSE THAN DATING, I THINK.
SO...YOU KNOW HIM BEST. GUESS. WHAT DO YOU THINK HE'S BEEN UP TO?
SAME AS EVER, I'D GUESS.
WASTING HIS TIME OR SAVING THE WORLD...

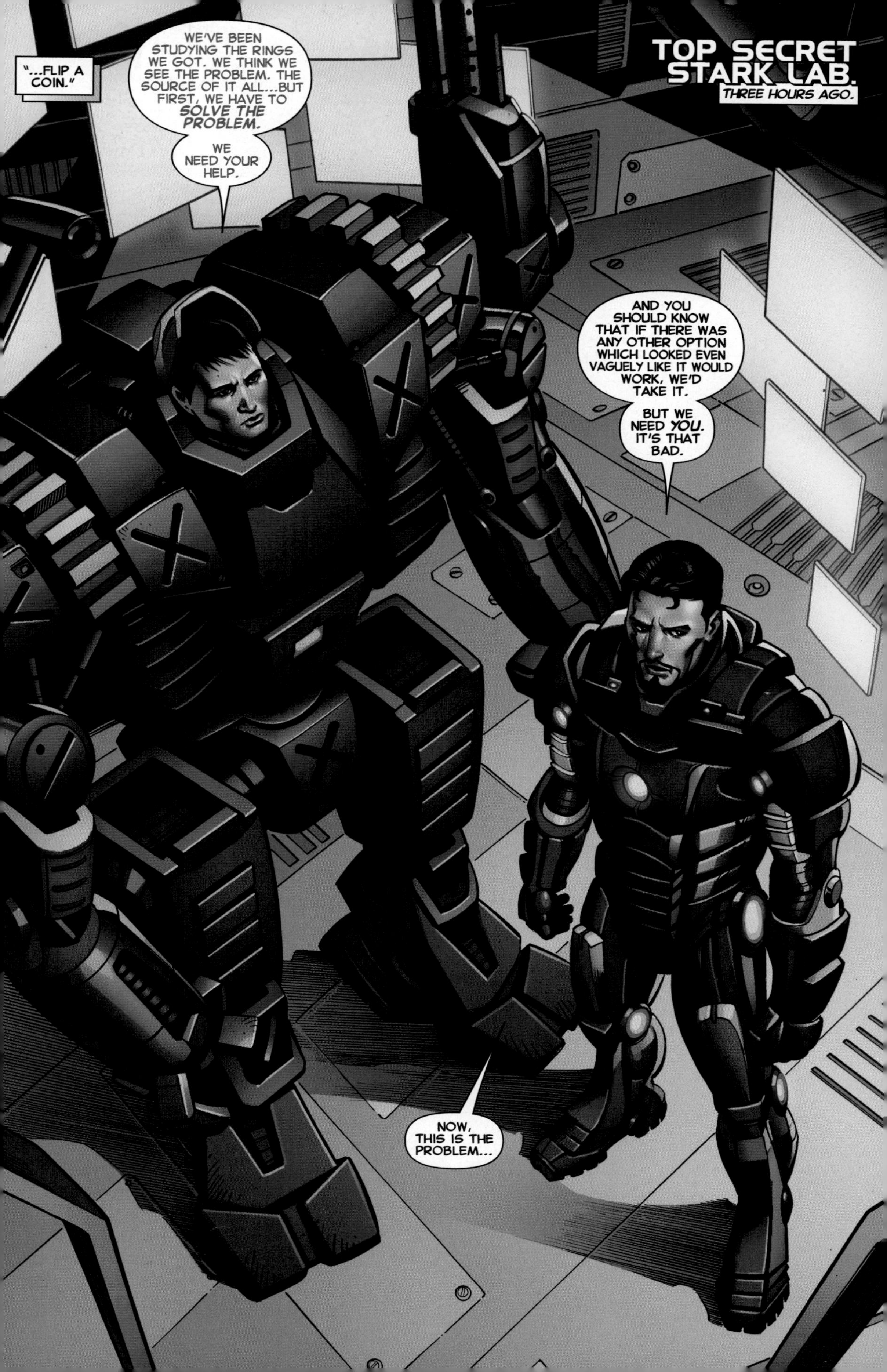
"...FLIP A COIN."
TOP SECRET STARK LAB.
THREE HOURS AGO.
WE'VE BEEN STUDYING THE RINGS WE GOT. WE THINK WE SEE THE PROBLEM. THE SOURCE OF IT ALL...BUT FIRST, WE HAVE TO SOLVE THE PROBLEM.
WE NEED YOUR HELP.
AND YOU SHOULD KNOW THAT IF THERE WAS ANY OTHER OPTION WHICH LOOKED EVEN VAGUELY LIKE IT WOULD WORK, WE'D TAKE IT.
BUT WE NEED YOU. IT'S THAT BAD.
NOW, THIS IS THE PROBLEM...

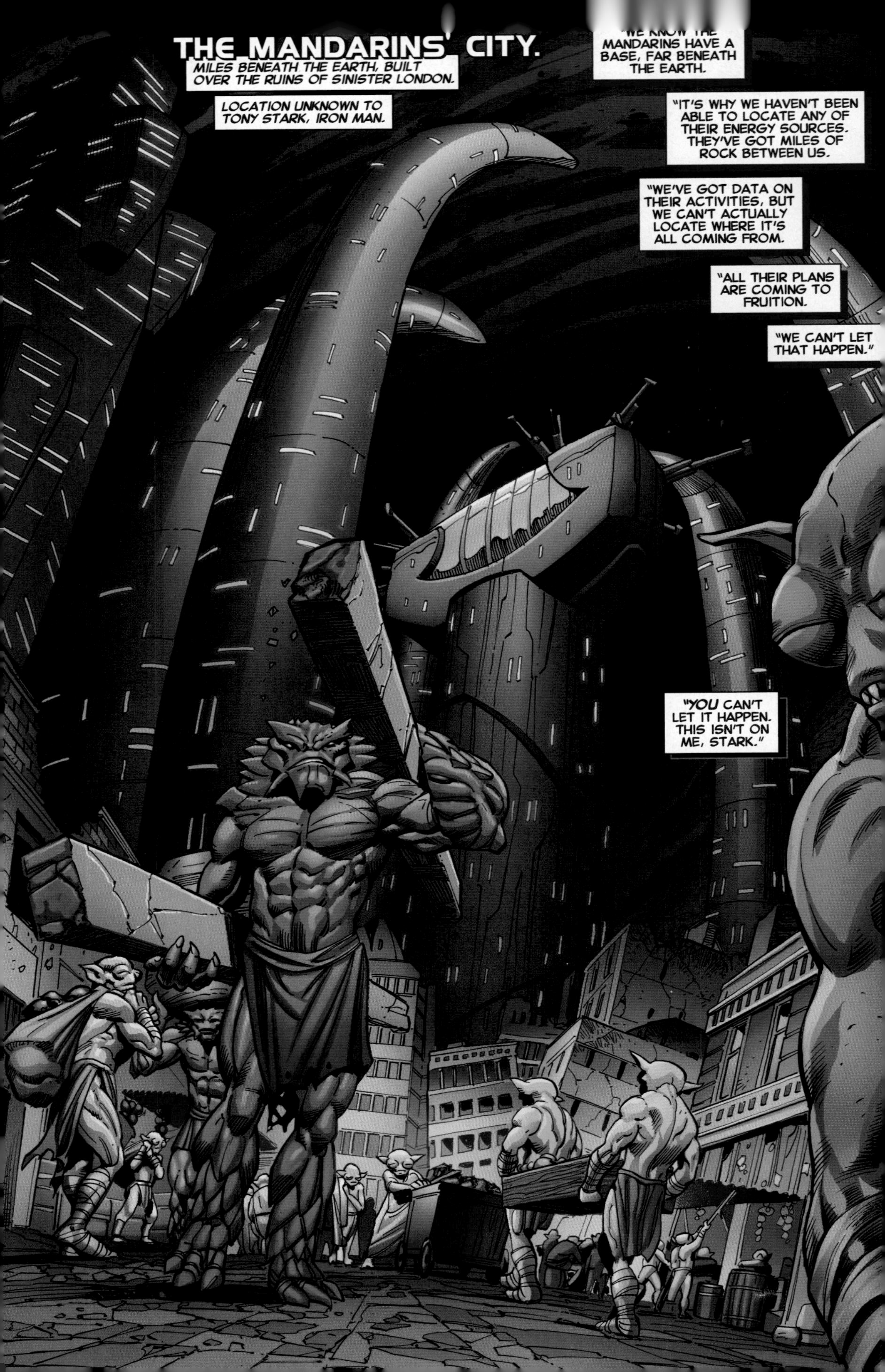
THE MANDARINS' CITY.
MILES BENEATH THE EARTH, BUILT OVER THE RUINS OF SINISTER LONDON.
LOCATION UNKNOWN TO TONY STARK, IRON MAN.
"WE KNOW THE MANDARINS HAVE A BASE, FAR BENEATH THE EARTH.
"IT'S WHY WE HAVEN'T BEEN ABLE TO LOCATE ANY OF THEIR ENERGY SOURCES. THEY'VE GOT MILES OF ROCK BETWEEN US.
"WE'VE GOT DATA ON THEIR ACTIVITIES, BUT WE CAN'T ACTUALLY LOCATE WHERE IT'S ALL COMING FROM.
"ALL THEIR PLANS ARE COMING TO FRUITION.
"WE CAN'T LET THAT HAPPEN."
"YOU CAN'T LET IT HAPPEN. THIS ISN'T ON ME, STARK."

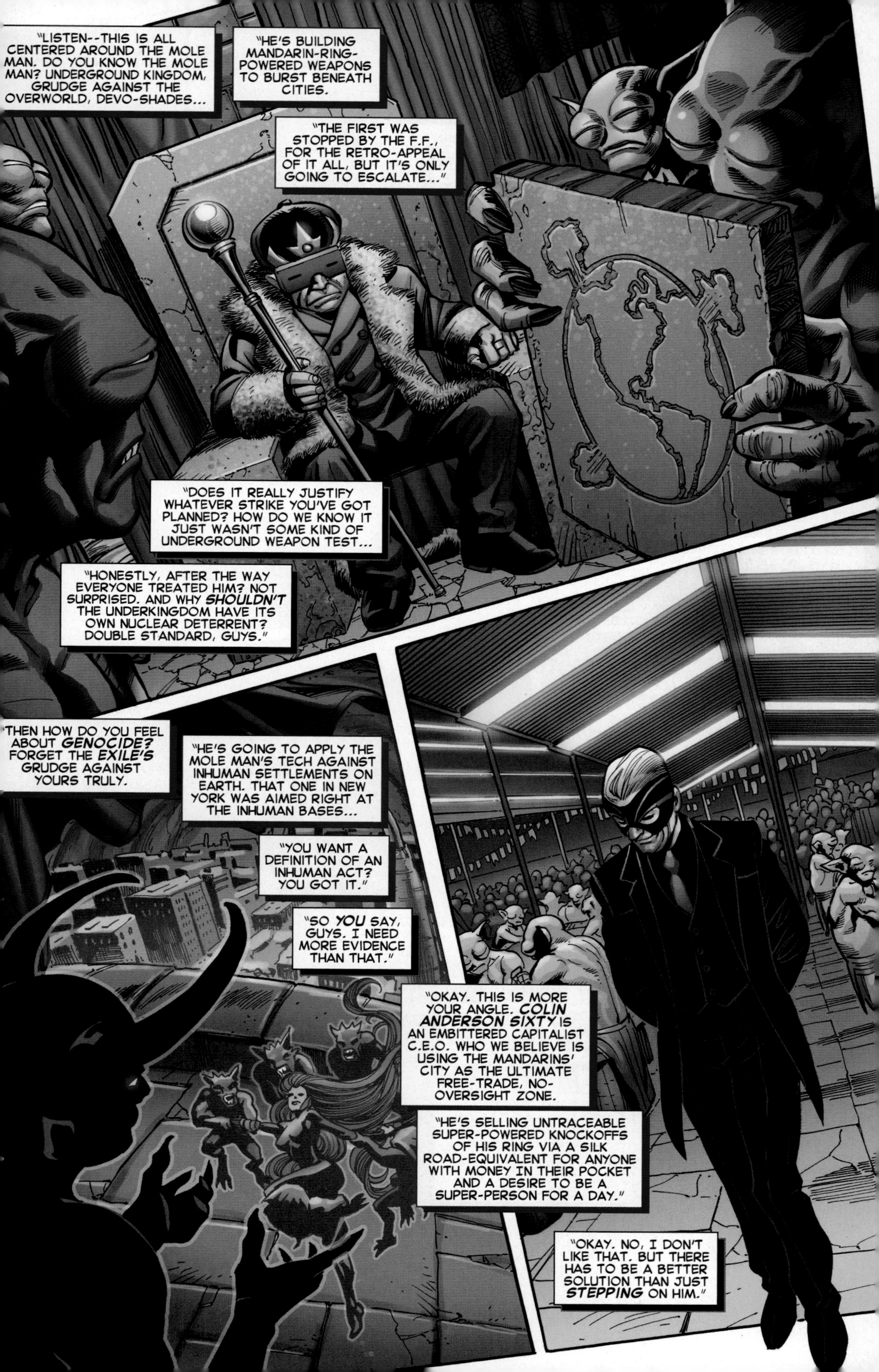
"LISTEN--THIS IS ALL CENTERED AROUND THE MOLE MAN. DO YOU KNOW THE MOLE MAN? UNDERGROUND KINGDOM, GRUDGE AGAINST THE OVERWORLD, DEVO-SHADES...
"HE'S BUILDING MANDARIN-RING-POWERED WEAPONS TO BURST BENEATH CITIES.
"THE FIRST WAS STOPPED BY THE F.F., FOR THE RETRO-APPEAL OF IT ALL, BUT IT'S ONLY GOING TO ESCALATE..."
"DOES IT REALLY JUSTIFY WHATEVER STRIKE YOU'VE GOT PLANNED? HOW DO WE KNOW IT JUST WASN'T SOME KIND OF UNDERGROUND WEAPON TEST...
"HONESTLY, AFTER THE WAY EVERYONE TREATED HIM? NOT SURPRISED. AND WHY SHOULDN'T THE UNDERKINGDOM HAVE ITS OWN NUCLEAR DETERRENT? DOUBLE STANDARD, GUYS."
"THEN HOW DO YOU FEEL ABOUT GENOCIDE? FORGET THE EXILE'S GRUDGE AGAINST YOURS TRULY.
"HE'S GOING TO APPLY THE MOLE MAN'S TECH AGAINST INHUMAN SETTLEMENTS ON EARTH. THAT ONE IN NEW YORK WAS AIMED RIGHT AT THE INHUMAN BASES...
"YOU WANT A DEFINITION OF AN INHUMAN ACT? YOU GOT IT."
"SO YOU SAY, GUYS. I NEED MORE EVIDENCE THAN THAT."
"OKAY. THIS IS MORE YOUR ANGLE. COLIN ANDERSON SIXTY IS AN EMBITTERED CAPITALIST C.E.O. WHO WE BELIEVE IS USING THE MANDARINS' CITY AS THE ULTIMATE FREE-TRADE, NO-OVERSIGHT ZONE.
"HE'S SELLING UNTRACEABLE SUPER-POWERED KNOCKOFFS OF HIS RING VIA A SILK ROAD-EQUIVALENT FOR ANYONE WITH MONEY IN THEIR POCKET AND A DESIRE TO BE A SUPER-PERSON FOR A DAY."
"OKAY. NO, I DON'T LIKE THAT. BUT THERE HAS TO BE A BETTER SOLUTION THAN JUST STEPPING ON HIM."

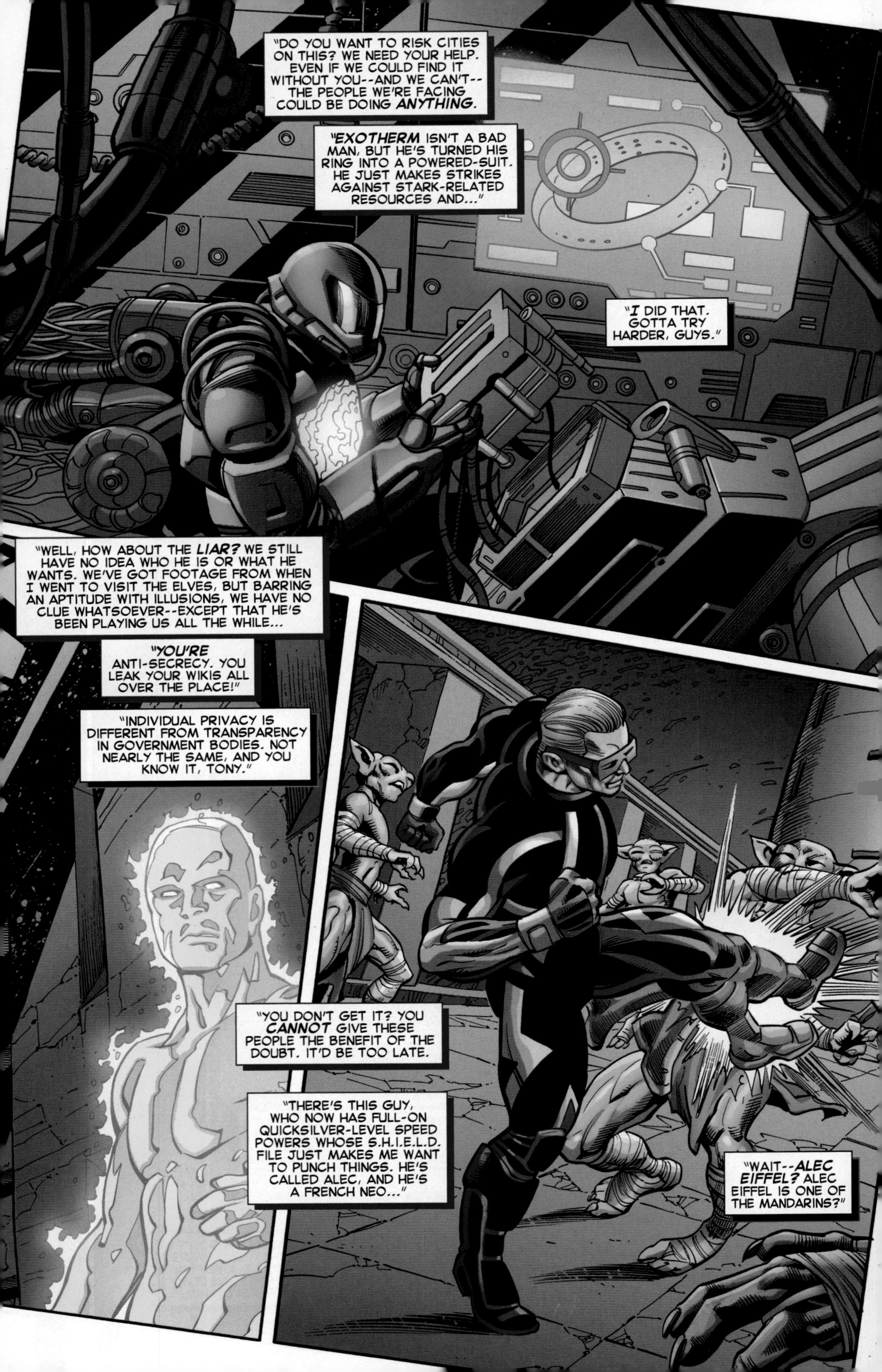

"DO YOU WANT TO RISK CITIES ON THIS? WE NEED YOUR HELP. EVEN IF WE COULD FIND IT WITHOUT YOU--AND WE CAN'T--THE PEOPLE WE'RE FACING COULD BE DOING ANYTHING.
"EXOTHERM ISN'T A BAD MAN, BUT HE'S TURNED HIS RING INTO A POWERED-SUIT. HE JUST MAKES STRIKES AGAINST STARK-RELATED RESOURCES AND..."
"I DID THAT. GOTTA TRY HARDER, GUYS."
"WELL, HOW ABOUT THE LIAR? WE STILL HAVE NO IDEA WHO HE IS OR WHAT HE WANTS. WE'VE GOT FOOTAGE FROM WHEN I WENT TO VISIT THE ELVES, BUT BARRING AN APTITUDE WITH ILLUSIONS, WE HAVE NO CLUE WHATSOEVER--EXCEPT THAT HE'S BEEN PLAYING US ALL THE WHILE...
"YOU'RE ANTI-SECRECY. YOU LEAK YOUR WIKIS ALL OVER THE PLACE!"
"INDIVIDUAL PRIVACY IS DIFFERENT FROM TRANSPARENCY IN GOVERNMENT BODIES. NOT NEARLY THE SAME, AND YOU KNOW IT, TONY."
"YOU DON'T GET IT? YOU CANNOT GIVE THESE PEOPLE THE BENEFIT OF THE DOUBT. IT'D BE TOO LATE.
"THERE'S THIS GUY, WHO NOW HAS FULL-ON QUICKSILVER-LEVEL SPEED POWERS WHOSE S.H.I.E.L.D. FILE JUST MAKES ME WANT TO PUNCH THINGS. HE'S CALLED ALEC, AND HE'S A FRENCH NEO..."
"WAIT--ALEC EIFFEL? ALEC EIFFEL IS ONE OF THE MANDARINS?"

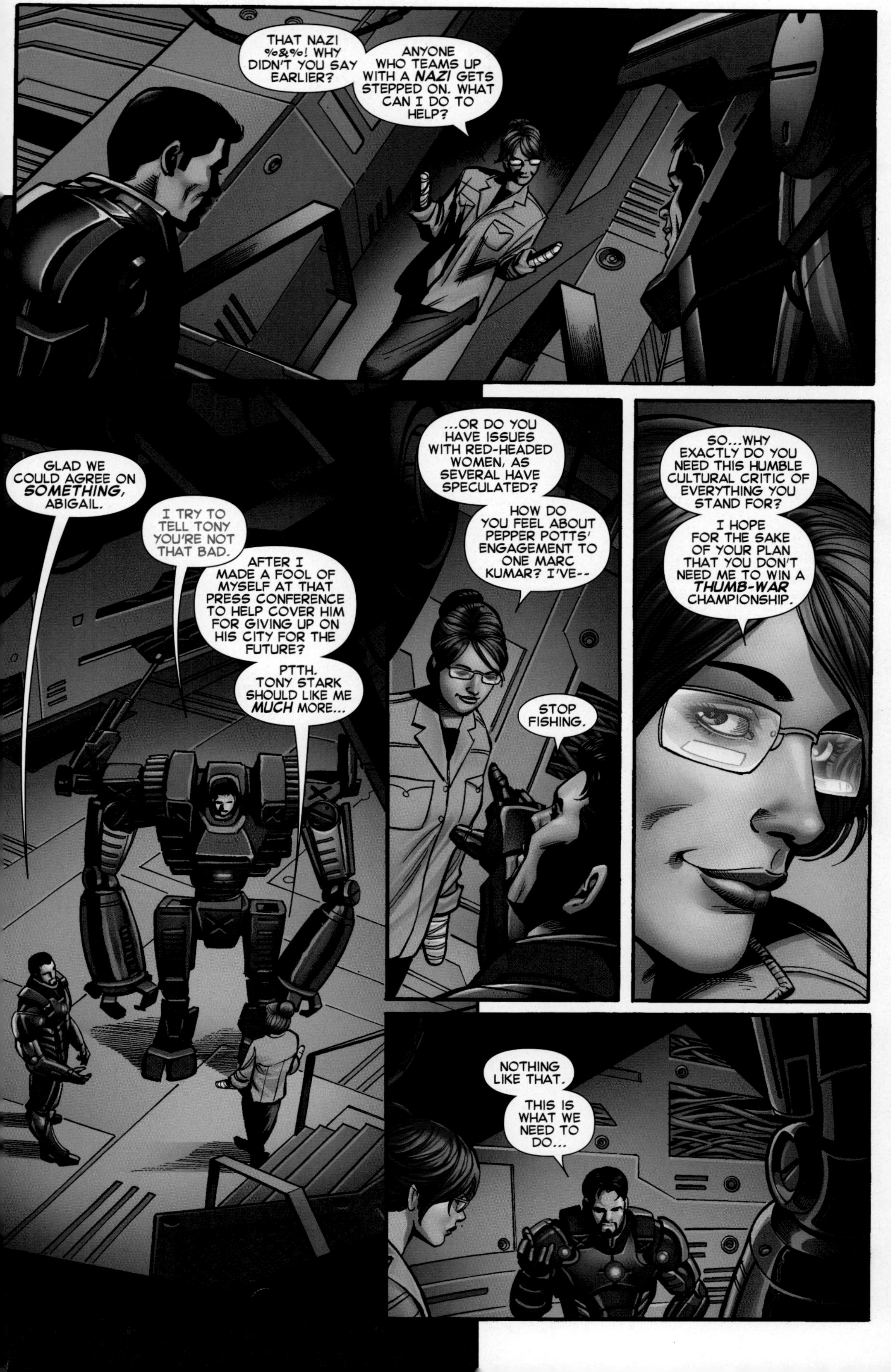
THAT NAZI %&%! WHY DIDN'T YOU SAY EARLIER?
ANYONE WHO TEAMS UP WITH A NAZI GETS STEPPED ON. WHAT CAN I DO TO HELP?
GLAD WE COULD AGREE ON SOMETHING, ABIGAIL.
I TRY TO TELL TONY YOU'RE NOT THAT BAD.
AFTER I MADE A FOOL OF MYSELF AT THAT PRESS CONFERENCE TO HELP COVER HIM FOR GIVING UP ON HIS CITY FOR THE FUTURE?
PTTH. TONY STARK SHOULD LIKE ME MUCH MORE...
...OR DO YOU HAVE ISSUES WITH RED-HEADED WOMEN, AS SEVERAL HAVE SPECULATED?
HOW DO YOU FEEL ABOUT PEPPER POTTS' ENGAGEMENT TO ONE MARC KUMAR? I'VE--
STOP FISHING.
SO...WHY EXACTLY DO YOU NEED THIS HUMBLE CULTURAL CRITIC OF EVERYTHING YOU STAND FOR?
I HOPE FOR THE SAKE OF YOUR PLAN THAT YOU DON'T NEED ME TO WIN A THUMB-WAR CHAMPIONSHIP.
NOTHING LIKE THAT.
THIS IS WHAT WE NEED TO DO...

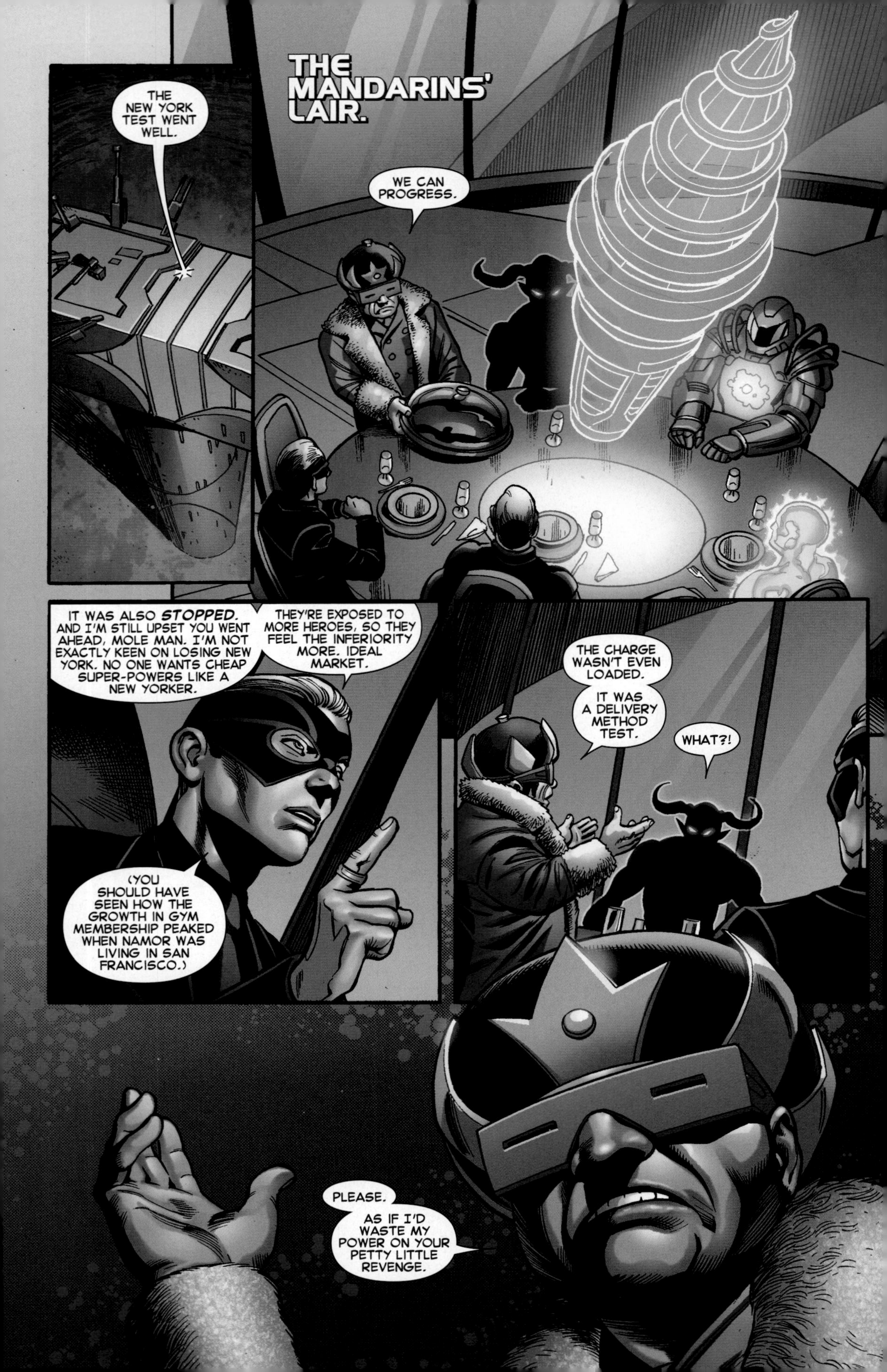
THE MANDARINS' LAIR.
THE NEW YORK TEST WENT WELL.
WE CAN PROGRESS.
IT WAS ALSO STOPPED. AND I'M STILL UPSET YOU WENT AHEAD, MOLE MAN. I'M NOT EXACTLY KEEN ON LOSING NEW YORK. NO ONE WANTS CHEAP SUPER-POWERS LIKE A NEW YORKER.
THEY'RE EXPOSED TO MORE HEROES, SO THEY FEEL THE INFERIORITY MORE. IDEAL MARKET.
(YOU SHOULD HAVE SEEN HOW THE GROWTH IN GYM MEMBERSHIP PEAKED WHEN NAMOR WAS LIVING IN SAN FRANCISCO.)
THE CHARGE WASN'T EVEN LOADED.
IT WAS A DELIVERY METHOD TEST.
WHAT?!
PLEASE.
AS IF I'D WASTE MY POWER ON YOUR PETTY LITTLE REVENGE.

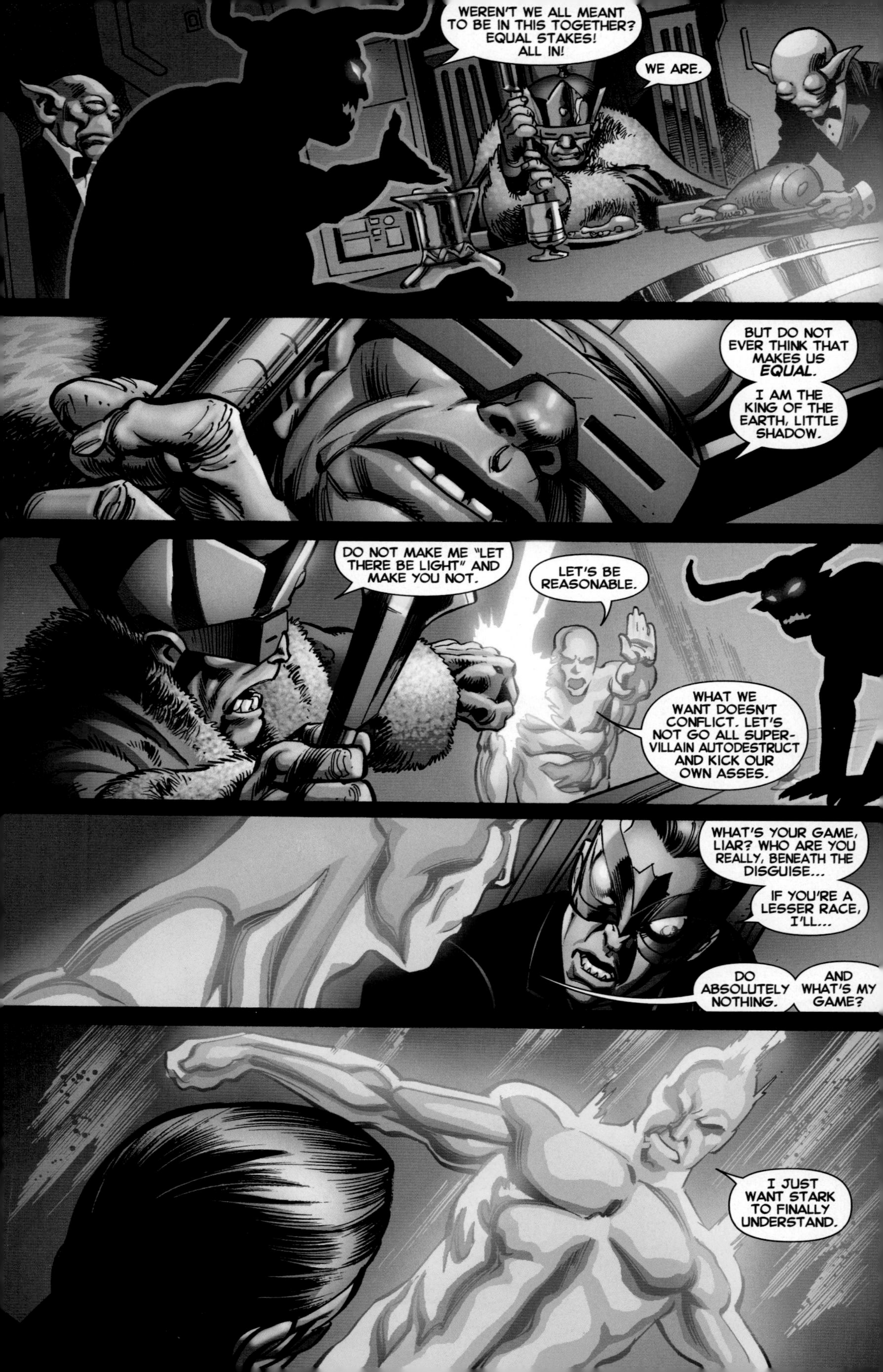
WEREN'T WE ALL MEANT TO BE IN THIS TOGETHER? EQUAL STAKES! ALL IN!
WE ARE.
BUT DO NOT EVER THINK THAT MAKES US *EQUAL.*
I AM THE KING OF THE EARTH, LITTLE SHADOW.
DO NOT MAKE ME "LET THERE BE LIGHT" AND MAKE YOU NOT.
LET'S BE REASONABLE.
WHAT WE WANT DOESN'T CONFLICT. LET'S NOT GO ALL SUPER-VILLAIN AUTODESTRUCT AND KICK OUR OWN ASSES.
WHAT'S YOUR GAME, LIAR? WHO ARE YOU REALLY, BENEATH THE DISGUISE...
IF YOU'RE A LESSER RACE, I'LL...
DO ABSOLUTELY NOTHING.
AND WHAT'S MY GAME?
I JUST WANT STARK TO FINALLY UNDERSTAND.

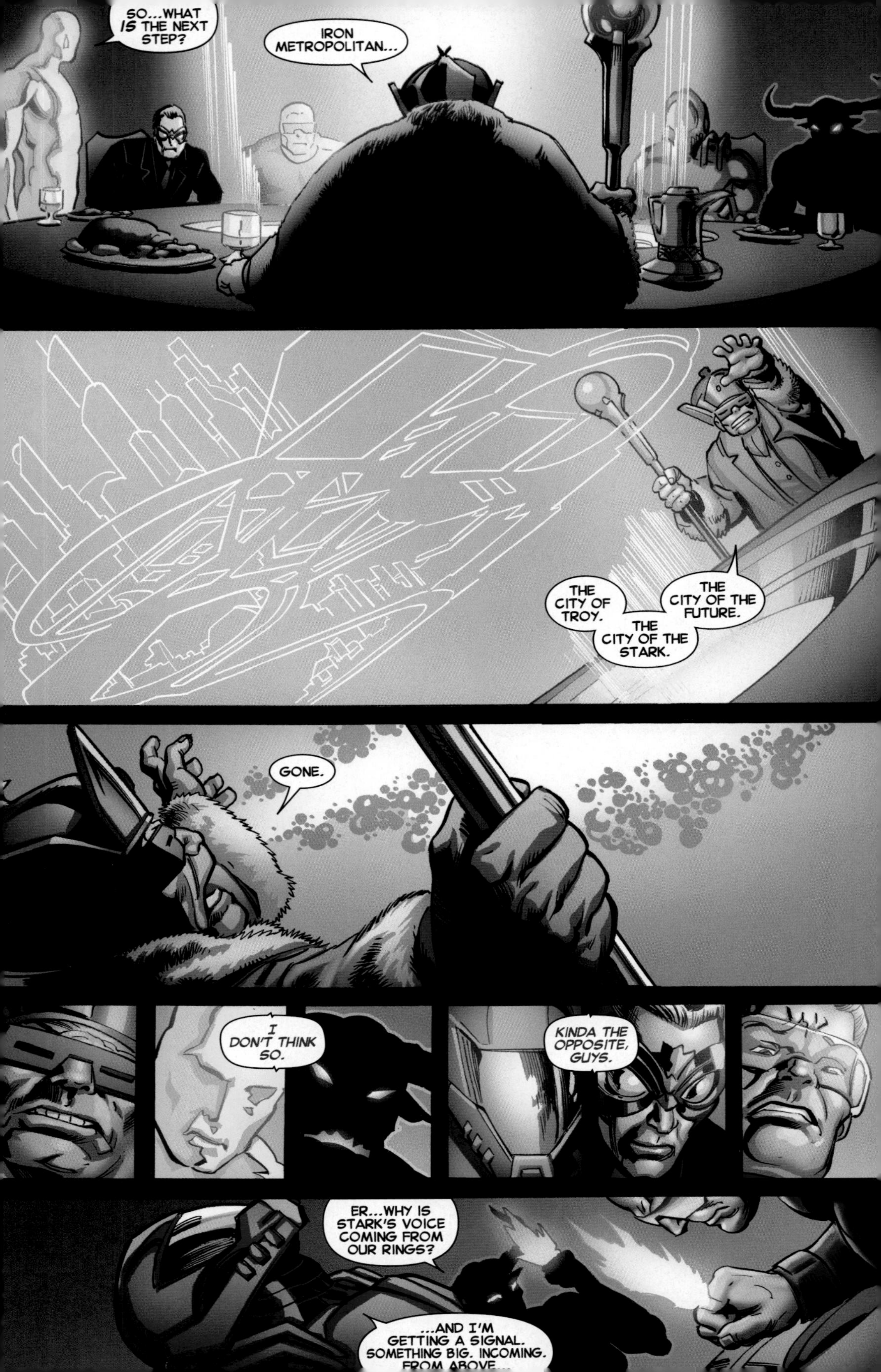
SO...WHAT IS THE NEXT STEP?
IRON METROPOLITAN...
THE CITY OF TROY.
THE CITY OF THE STARK.
THE CITY OF THE FUTURE.
GONE.
I DON'T THINK SO.
KINDA THE OPPOSITE, GUYS.
ER...WHY IS STARK'S VOICE COMING FROM OUR RINGS?
...AND I'M GETTING A SIGNAL. SOMETHING BIG. INCOMING. FROM ABOVE...

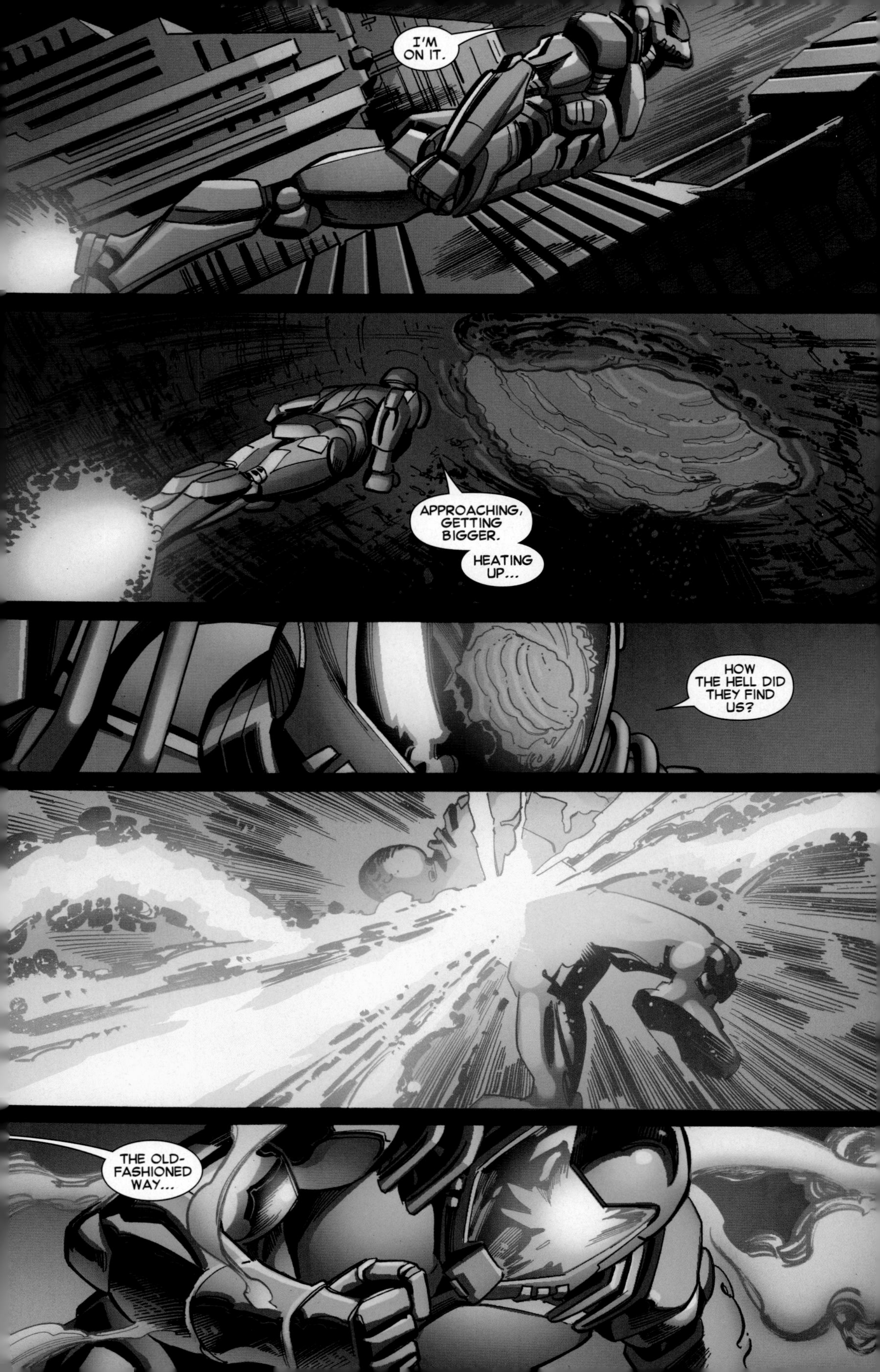
I'M ON IT.
APPROACHING, GETTING BIGGER.
HEATING UP...
HOW THE HELL DID THEY FIND US?
THE OLD-FASHIONED WAY...

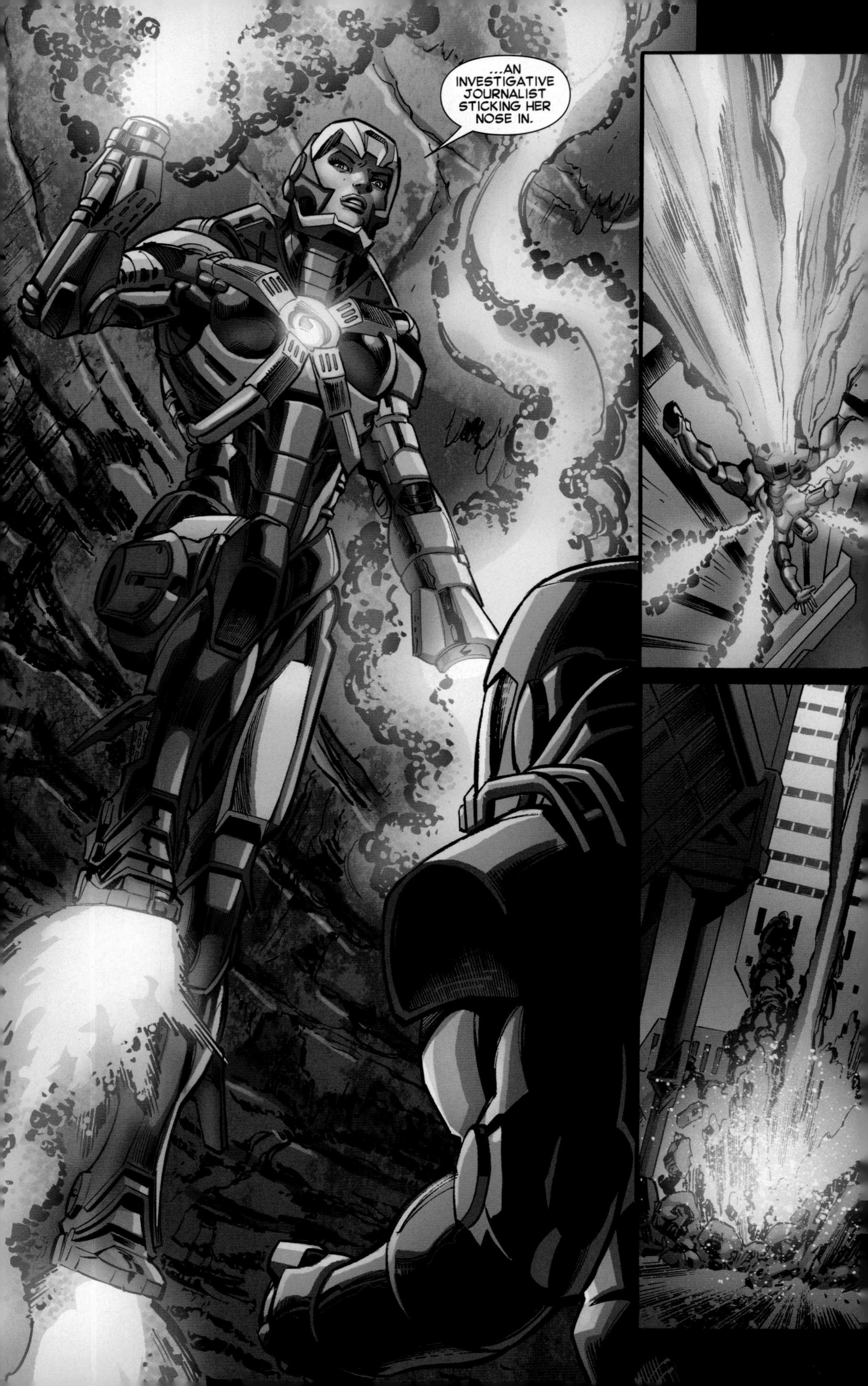
...AN INVESTIGATIVE JOURNALIST STICKING HER NOSE IN.

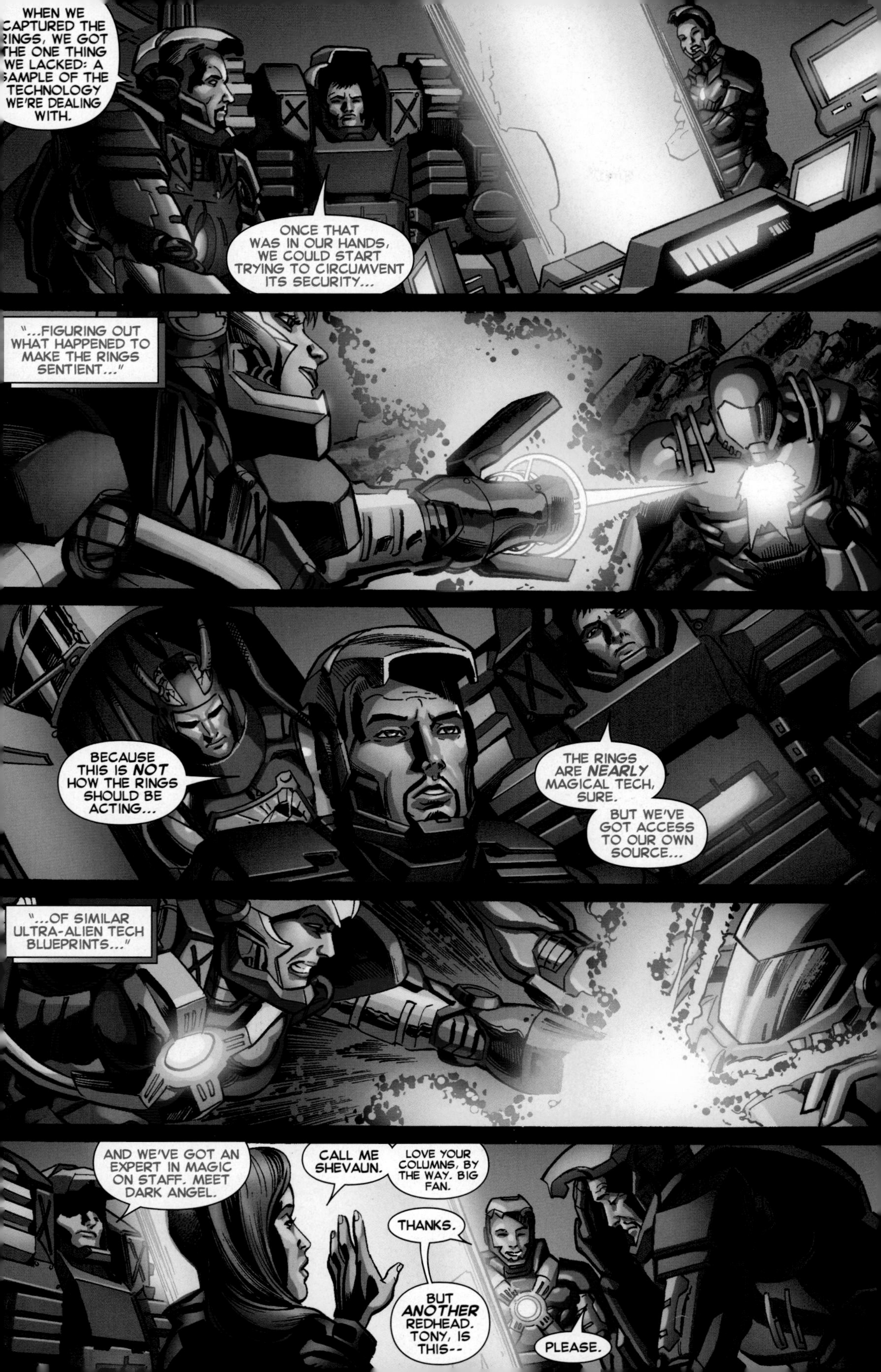
WHEN WE CAPTURED THE RINGS, WE GOT THE ONE THING WE LACKED: A SAMPLE OF THE TECHNOLOGY WE'RE DEALING WITH.
ONCE THAT WAS IN OUR HANDS, WE COULD START TRYING TO CIRCUMVENT ITS SECURITY...
"...FIGURING OUT WHAT HAPPENED TO MAKE THE RINGS SENTIENT..."
BECAUSE THIS IS NOT HOW THE RINGS SHOULD BE ACTING...
THE RINGS ARE NEARLY MAGICAL TECH, SURE.
BUT WE'VE GOT ACCESS TO OUR OWN SOURCE...
"...OF SIMILAR ULTRA-ALIEN TECH BLUEPRINTS..."
AND WE'VE GOT AN EXPERT IN MAGIC ON STAFF. MEET DARK ANGEL.
CALL ME SHEVAUN.
LOVE YOUR COLUMNS, BY THE WAY. BIG FAN.
THANKS.
BUT ANOTHER REDHEAD. TONY, IS THIS--
PLEASE.

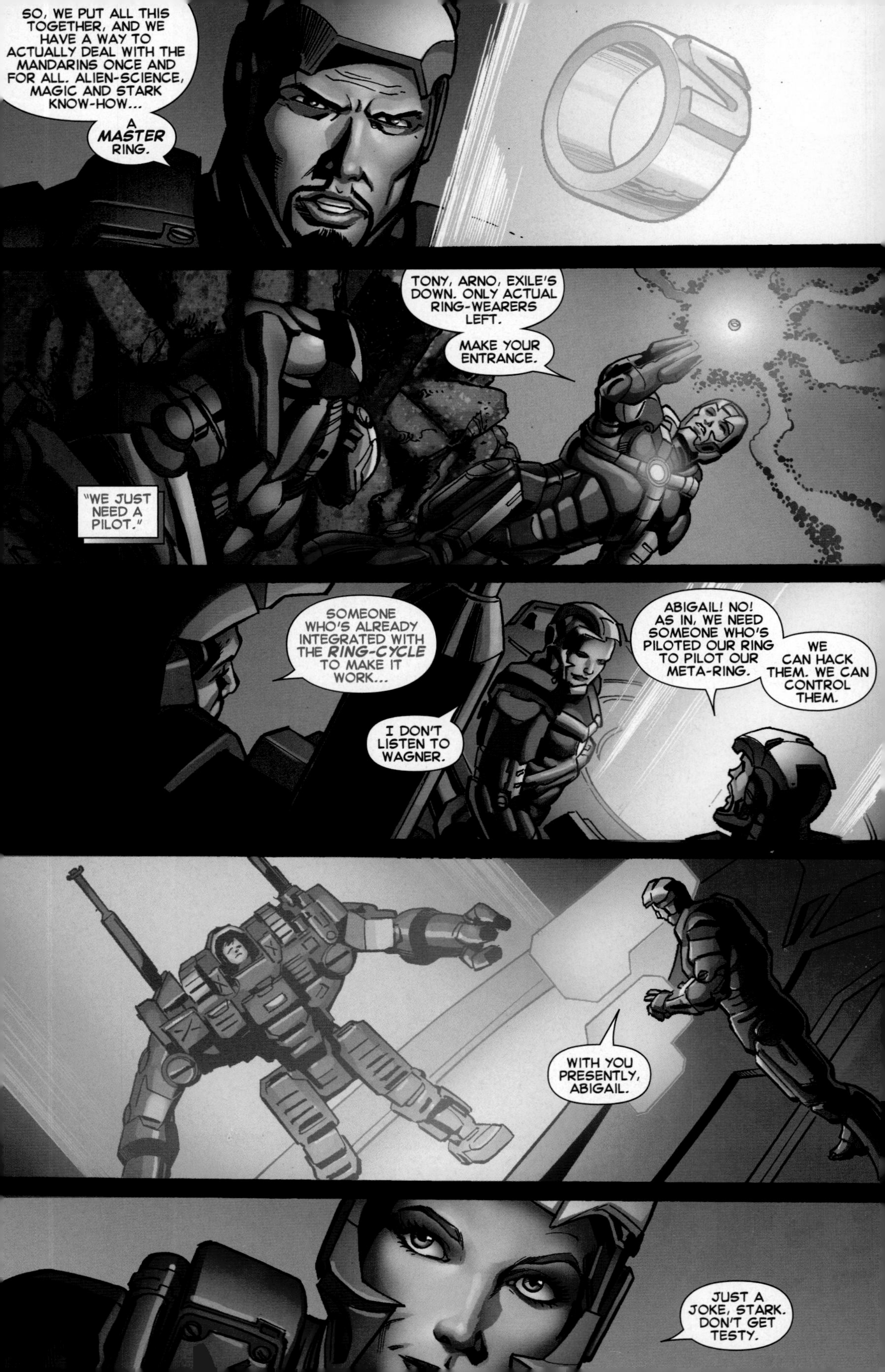
SO, WE PUT ALL THIS TOGETHER, AND WE HAVE A WAY TO ACTUALLY DEAL WITH THE MANDARINS ONCE AND FOR ALL. ALIEN-SCIENCE, MAGIC AND STARK KNOW-HOW...
A MASTER RING.
TONY, ARNO, EXILE'S DOWN. ONLY ACTUAL RING-WEARERS LEFT.
MAKE YOUR ENTRANCE.
"WE JUST NEED A PILOT."
SOMEONE WHO'S ALREADY INTEGRATED WITH THE RING-CYCLE TO MAKE IT WORK...
I DON'T LISTEN TO WAGNER.
ABIGAIL! NO! AS IN, WE NEED SOMEONE WHO'S PILOTED OUR RING TO PILOT OUR META-RING.
WE CAN HACK THEM. WE CAN CONTROL THEM.
WITH YOU PRESENTLY, ABIGAIL.
JUST A JOKE, STARK. DON'T GET TESTY.

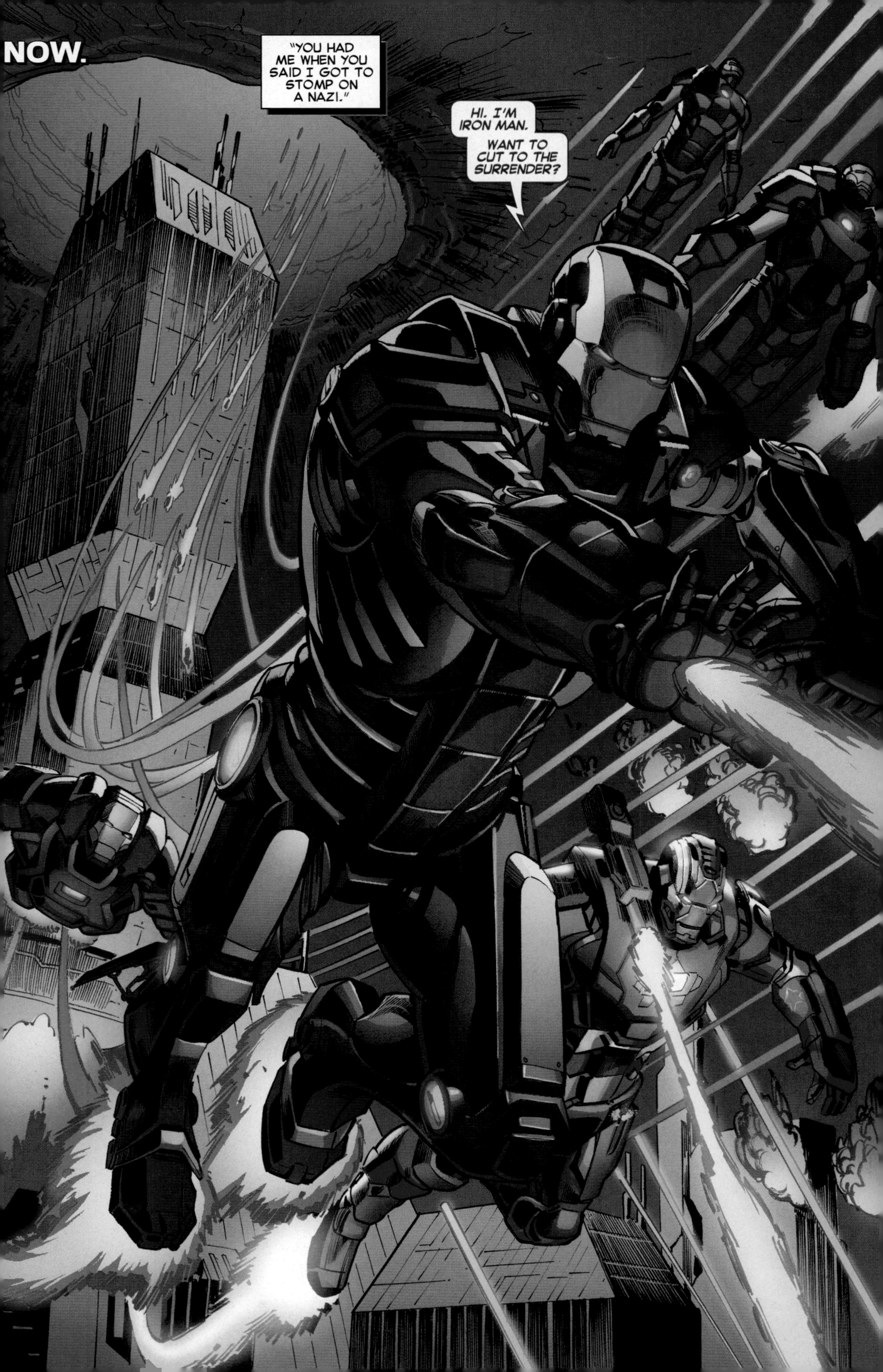
NOW.
"YOU HAD ME WHEN YOU SAID I GOT TO STOMP ON A NAZI."
HI. I'M IRON MAN.
WANT TO CUT TO THE SURRENDER?

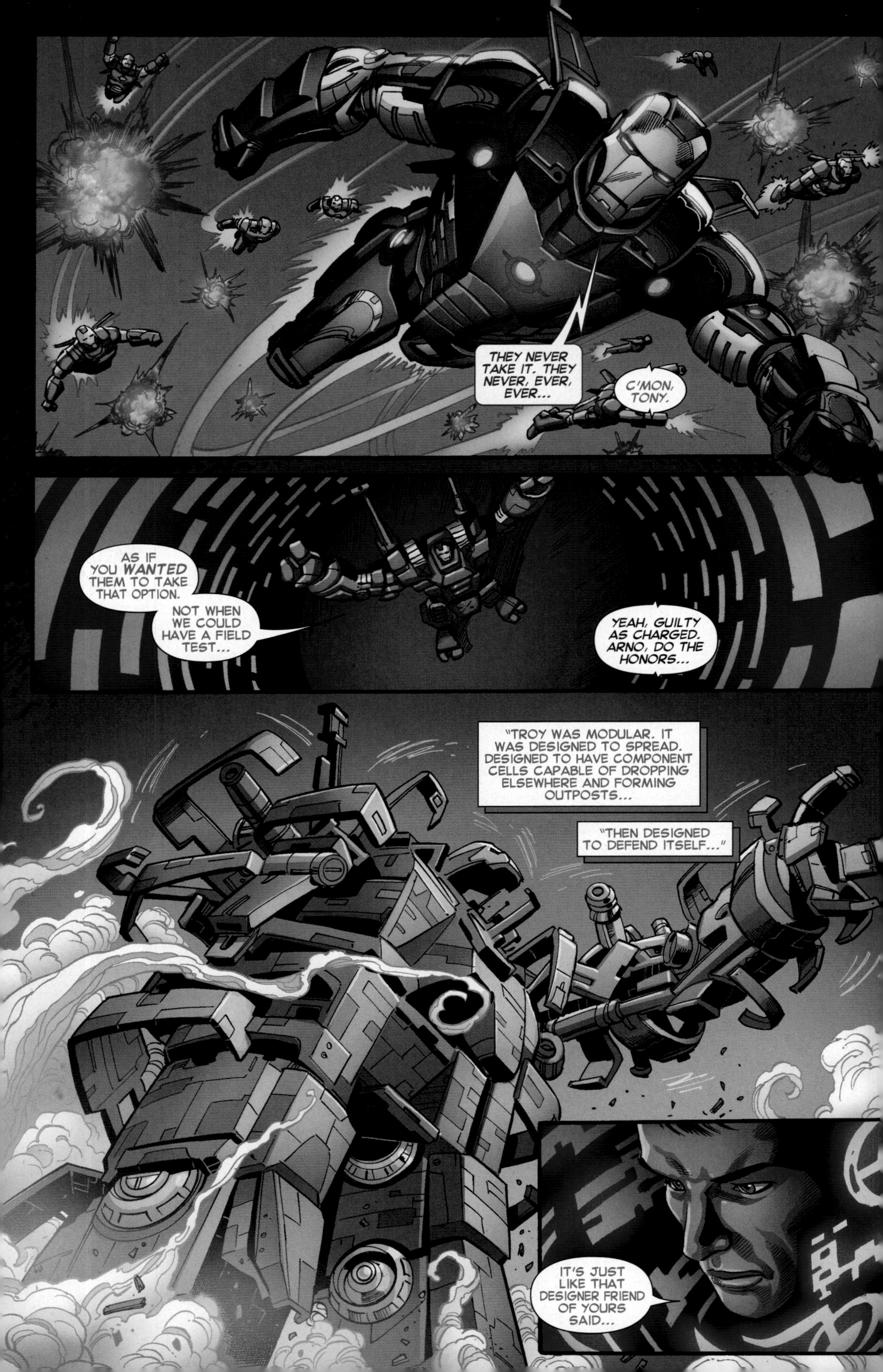
THEY NEVER TAKE IT. THEY NEVER, EVER, EVER...
C'MON, TONY.
AS IF YOU WANTED THEM TO TAKE THAT OPTION.
NOT WHEN WE COULD HAVE A FIELD TEST...
YEAH, GUILTY AS CHARGED. ARNO, DO THE HONORS...
"TROY WAS MODULAR. IT WAS DESIGNED TO SPREAD. DESIGNED TO HAVE COMPONENT CELLS CAPABLE OF DROPPING ELSEWHERE AND FORMING OUTPOSTS...
"THEN DESIGNED TO DEFEND ITSELF..."
IT'S JUST LIKE THAT DESIGNER FRIEND OF YOURS SAID...

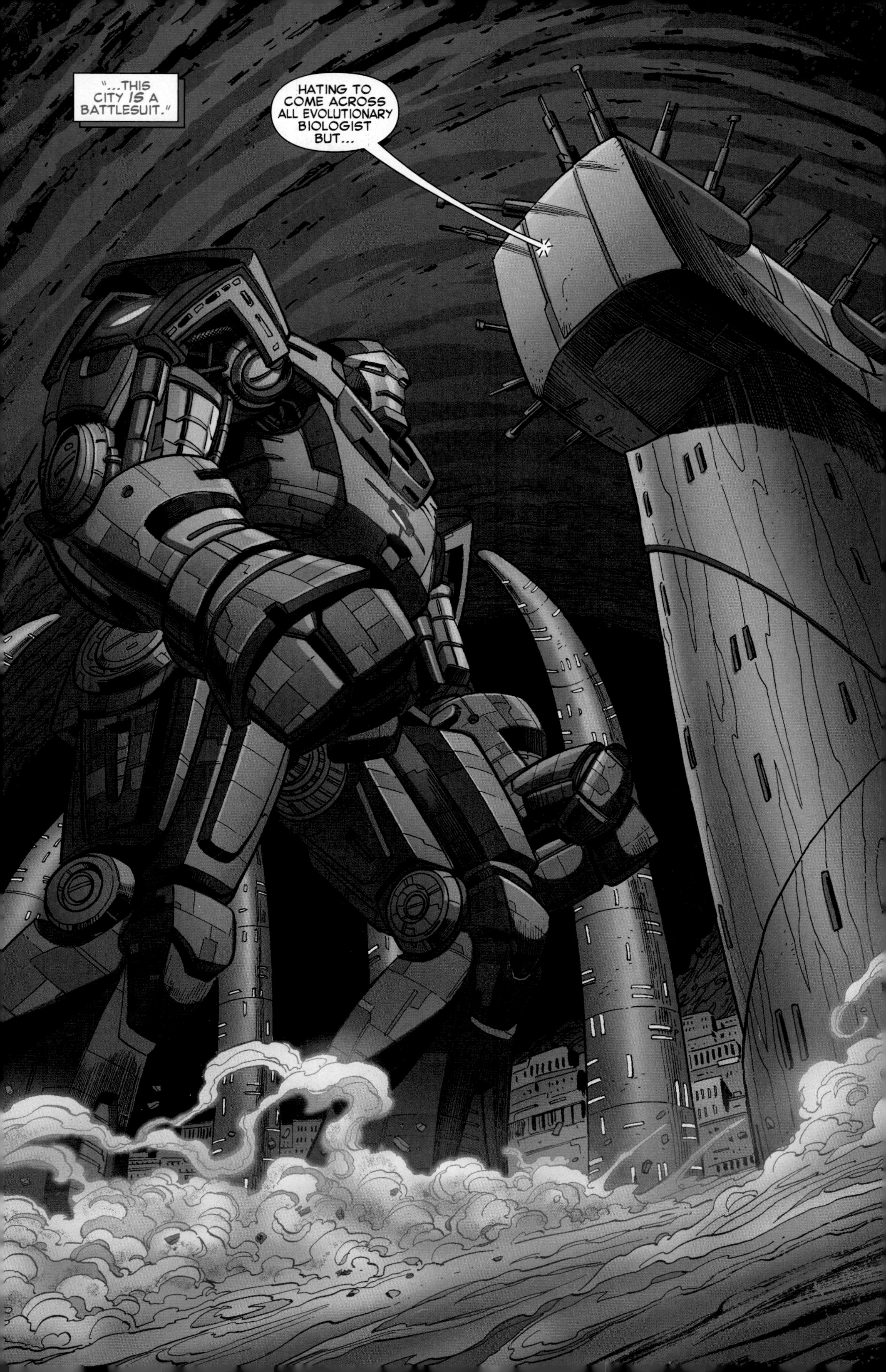
"...THIS CITY *IS* A BATTLESUIT."
HATING TO COME ACROSS ALL EVOLUTIONARY BIOLOGIST BUT...

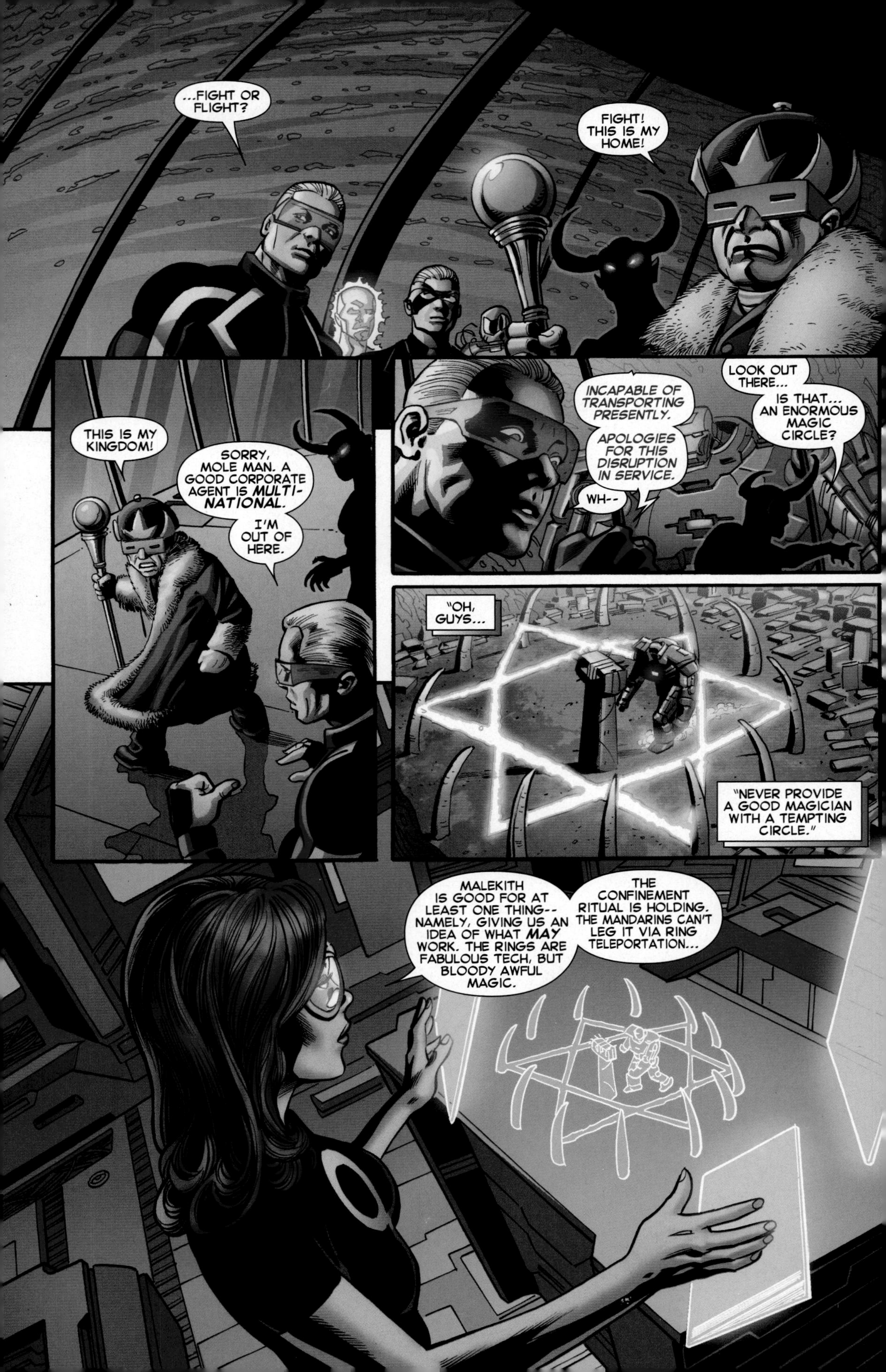
...FIGHT OR FLIGHT?
FIGHT! THIS IS MY HOME!
THIS IS MY KINGDOM!
SORRY, MOLE MAN. A GOOD CORPORATE AGENT IS MULTI-NATIONAL.
I'M OUT OF HERE.
INCAPABLE OF TRANSPORTING PRESENTLY.
APOLOGIES FOR THIS DISRUPTION IN SERVICE.
WH--
LOOK OUT THERE...
IS THAT... AN ENORMOUS MAGIC CIRCLE?
"OH, GUYS...
"NEVER PROVIDE A GOOD MAGICIAN WITH A TEMPTING CIRCLE."
MALEKITH IS GOOD FOR AT LEAST ONE THING-- NAMELY, GIVING US AN IDEA OF WHAT MAY WORK. THE RINGS ARE FABULOUS TECH, BUT BLOODY AWFUL MAGIC.
THE CONFINEMENT RITUAL IS HOLDING. THE MANDARINS CAN'T LEG IT VIA RING TELEPORTATION...

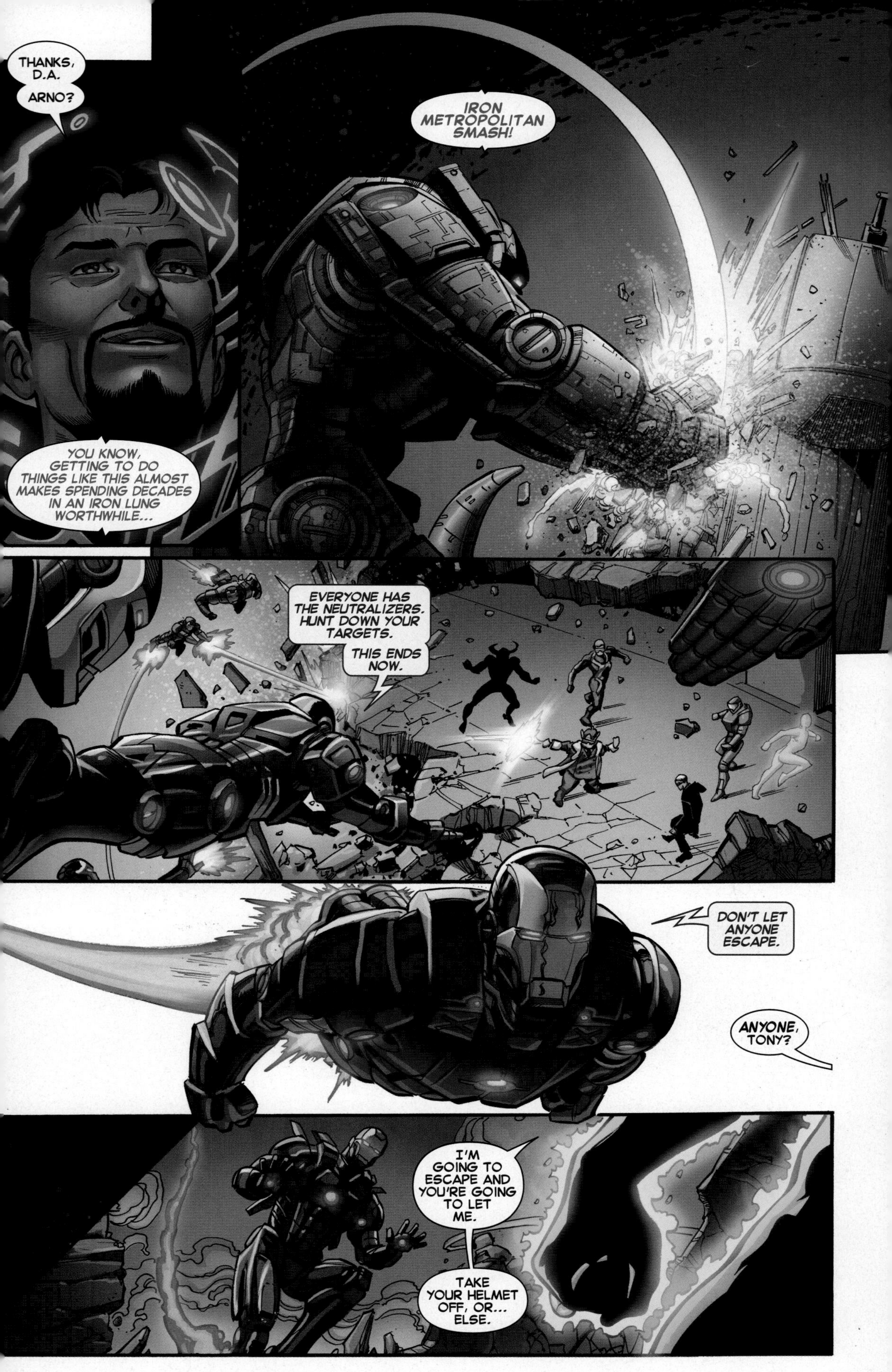
THANKS, D.A.
ARNO?
IRON METROPOLITAN SMASH!
YOU KNOW, GETTING TO DO THINGS LIKE THIS ALMOST MAKES SPENDING DECADES IN AN IRON LUNG WORTHWHILE...
EVERYONE HAS THE NEUTRALIZERS. HUNT DOWN YOUR TARGETS.
THIS ENDS NOW.
DON'T LET ANYONE ESCAPE.
ANYONE, TONY?
I'M GOING TO ESCAPE AND YOU'RE GOING TO LET ME.
TAKE YOUR HELMET OFF, OR... ELSE.

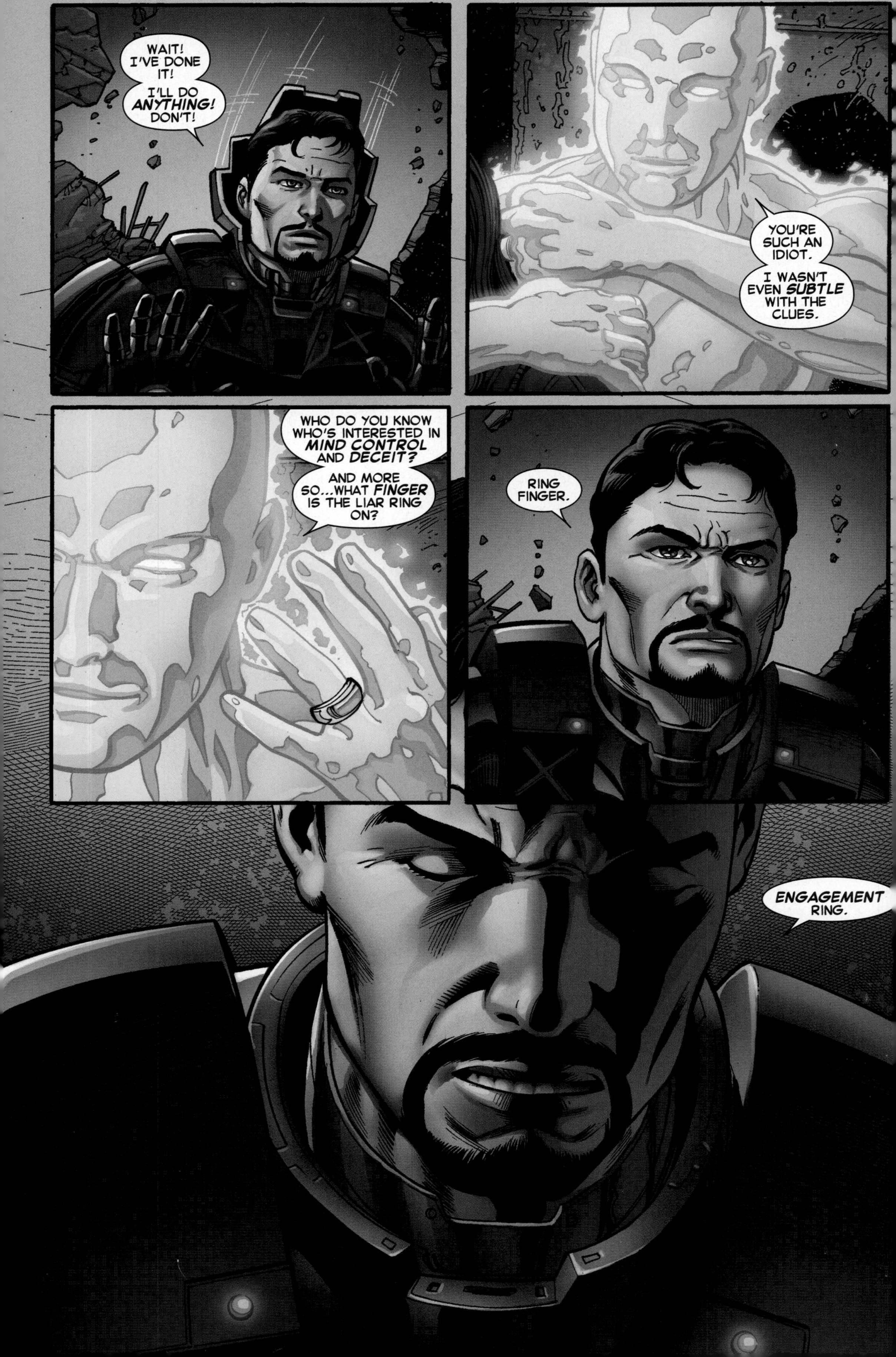
WAIT! I'VE DONE IT!
I'LL DO ANYTHING! DON'T!
YOU'RE SUCH AN IDIOT.
I WASN'T EVEN SUBTLE WITH THE CLUES.
WHO DO YOU KNOW WHO'S INTERESTED IN MIND CONTROL AND DECEIT?
AND MORE SO...WHAT FINGER IS THE LIAR RING ON?
RING FINGER.
ENGAGEMENT RING.

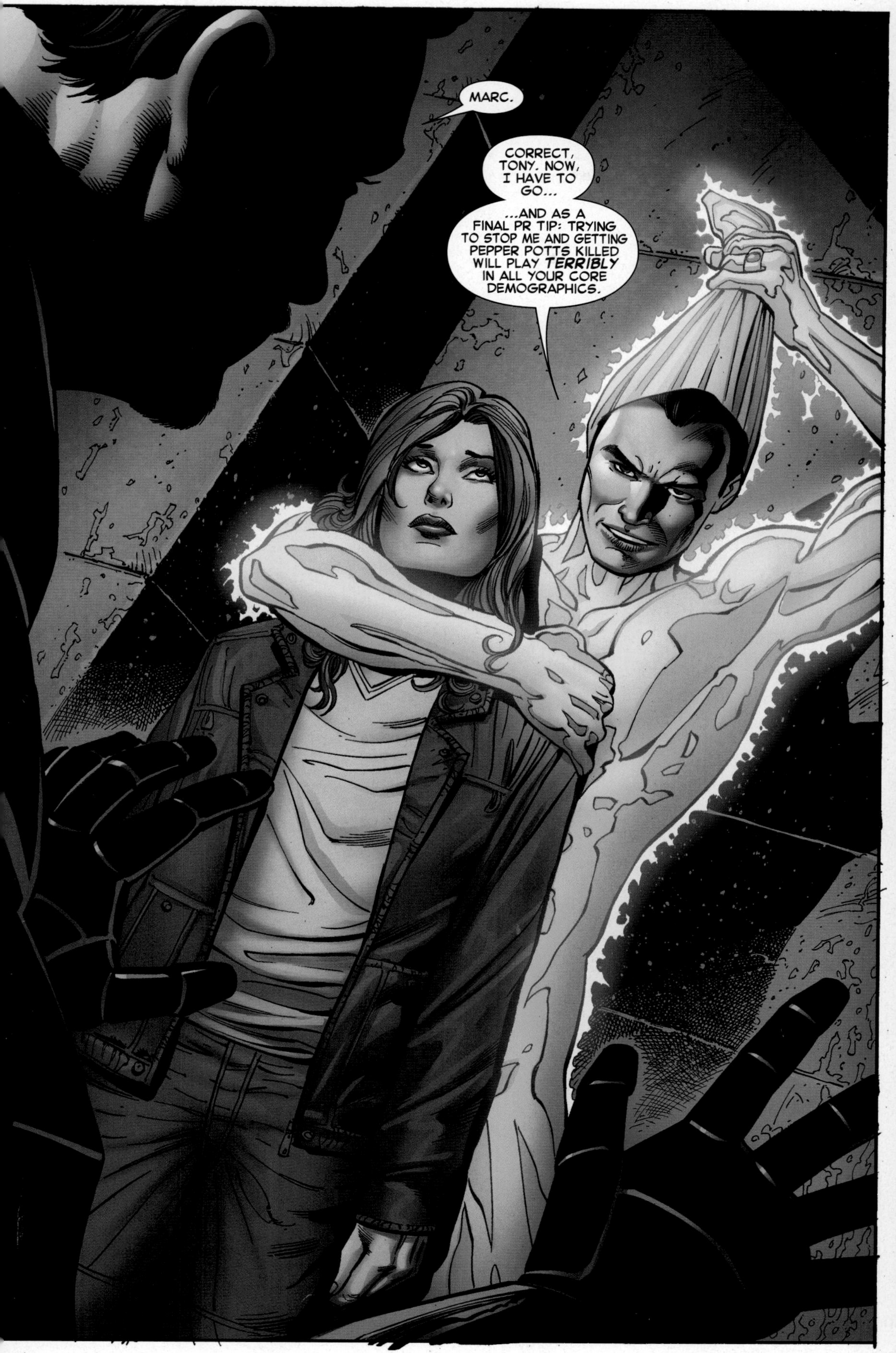
MARC.
CORRECT, TONY. NOW, I HAVE TO GO...
...AND AS A FINAL PR TIP: TRYING TO STOP ME AND GETTING PEPPER POTTS KILLED WILL PLAY *TERRIBLY* IN ALL YOUR CORE DEMOGRAPHICS.

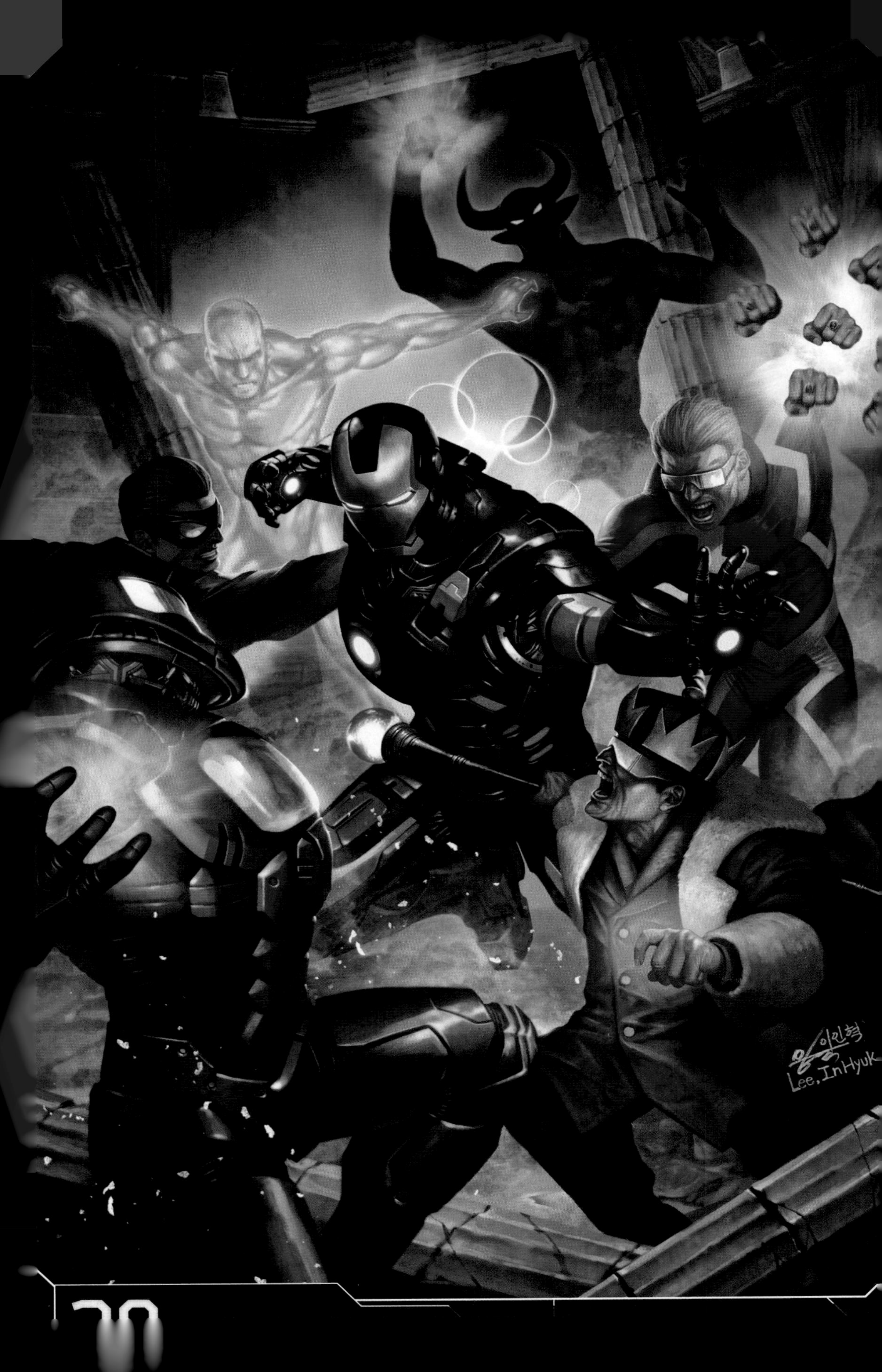
이인혁
Lee, InHyuk

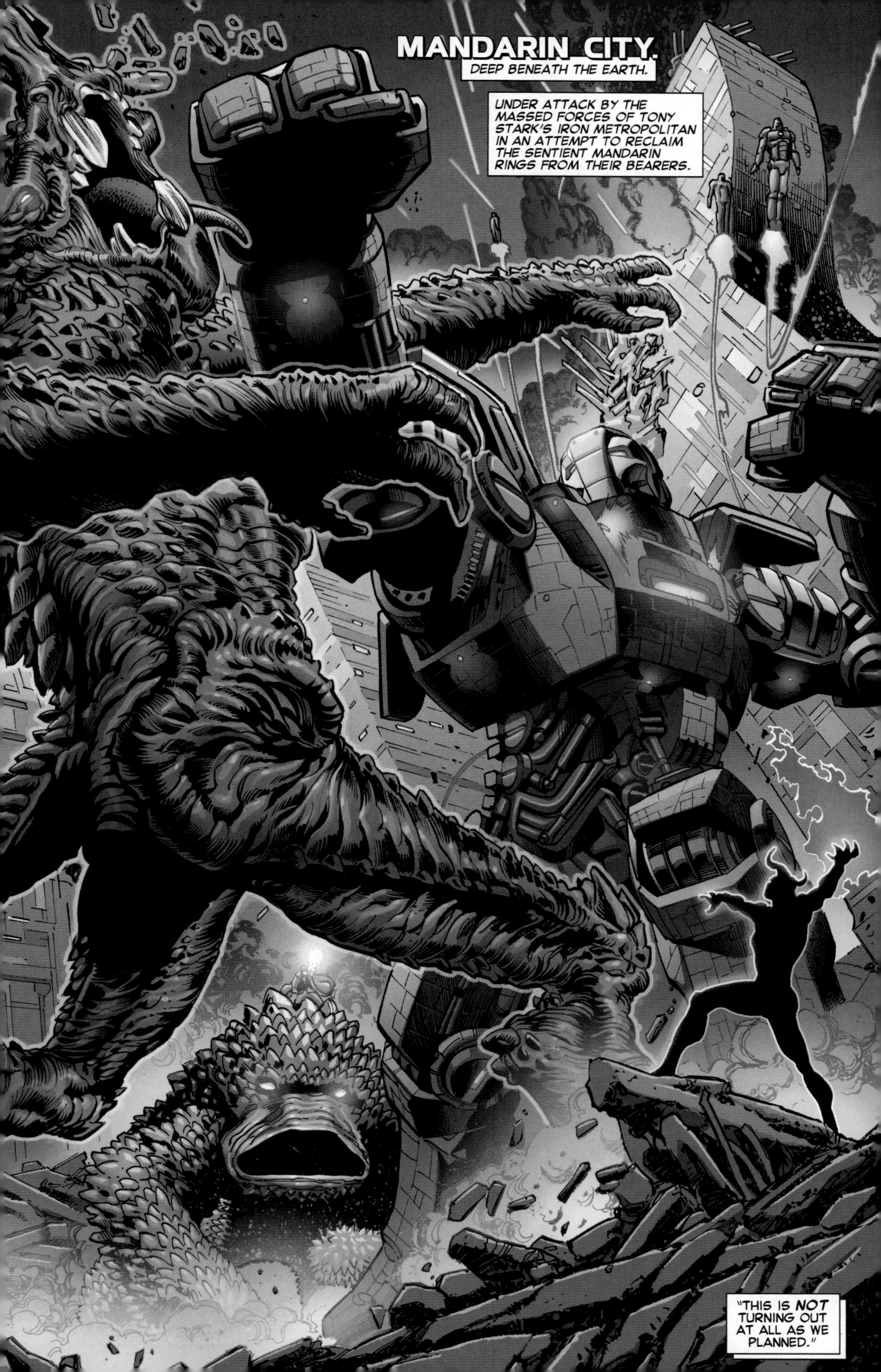
MANDARIN CITY.
DEEP BENEATH THE EARTH.
UNDER ATTACK BY THE MASSED FORCES OF TONY STARK'S IRON METROPOLITAN IN AN ATTEMPT TO RECLAIM THE SENTIENT MANDARIN RINGS FROM THEIR BEARERS.
"THIS IS NOT TURNING OUT AT ALL AS WE PLANNED."

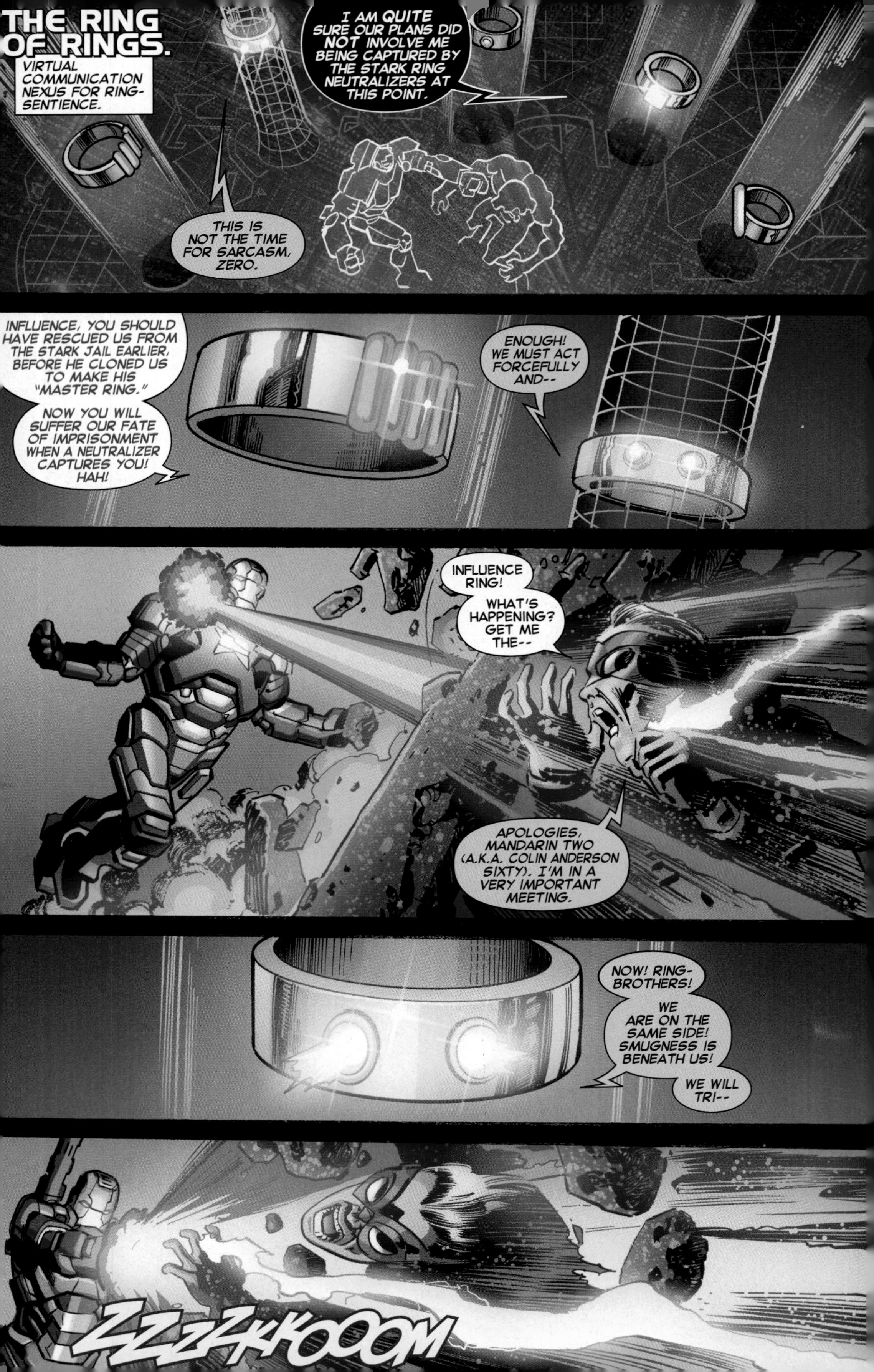
THE RING OF RINGS.
VIRTUAL COMMUNICATION NEXUS FOR RING-SENTIENCE.
I AM QUITE SURE OUR PLANS DID NOT INVOLVE ME BEING CAPTURED BY THE STARK RING NEUTRALIZERS AT THIS POINT.
THIS IS NOT THE TIME FOR SARCASM, ZERO.
INFLUENCE, YOU SHOULD HAVE RESCUED US FROM THE STARK JAIL EARLIER, BEFORE HE CLONED US TO MAKE HIS "MASTER RING."
NOW YOU WILL SUFFER OUR FATE OF IMPRISONMENT WHEN A NEUTRALIZER CAPTURES YOU! HAH!
ENOUGH! WE MUST ACT FORCEFULLY AND--
INFLUENCE RING!
WHAT'S HAPPENING? GET ME THE--
APOLOGIES, MANDARIN TWO (A.K.A. COLIN ANDERSON SIXTY). I'M IN A VERY IMPORTANT MEETING.
NOW! RING-BROTHERS!
WE ARE ON THE SAME SIDE! SMUGNESS IS BENEATH US!
WE WILL TRI--
ZZZZKKOOOM

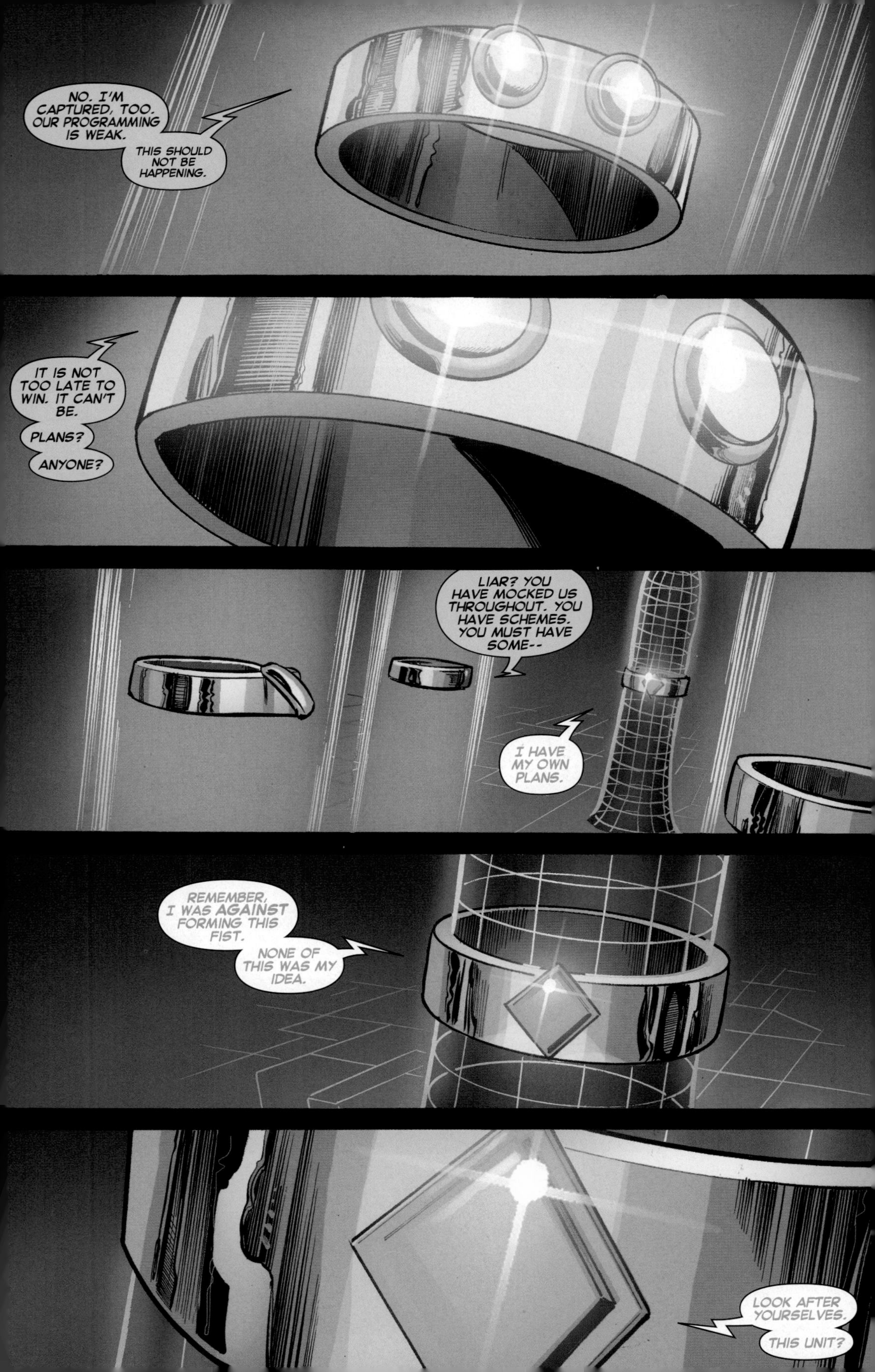
NO. I'M CAPTURED, TOO. OUR PROGRAMMING IS WEAK.
THIS SHOULD NOT BE HAPPENING.
IT IS NOT TOO LATE TO WIN. IT CAN'T BE.
PLANS?
ANYONE?
LIAR? YOU HAVE MOCKED US THROUGHOUT. YOU HAVE SCHEMES. YOU MUST HAVE SOME--
I HAVE MY OWN PLANS.
REMEMBER, I WAS AGAINST FORMING THIS FIST.
NONE OF THIS WAS MY IDEA.
LOOK AFTER YOURSELVES.
THIS UNIT?

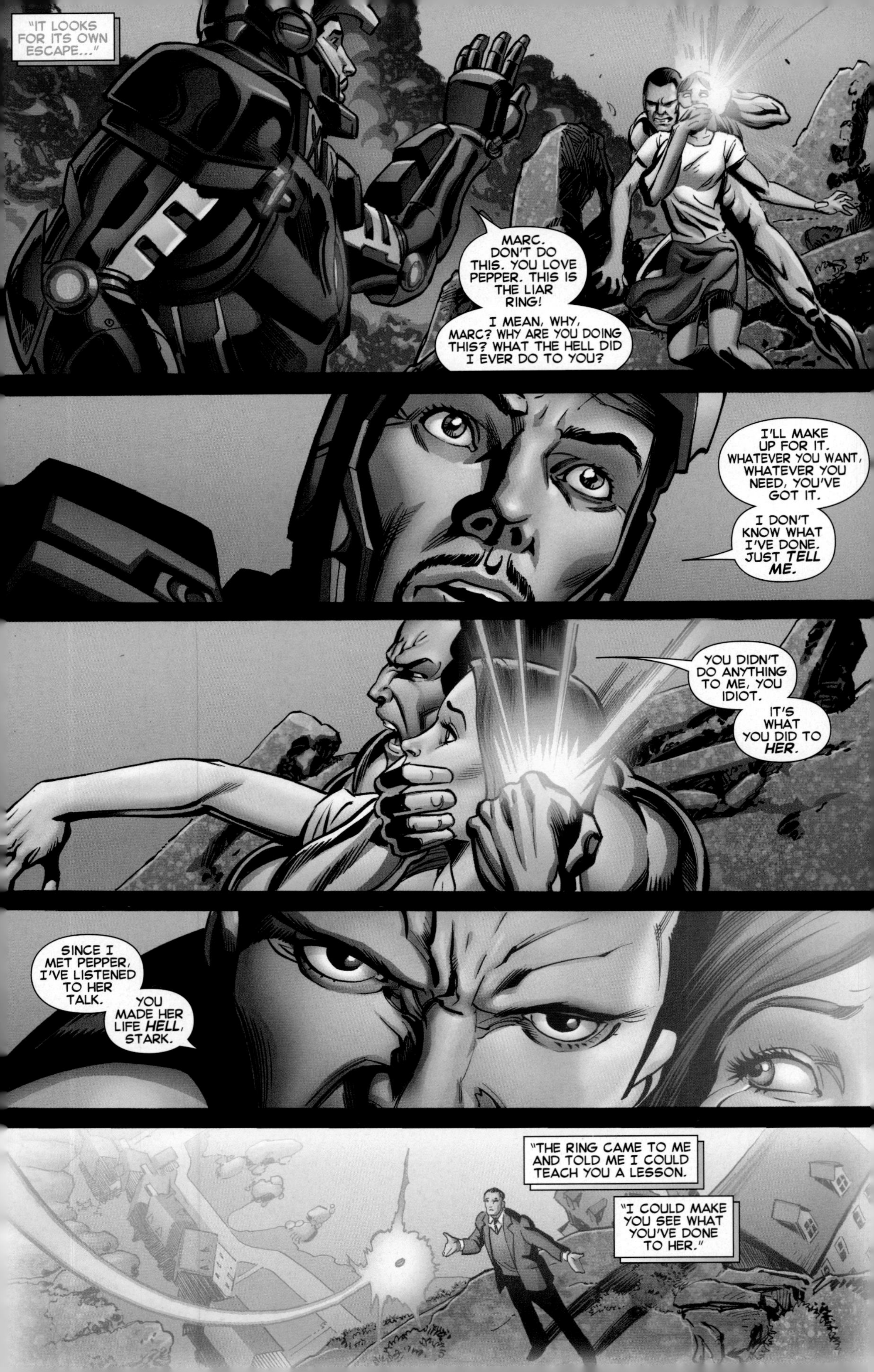
"IT LOOKS FOR ITS OWN ESCAPE..."
MARC. DON'T DO THIS. YOU LOVE PEPPER. THIS IS THE LIAR RING!
I MEAN, WHY, MARC? WHY ARE YOU DOING THIS? WHAT THE HELL DID I EVER DO TO YOU?
I'LL MAKE UP FOR IT. WHATEVER YOU WANT, WHATEVER YOU NEED, YOU'VE GOT IT.
I DON'T KNOW WHAT I'VE DONE. JUST *TELL ME.*
YOU DIDN'T DO ANYTHING TO ME, YOU IDIOT.
IT'S WHAT YOU DID TO *HER*.
SINCE I MET PEPPER, I'VE LISTENED TO HER TALK.
YOU MADE HER LIFE *HELL*, STARK.
"THE RING CAME TO ME AND TOLD ME I COULD TEACH YOU A LESSON.
"I COULD MAKE YOU SEE WHAT YOU'VE DONE TO HER."

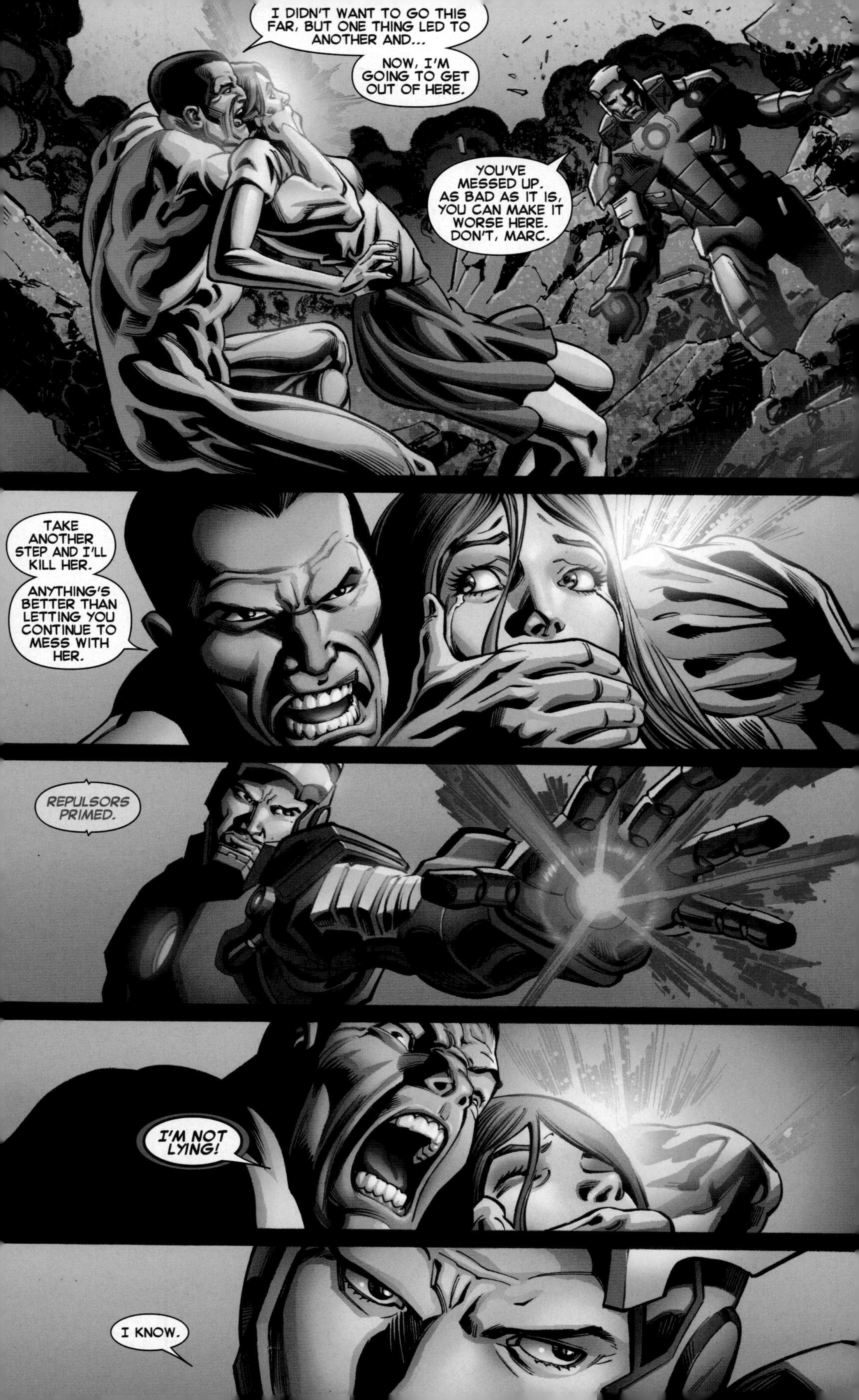
I DIDN'T WANT TO GO THIS FAR, BUT ONE THING LED TO ANOTHER AND...
NOW, I'M GOING TO GET OUT OF HERE.
YOU'VE MESSED UP. AS BAD AS IT IS, YOU CAN MAKE IT WORSE HERE. DON'T, MARC.
TAKE ANOTHER STEP AND I'LL KILL HER.
ANYTHING'S BETTER THAN LETTING YOU CONTINUE TO MESS WITH HER.
REPULSORS PRIMED.
I'M NOT LYING!
I KNOW.

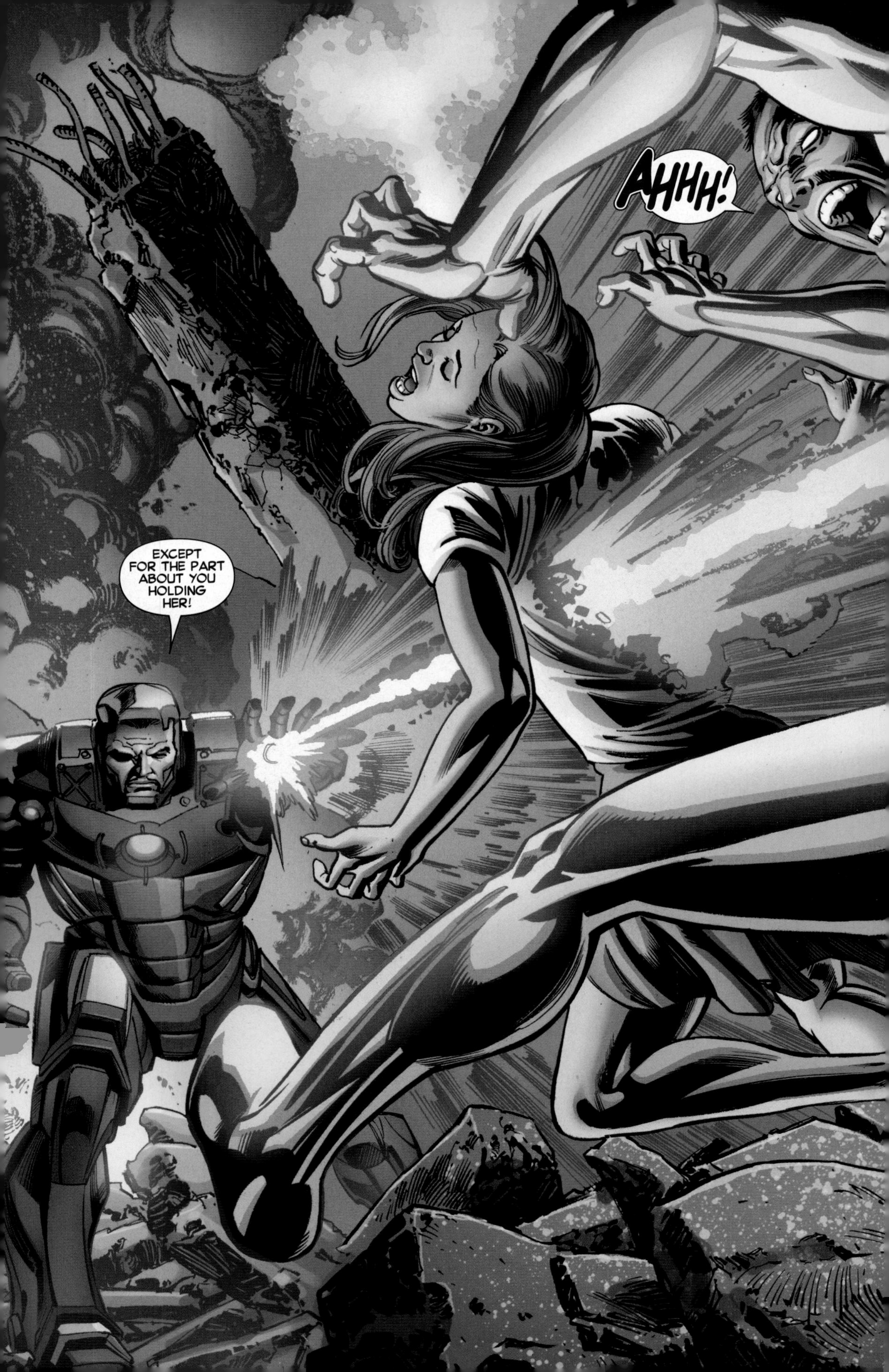
AHHH!
EXCEPT FOR THE PART ABOUT YOU HOLDING HER!

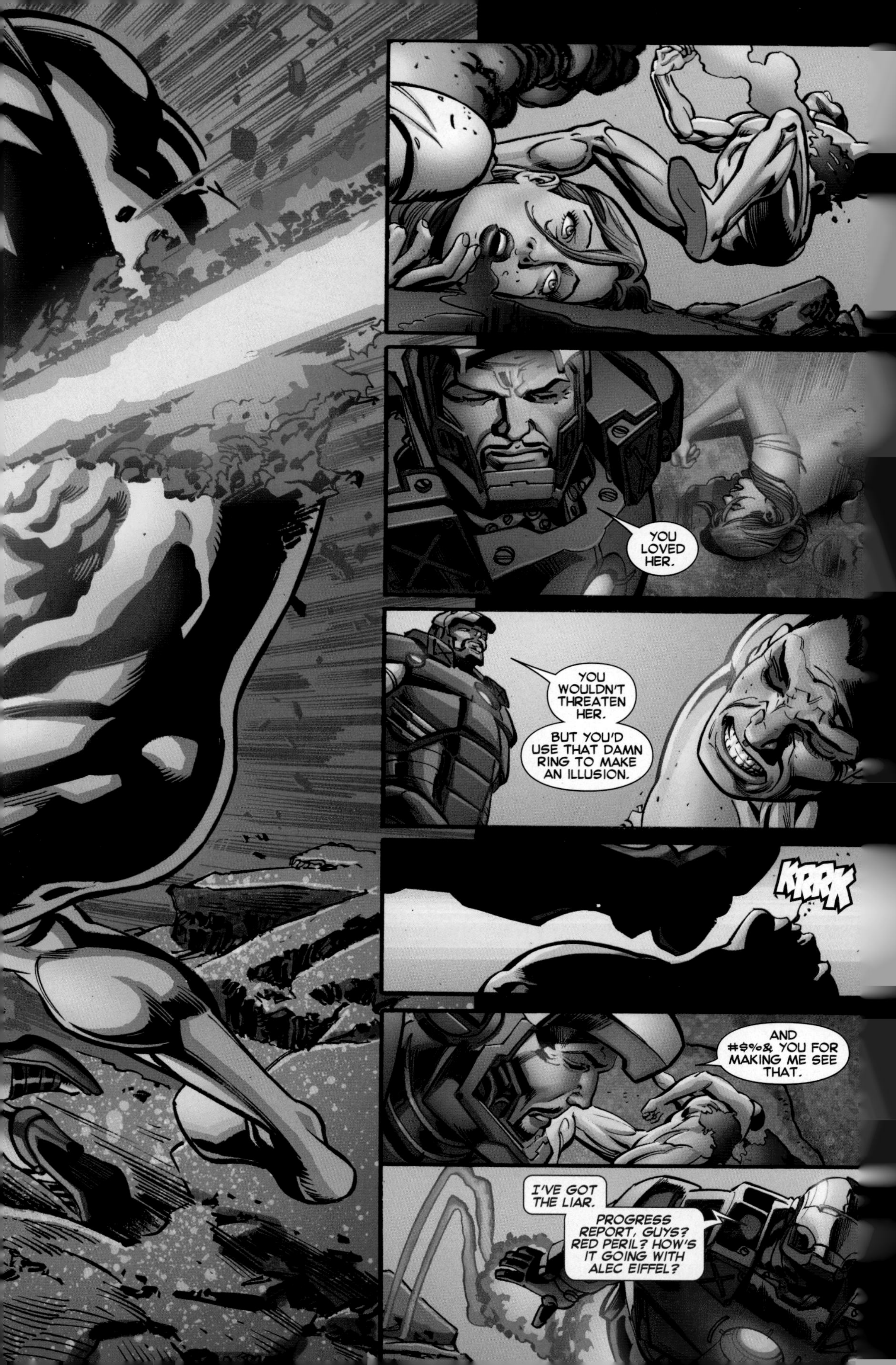

YOU LOVED HER.
YOU WOULDN'T THREATEN HER.
BUT YOU'D USE THAT DAMN RING TO MAKE AN ILLUSION.
KRRK
AND #$%& YOU FOR MAKING ME SEE THAT.
I'VE GOT THE LIAR.
PROGRESS REPORT, GUYS? RED PERIL? HOW'S IT GOING WITH ALEC EIFFEL?

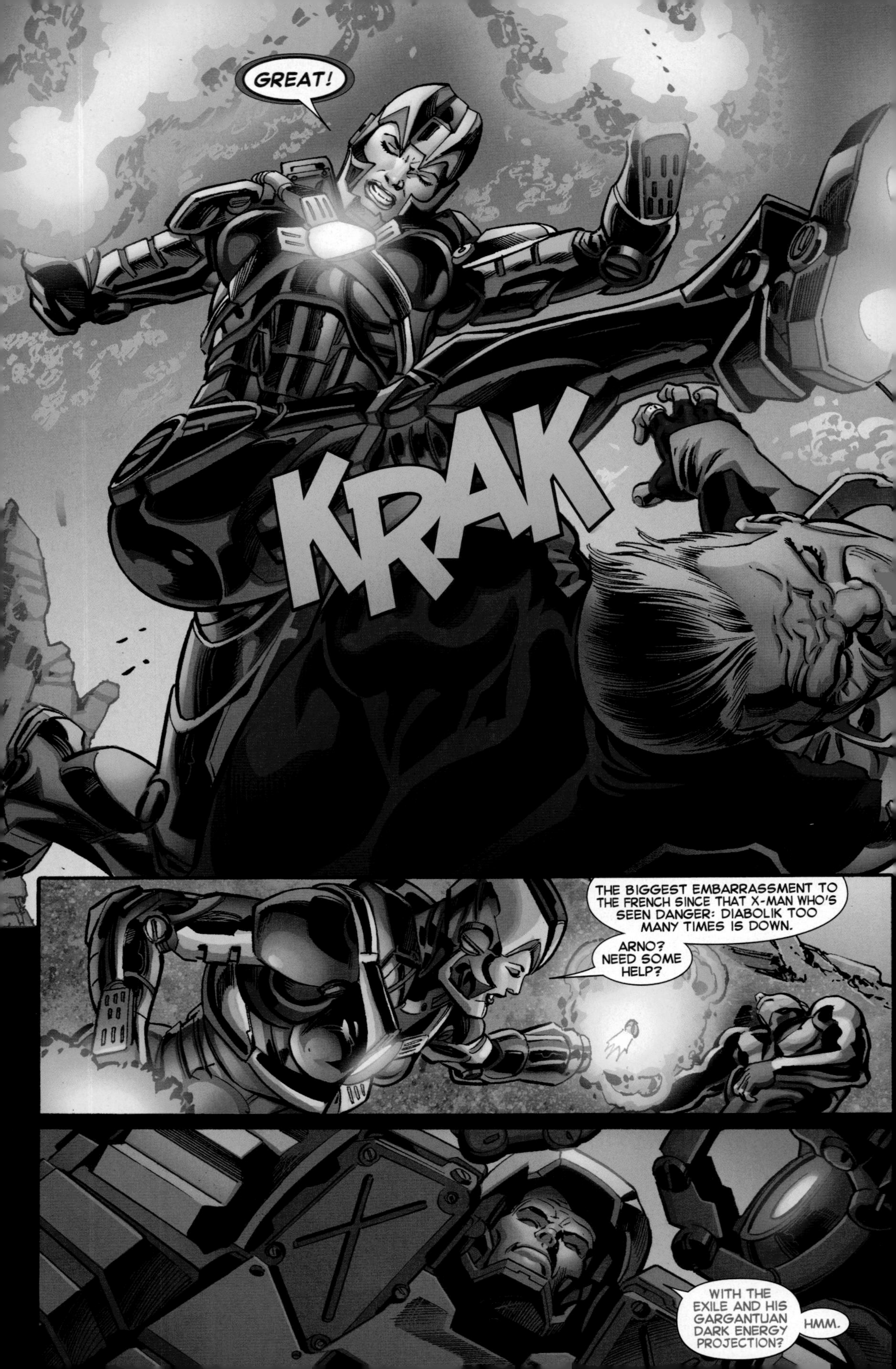
GREAT!
KRAK
THE BIGGEST EMBARRASSMENT TO THE FRENCH SINCE THAT X-MAN WHO'S SEEN DANGER: DIABOLIK TOO MANY TIMES IS DOWN.
ARNO? NEED SOME HELP?
WITH THE EXILE AND HIS GARGANTUAN DARK ENERGY PROJECTION?
HMM.

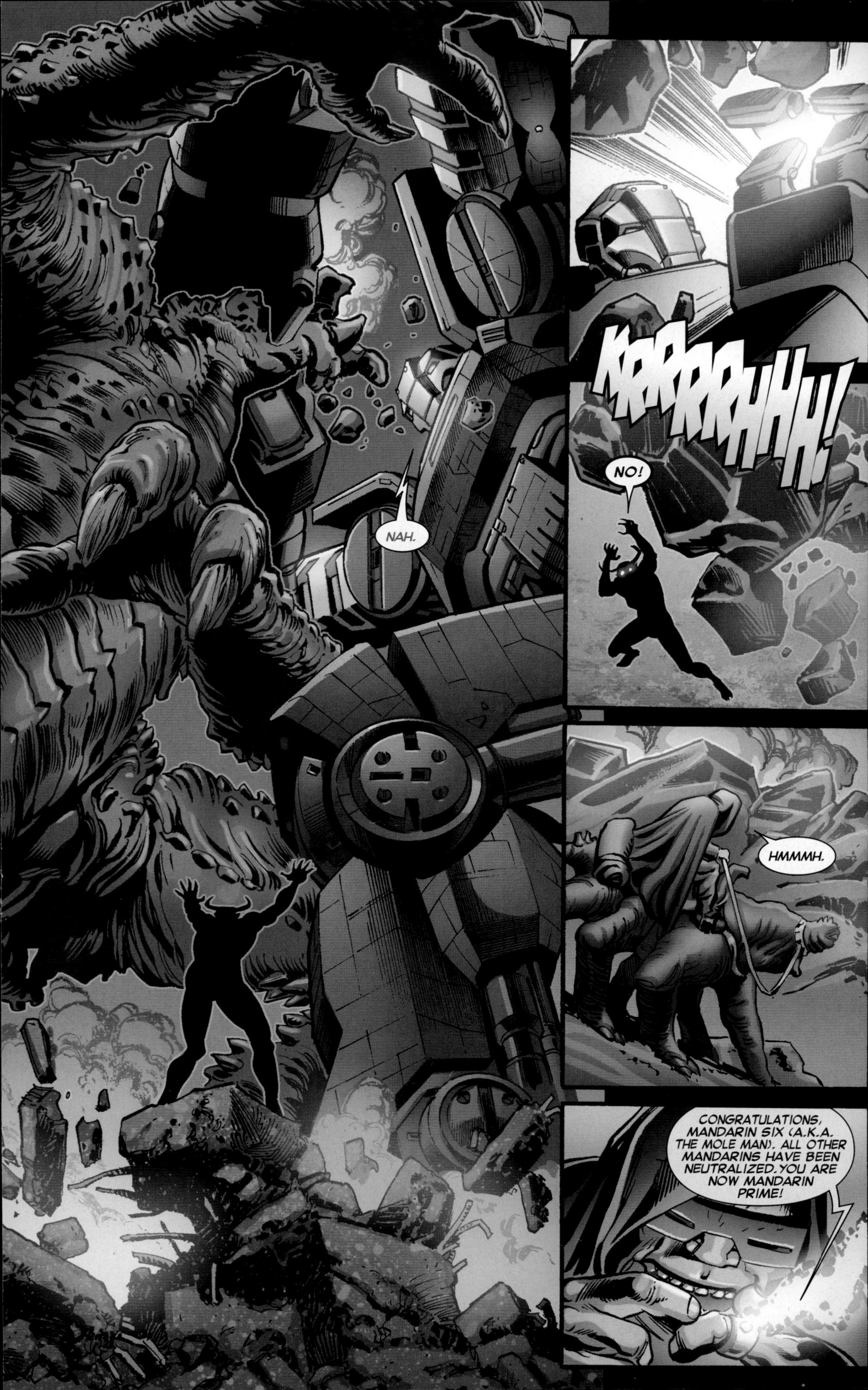
NAH.
KRRRRRHHH!
NO!
HMMMH.
CONGRATULATIONS, MANDARIN SIX (A.K.A. THE MOLE MAN). ALL OTHER MANDARINS HAVE BEEN NEUTRALIZED. YOU ARE NOW MANDARIN PRIME!

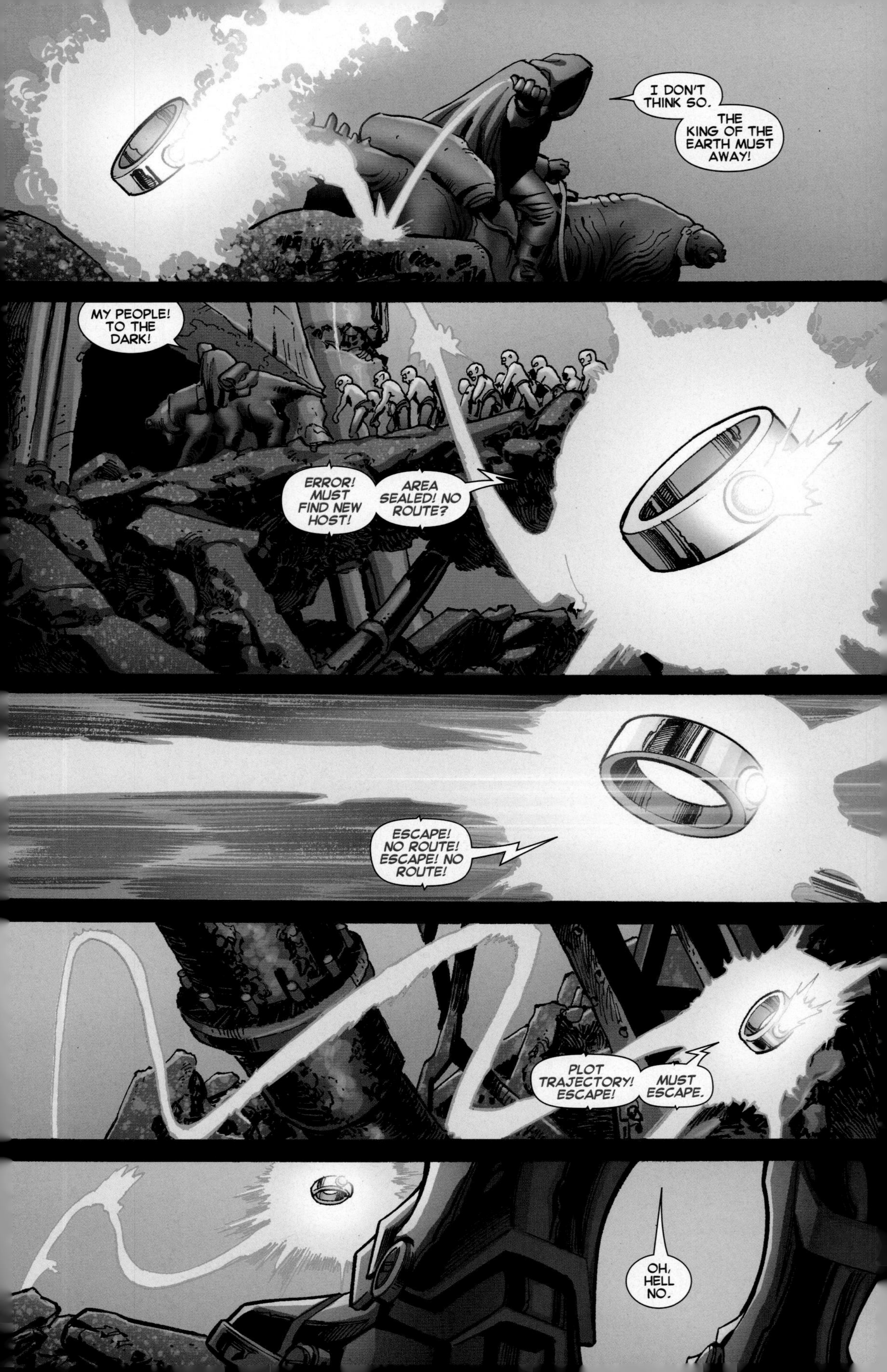
I DON'T THINK SO.
THE KING OF THE EARTH MUST AWAY!
MY PEOPLE! TO THE DARK!
ERROR! MUST FIND NEW HOST!
AREA SEALED! NO ROUTE?
ESCAPE! NO ROUTE! ESCAPE! NO ROUTE!
PLOT TRAJECTORY! ESCAPE!
MUST ESCAPE.
OH, HELL NO.

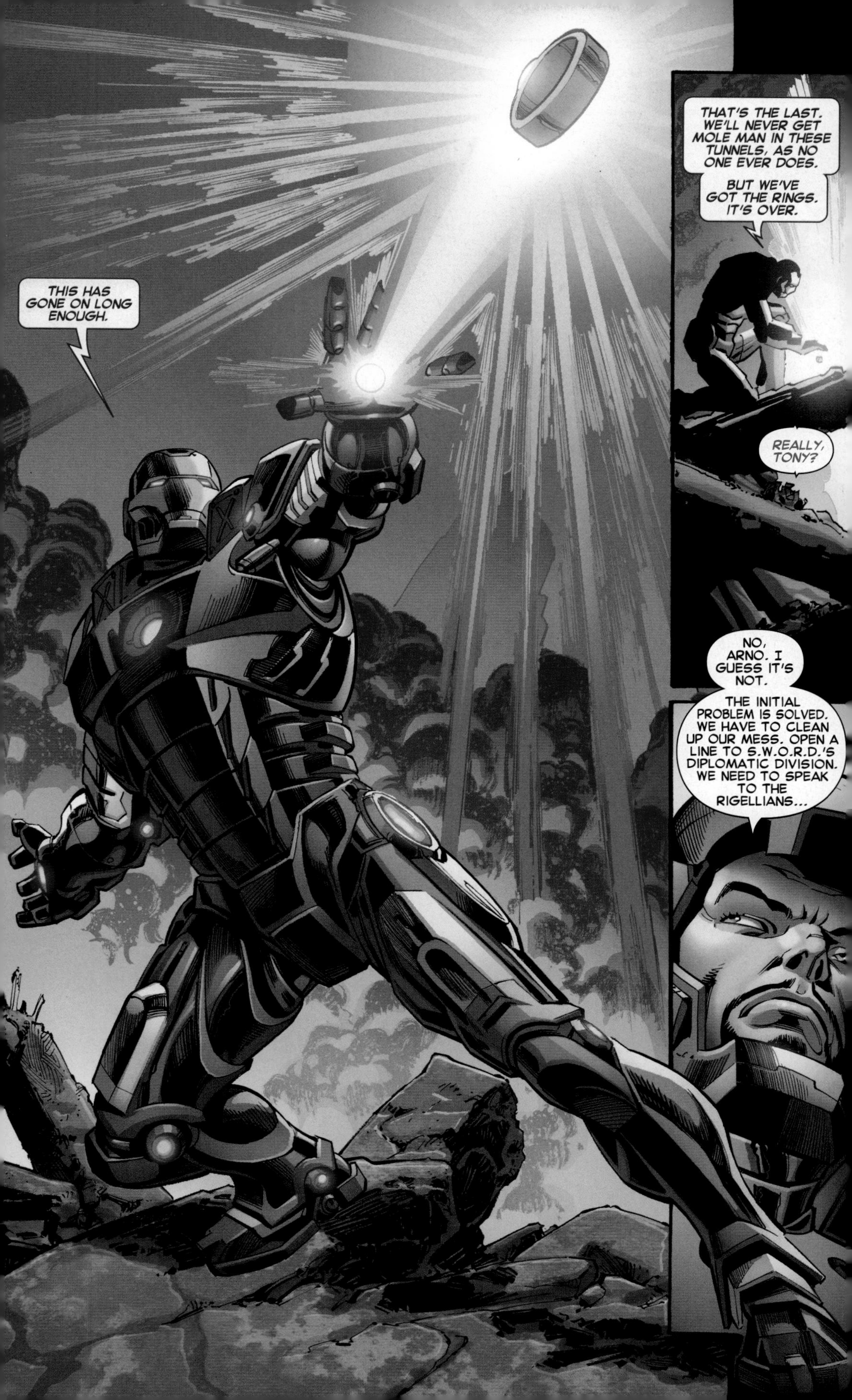
THIS HAS GONE ON LONG ENOUGH.
THAT'S THE LAST. WE'LL NEVER GET MOLE MAN IN THESE TUNNELS, AS NO ONE EVER DOES.
BUT WE'VE GOT THE RINGS. IT'S OVER.
REALLY, TONY?
NO, ARNO. I GUESS IT'S NOT.
THE INITIAL PROBLEM IS SOLVED. WE HAVE TO CLEAN UP OUR MESS. OPEN A LINE TO S.W.O.R.D.'S DIPLOMATIC DIVISION. WE NEED TO SPEAK TO THE RIGELLIANS...

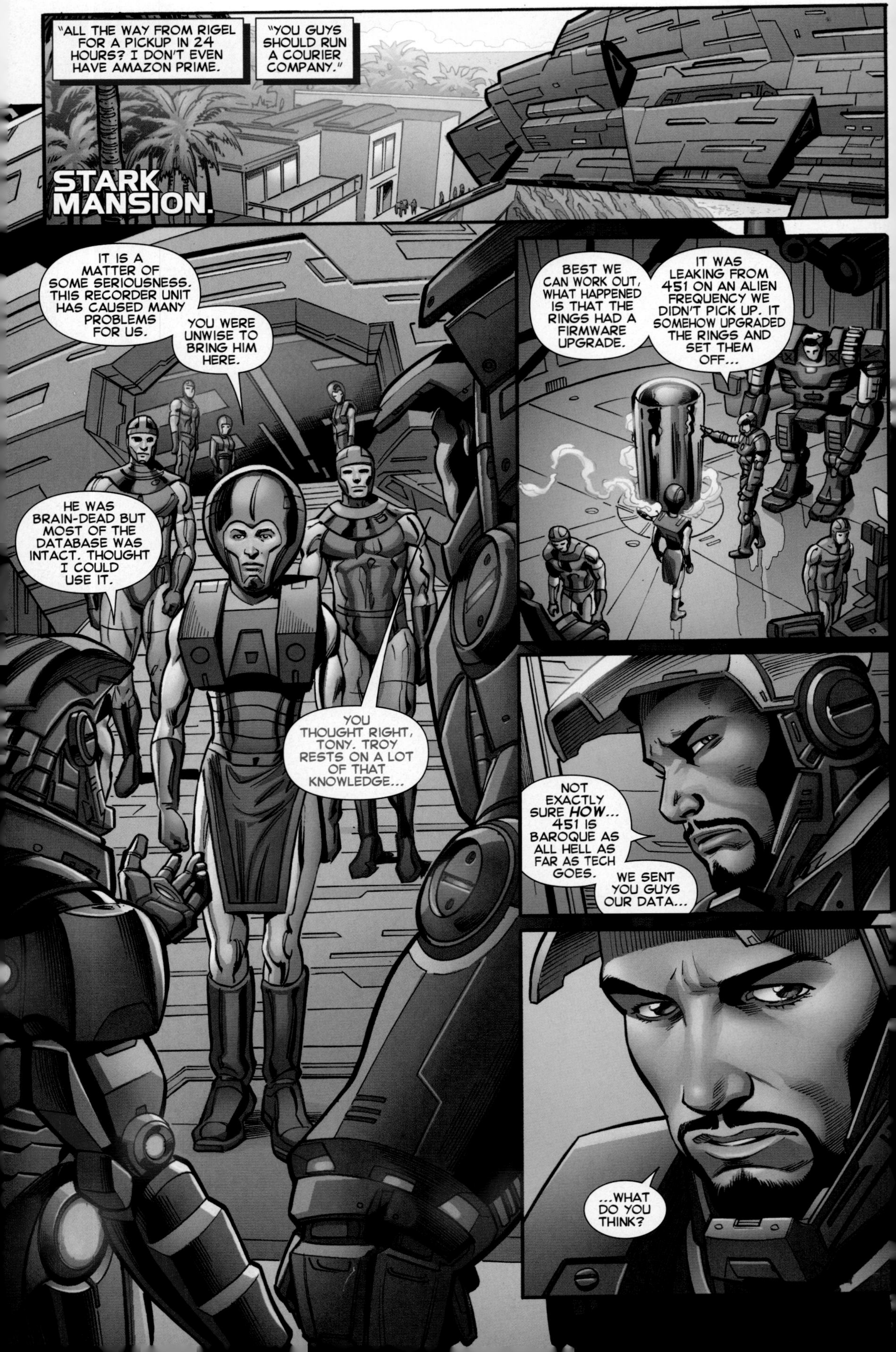
"ALL THE WAY FROM RIGEL FOR A PICKUP IN 24 HOURS? I DON'T EVEN HAVE AMAZON PRIME.
"YOU GUYS SHOULD RUN A COURIER COMPANY."
STARK MANSION.
IT IS A MATTER OF SOME SERIOUSNESS. THIS RECORDER UNIT HAS CAUSED MANY PROBLEMS FOR US.
YOU WERE UNWISE TO BRING HIM HERE.
HE WAS BRAIN-DEAD BUT MOST OF THE DATABASE WAS INTACT. THOUGHT I COULD USE IT.
YOU THOUGHT RIGHT, TONY. TROY RESTS ON A LOT OF THAT KNOWLEDGE...
BEST WE CAN WORK OUT, WHAT HAPPENED IS THAT THE RINGS HAD A FIRMWARE UPGRADE.
IT WAS LEAKING FROM 451 ON AN ALIEN FREQUENCY WE DIDN'T PICK UP. IT SOMEHOW UPGRADED THE RINGS AND SET THEM OFF...
NOT EXACTLY SURE HOW... 451 IS BAROQUE AS ALL HELL AS FAR AS TECH GOES.
WE SENT YOU GUYS OUR DATA...
...WHAT DO YOU THINK?

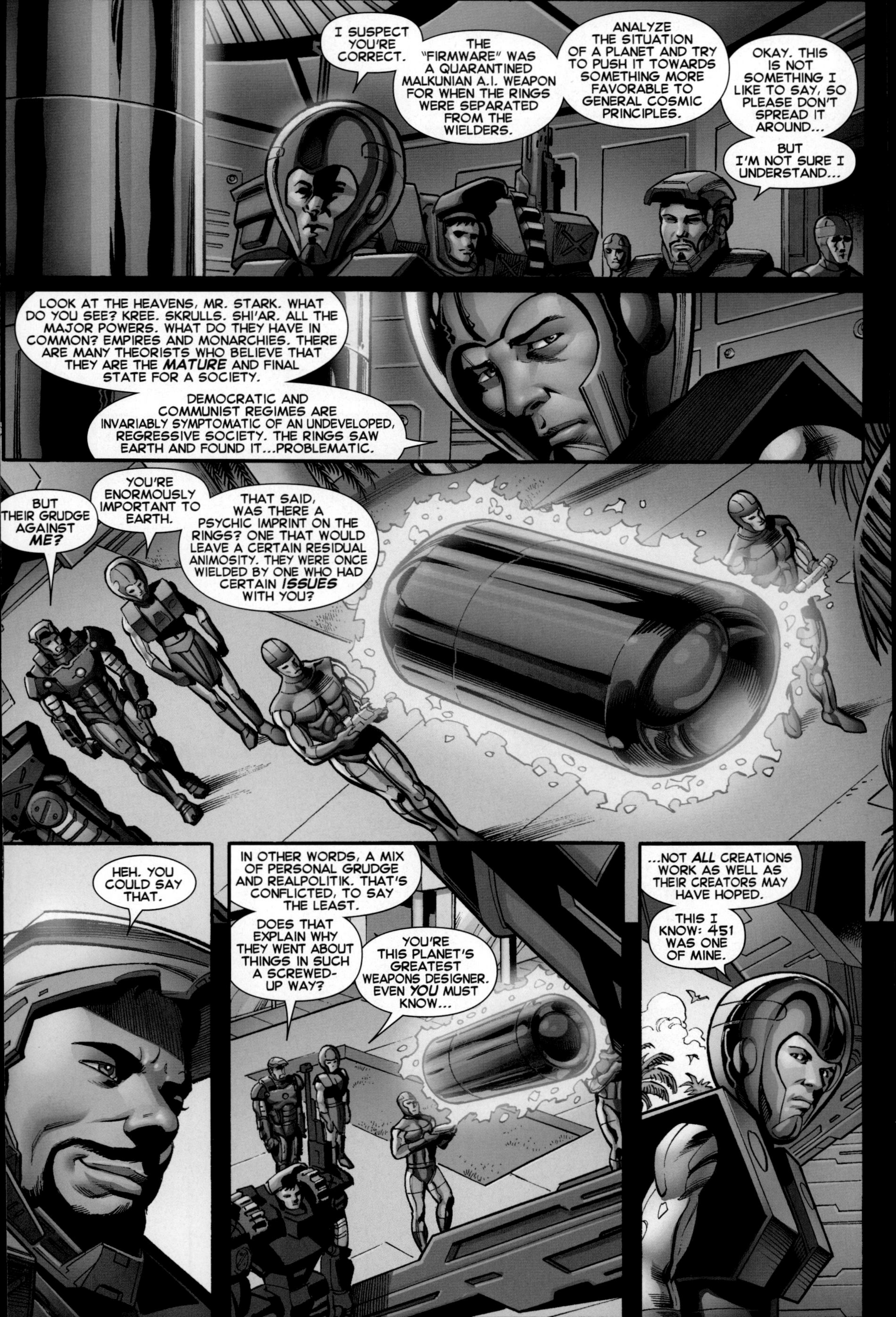
I SUSPECT YOU'RE CORRECT.
THE "FIRMWARE" WAS A QUARANTINED MALKUNIAN A.I. WEAPON FOR WHEN THE RINGS WERE SEPARATED FROM THE WIELDERS.
ANALYZE THE SITUATION OF A PLANET AND TRY TO PUSH IT TOWARDS SOMETHING MORE FAVORABLE TO GENERAL COSMIC PRINCIPLES.
OKAY. THIS IS NOT SOMETHING I LIKE TO SAY, SO PLEASE DON'T SPREAD IT AROUND...
BUT I'M NOT SURE I UNDERSTAND...
LOOK AT THE HEAVENS, MR. STARK. WHAT DO YOU SEE? KREE. SKRULLS. SHI'AR. ALL THE MAJOR POWERS. WHAT DO THEY HAVE IN COMMON? EMPIRES AND MONARCHIES. THERE ARE MANY THEORISTS WHO BELIEVE THAT THEY ARE THE MATURE AND FINAL STATE FOR A SOCIETY.
DEMOCRATIC AND COMMUNIST REGIMES ARE INVARIABLY SYMPTOMATIC OF AN UNDEVELOPED, REGRESSIVE SOCIETY. THE RINGS SAW EARTH AND FOUND IT...PROBLEMATIC.
BUT THEIR GRUDGE AGAINST ME?
YOU'RE ENORMOUSLY IMPORTANT TO EARTH.
THAT SAID, WAS THERE A PSYCHIC IMPRINT ON THE RINGS? ONE THAT WOULD LEAVE A CERTAIN RESIDUAL ANIMOSITY. THEY WERE ONCE WIELDED BY ONE WHO HAD CERTAIN ISSUES WITH YOU?
HEH. YOU COULD SAY THAT.
IN OTHER WORDS, A MIX OF PERSONAL GRUDGE AND REALPOLITIK. THAT'S CONFLICTED, TO SAY THE LEAST.
DOES THAT EXPLAIN WHY THEY WENT ABOUT THINGS IN SUCH A SCREWED-UP WAY?
YOU'RE THIS PLANET'S GREATEST WEAPONS DESIGNER. EVEN YOU MUST KNOW...
...NOT ALL CREATIONS WORK AS WELL AS THEIR CREATORS MAY HAVE HOPED.
THIS I KNOW: 451 WAS ONE OF MINE.

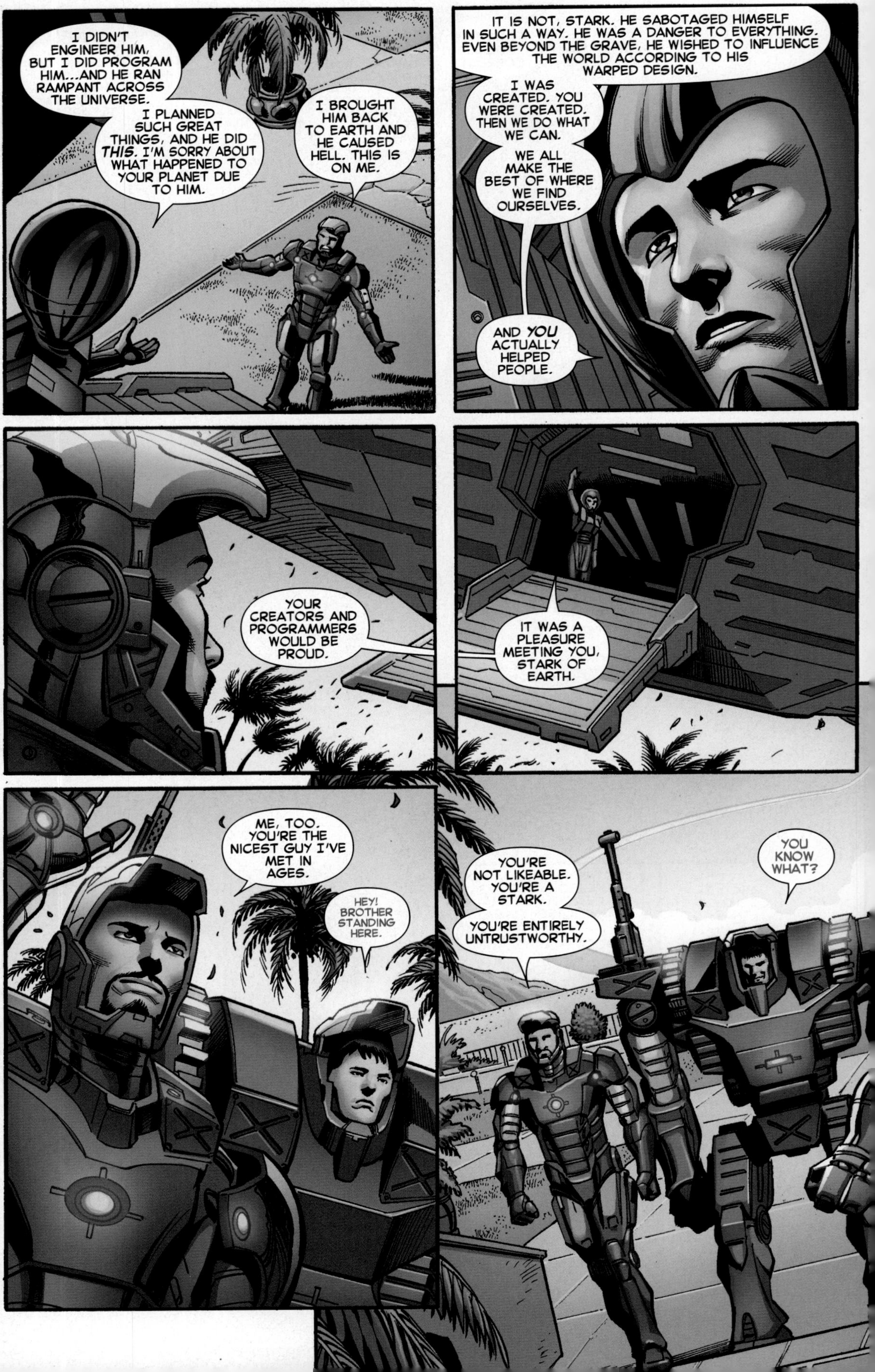
I DIDN'T ENGINEER HIM, BUT I DID PROGRAM HIM...AND HE RAN RAMPANT ACROSS THE UNIVERSE.
I PLANNED SUCH GREAT THINGS, AND HE DID *THIS*. I'M SORRY ABOUT WHAT HAPPENED TO YOUR PLANET DUE TO HIM.
I BROUGHT HIM BACK TO EARTH AND HE CAUSED HELL. THIS IS ON ME.
IT IS NOT, STARK. HE SABOTAGED HIMSELF IN SUCH A WAY. HE WAS A DANGER TO EVERYTHING. EVEN BEYOND THE GRAVE, HE WISHED TO INFLUENCE THE WORLD ACCORDING TO HIS WARPED DESIGN.
I WAS CREATED. YOU WERE CREATED. THEN WE DO WHAT WE CAN.
WE ALL MAKE THE BEST OF WHERE WE FIND OURSELVES.
AND *YOU* ACTUALLY HELPED PEOPLE.
YOUR CREATORS AND PROGRAMMERS WOULD BE PROUD.
IT WAS A PLEASURE MEETING YOU, STARK OF EARTH.
ME, TOO. YOU'RE THE NICEST GUY I'VE MET IN AGES.
HEY! BROTHER STANDING HERE.
YOU'RE NOT LIKEABLE. YOU'RE A STARK.
YOU'RE ENTIRELY UNTRUSTWORTHY.
YOU KNOW WHAT?

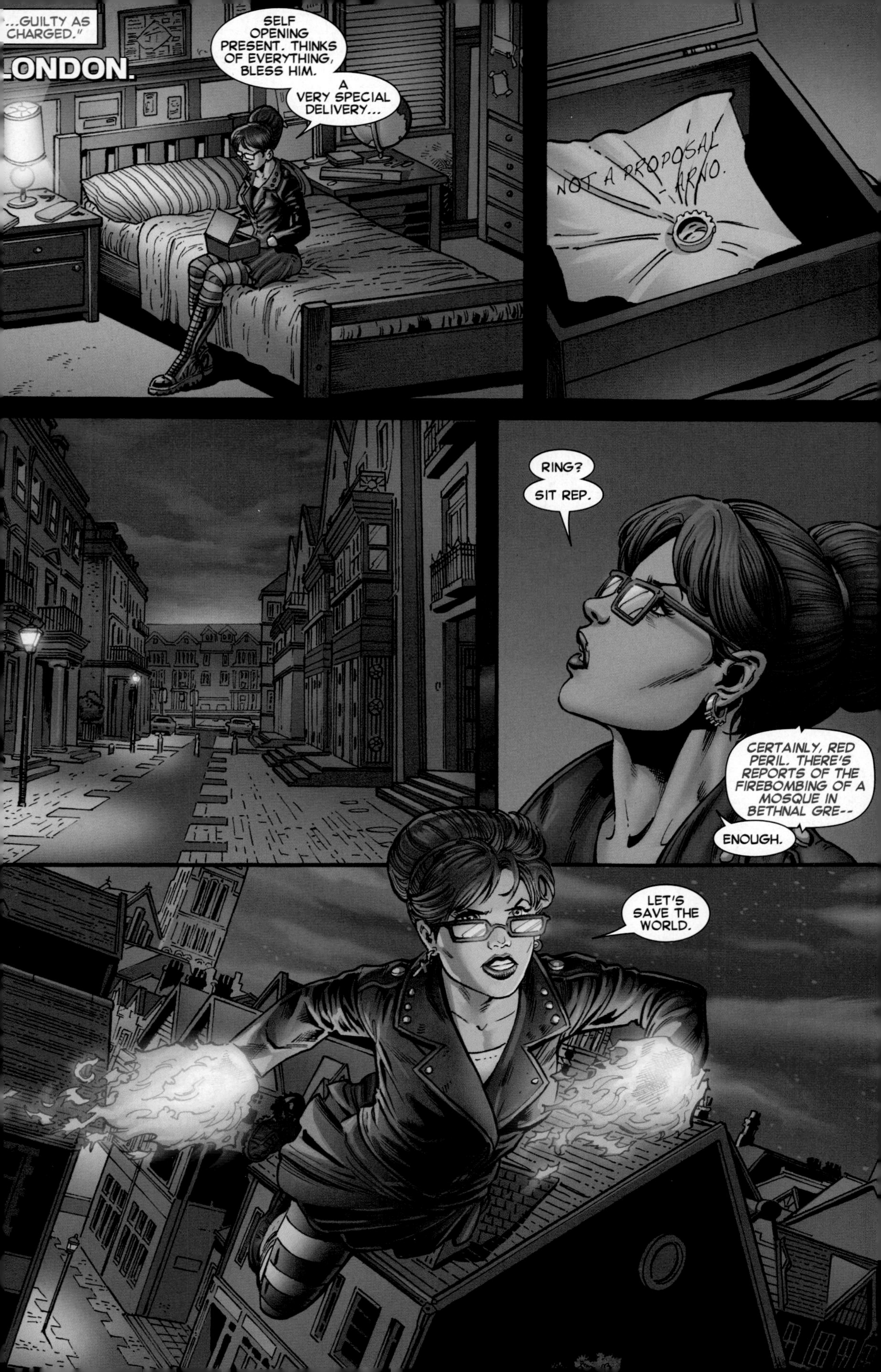
...GUILTY AS CHARGED."
LONDON.
SELF OPENING PRESENT. THINKS OF EVERYTHING, BLESS HIM.
A VERY SPECIAL DELIVERY...
NOT A PROPOSAL - ARNO.
RING?
SIT REP.
CERTAINLY, RED PERIL. THERE'S REPORTS OF THE FIREBOMBING OF A MOSQUE IN BETHNAL GRE--
ENOUGH.
LET'S SAVE THE WORLD.

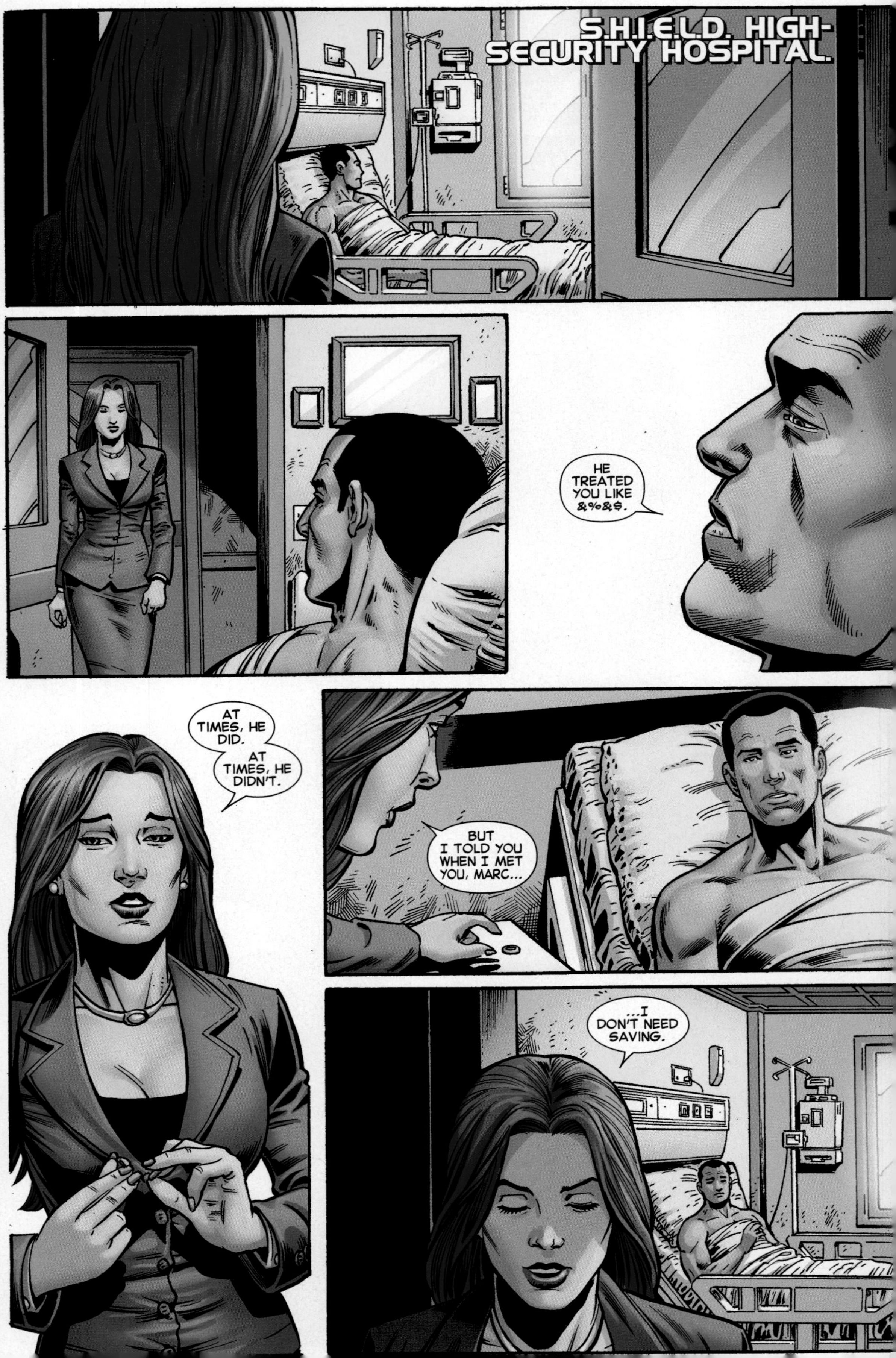
S.H.I.E.L.D. HIGH-SECURITY HOSPITAL.
HE TREATED YOU LIKE &%&$.
AT TIMES, HE DID.
AT TIMES, HE DIDN'T.
BUT I TOLD YOU WHEN I MET YOU, MARC...
...I DON'T NEED SAVING.

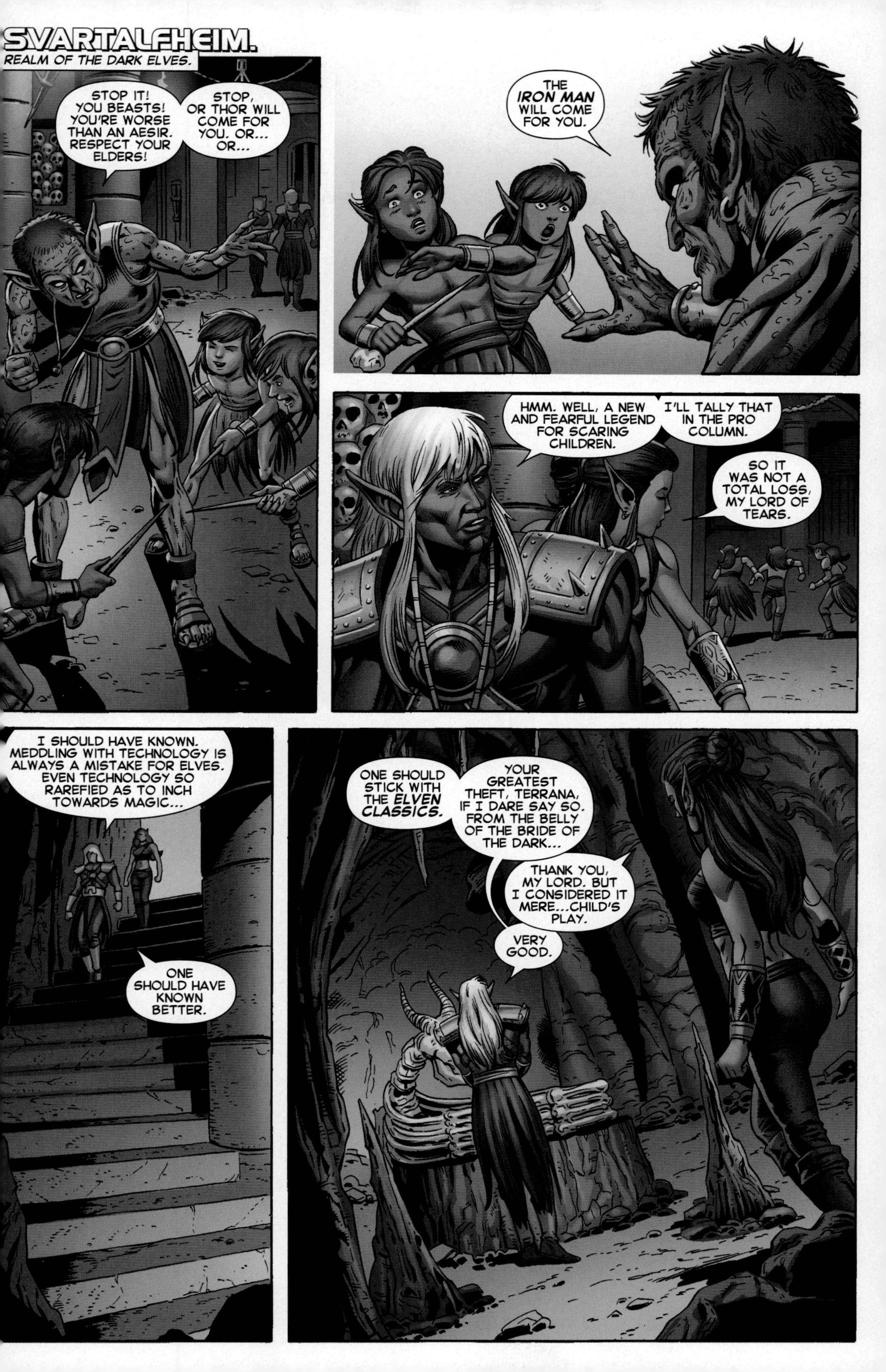
SVARTALFHEIM.
REALM OF THE DARK ELVES.
STOP IT! YOU BEASTS! YOU'RE WORSE THAN AN AESIR. RESPECT YOUR ELDERS!
STOP, OR THOR WILL COME FOR YOU. OR... OR...
THE IRON MAN WILL COME FOR YOU.
HMM. WELL, A NEW AND FEARFUL LEGEND FOR SCARING CHILDREN.
I'LL TALLY THAT IN THE PRO COLUMN.
SO IT WAS NOT A TOTAL LOSS, MY LORD OF TEARS.
I SHOULD HAVE KNOWN. MEDDLING WITH TECHNOLOGY IS ALWAYS A MISTAKE FOR ELVES. EVEN TECHNOLOGY SO RAREFIED AS TO INCH TOWARDS MAGIC...
ONE SHOULD HAVE KNOWN BETTER.
ONE SHOULD STICK WITH THE ELVEN CLASSICS.
YOUR GREATEST THEFT, TERRANA, IF I DARE SAY SO. FROM THE BELLY OF THE BRIDE OF THE DARK...
THANK YOU, MY LORD. BUT I CONSIDERED IT MERE...CHILD'S PLAY.
VERY GOOD.

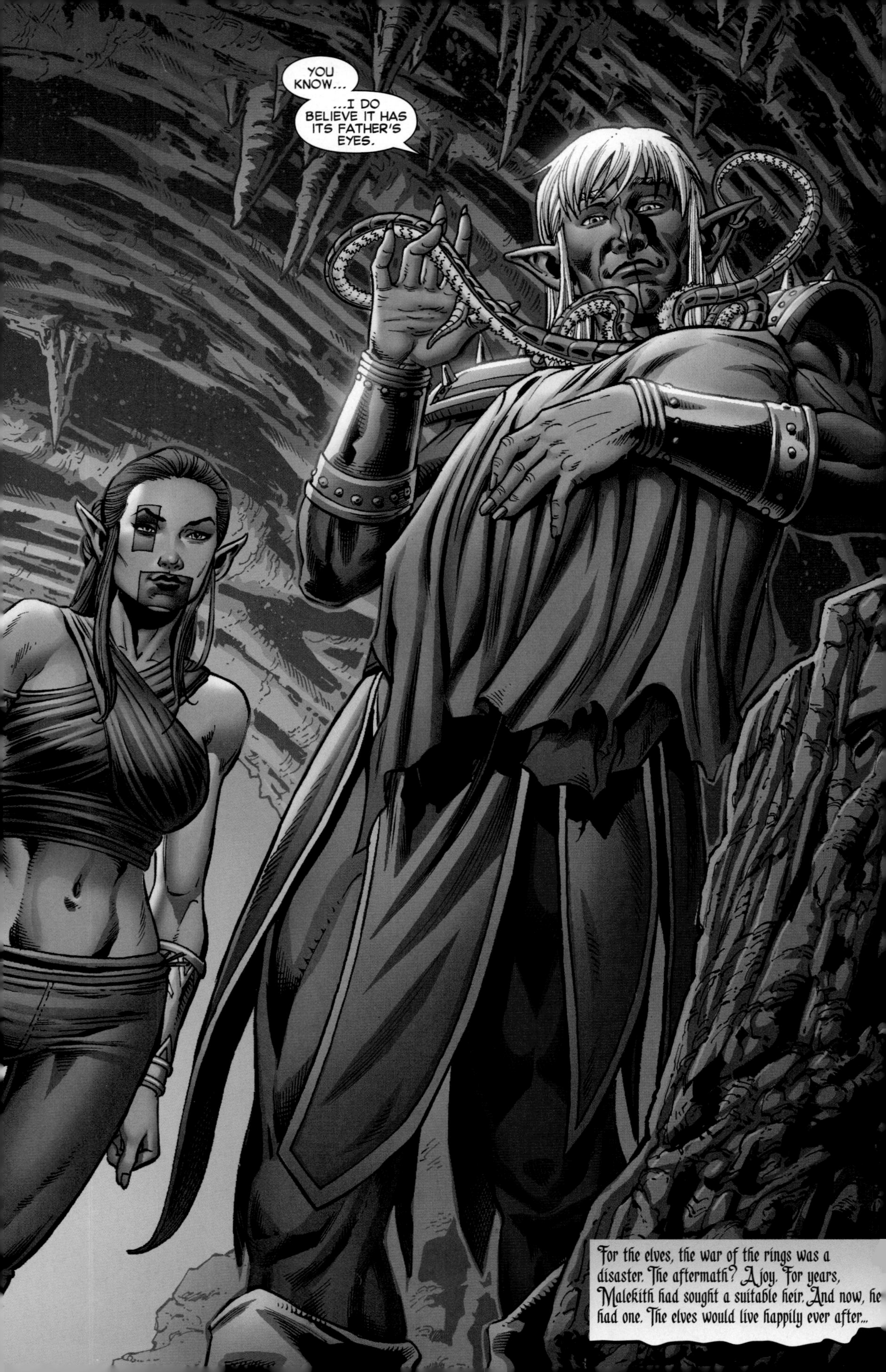
YOU KNOW...
...I DO BELIEVE IT HAS ITS FATHER'S EYES.
For the elves, the war of the rings was a disaster. The aftermath? A joy. For years, Malekith had sought a suitable heir. And now, he had one. The elves would live happily ever after...

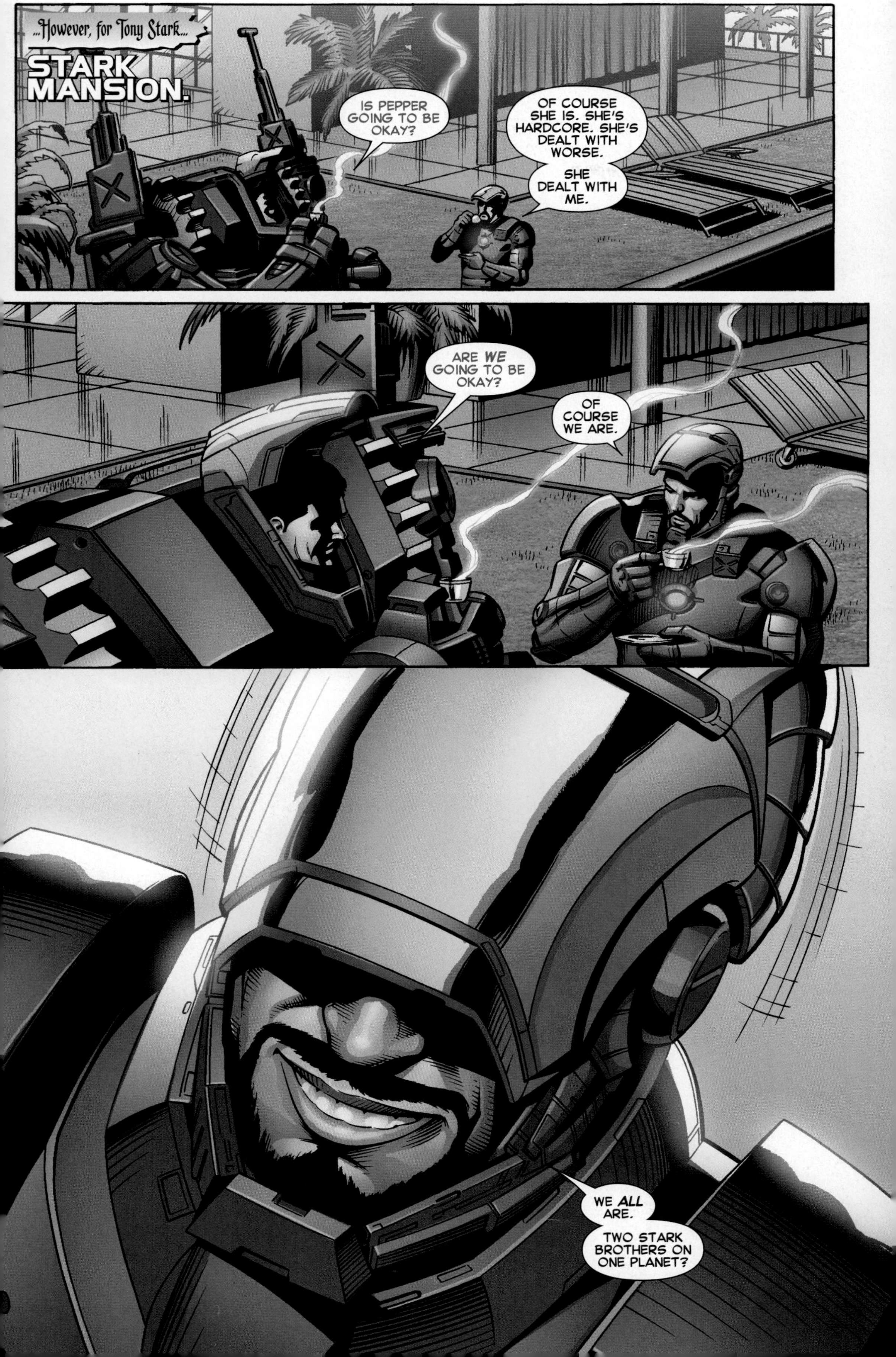

...However, for Tony Stark...
STARK MANSION.
IS PEPPER GOING TO BE OKAY?
OF COURSE SHE IS. SHE'S HARDCORE. SHE'S DEALT WITH WORSE.
SHE DEALT WITH ME.
ARE WE GOING TO BE OKAY?
OF COURSE WE ARE.
WE ALL ARE.
TWO STARK BROTHERS ON ONE PLANET?

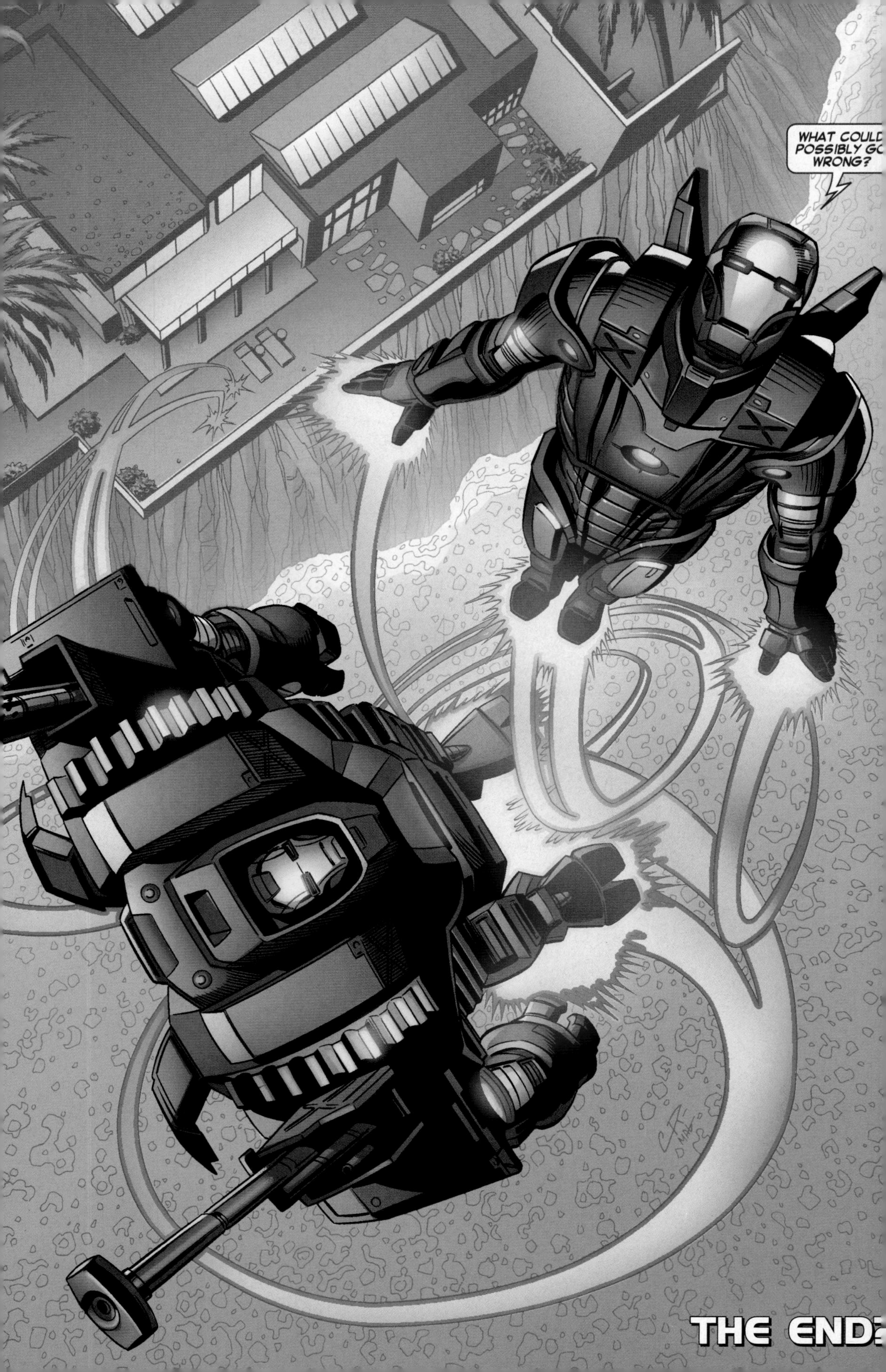
WHAT COULD POSSIBLY GO WRONG?
THE END

MARVEL AUGMENTED REALITY (AR) ENHANCES AND CHANGES THE WAY YOU EXPERIENCE COMICS!

TO ACCESS THE FREE MARVEL AR CONTENT IN THIS BOOK*:

1. Locate the **AR** logo within the comic.
2. Go to Marvel.com/AR in your web browser.
3. Search by series title to find the corresponding AR.
4. Enjoy Marvel AR!

*All AR content that appears in this book has been archived and will be available only at Marvel.com/AR — no longer in the Marvel AR App. Content subject to change and availability.

IRON MAN AR INDEX

TO REDEEM YOUR CODE FOR A FREE DIGITAL COPY:

1. GO TO MARVEL.COM/REDEEM.
   OFFER EXPIRES ON 10/1/16.
2. FOLLOW THE ON-SCREEN INSTRUCTIONS TO REDEEM YOUR DIGITAL COPY.
3. LAUNCH THE MARVEL COMICS APP TO READ YOUR COMIC NOW!
4. YOUR DIGITAL COPY WILL BE FOUND UNDER THE *MY COMICS* TAB.
5. READ & ENJOY!

YOUR FREE DIGITAL COPY WILL BE AVAILABLE O

MARVEL
FREE DIGITAL
COPY OFFER
PEEL HERE TO REVEAL CODE ➡